Lectionary Texts
Year C

The Church Hymnal Corporation
800 Second Avenue, New York, N.Y. 10017

*The Church Hymnal Corporation wishes to express its
appreciation to The National Council of Churches for permission
to use the texts, to the Reverend Leo Malania for editing this
volume, to Brother Howard E. Galley, C.A., for editorial
assistance and advice, to Nelson Gruppo for the layout and design,
and to Frank Hemlin for editorial coordination.*

ISBN 0-89869-008-0 Reader's Edition
0-89869-009-9 Pew Edition

Introduction

Lectionary Texts is published in three separate volumes for Years A, B, and C. The selection of the readings is in strict accordance with The Lectionary of *The Book of Common Prayer*, pages 889-925, and pages 288-291 for the Great Vigil of Easter. The texts of the readings have been drawn from *The Common Bible* (Revised Standard Version, an Ecumenical Edition), whose accuracy and wide ecumenical acceptance are generally recognized. The texts in this book may, of course, be replaced by corresponding passages from any of the other versions of the Bible authorized for public worship in this Church.

The readings have been edited for liturgical use in accordance with the suggestions in *The Book of Common Prayer*, page 888. All alternatives cited have been included. In only a very few cases where exactly the same passages are to be read, rather than reprinting an entire passage, page references to a preceding or following page are given.

All optional passages have also been included. Those which may be omitted (cited in parentheses in the Lectionary), have been set off in separate indented paragraphs, and marked with a vertical bar line at the margin. In some of the passages, an opening phrase needed to clarify the context is printed in italics and set off in brackets. These italicized words should be omitted when the preceding section is read and the continuity of the entire reading is clear. An example will be found on page 51, where the optional passage ends with an incomplete clause continued in the following passage. When the optional passage is omitted, the italicized words are needed to make the context clear. Unless otherwise indicated, all page numbers refer to *The Book of Common Prayer*.

In this book, citations from the Psalter are placed at the point where psalmody is normally used in the celebration of the Holy Eucharist, i.e., following the Old Testament Lesson. When the readings are used at a principal service of Morning or Evening Prayer, the Psalm is read at the place appointed in the service, i.e., before the Lessons. When used at the Office, the longer version of the Psalm is to be preferred. The shorter form is intended to be sung at the Eucharist.

The Church Hymnal Corporation wishes to record its deep appreciation to all who welcomed the publication of *Lectionary Texts: Year A* and *Lectionary Texts: Year B,* especially to those who made valuable suggestions for improving subsequent volumes in this series. To the extent possible, these suggestions have been incorporated in the present volume. An added improvement in this volume is the identification of the day or week in the footlines.

The publishers hope that this book will enrich participation in worship by all the people, and will assist the clergy and other ministers in worthily proclaiming the Word of God at the principal service of Sundays and major Holy Days.

Lectionary Texts: Year C

First Sunday of Advent

A Reading (Lesson) from the Book of Zechariah [14:4-9]

On the day of the Lord his feet shall stand on the Mount of
Olives which lies before Jerusalem on the east; and the
Mount of Olives shall be split in two from east to west by a
very wide valley; so that one half of the Mount shall
withdraw northward, and the other half southward. And
the valley of my mountains shall be stopped up, for the
valley of the mountains shall touch the side of it; and you
shall flee as you fled from the earthquake in the days of
Uzzi'ah king of Judah. Then the Lord your God will come,
and all the holy ones with him. On that day there shall be
neither cold nor frost. And there shall be continuous day (it
is known to the Lord), not day and not night, for at
evening time there shall be light. On that day living waters
shall flow out from Jerusalem, half of them to the eastern
sea and half of them to the western sea; it shall continue in
summer as in winter. And the Lord will become king over
all the earth; on that day the Lord will be one and his
name one.

Psalm 50 [page 654]   or   *50:1-6* [page 654]

*A Reading (Lesson) from the First Letter of Paul
to the Thessalonians* [3:9-13]

What thanksgiving can we render to God for you, for all
the joy which we feel for your sake before our God,

praying earnestly night and day that we may see you face to face and supply what is lacking in your faith? Now may our God and Father himself, and our Lord Jesus, direct our way to you; and may the Lord make you increase and abound in love to one another and to all men, as we do to you, so that he may establish your hearts unblamable in holiness before our God and Father, at the coming of our Lord Jesus with all his saints.

✝ *The Holy Gospel of Our Lord Jesus Christ According to Luke* [21:25-31]

Jesus said,"There will be signs in sun and moon and stars, and upon the earth distress of nations in perplexity at the roaring of the sea and the waves, men fainting with fear and with foreboding of what is coming on the world; for the powers of the heavens will be shaken. And then they will see the Son of man coming in a cloud with power and great glory. Now when these things begin to take place, look up and raise your heads, because your redemption is drawing near." And he told them a parable: "Look at the fig tree, and all the trees; as soon as they come out in leaf, you see for yourselves and know that the summer is already near. So also, when you see these things taking place, you know that the kingdom of God is near."

Second Sunday of Advent

A Reading (Lesson) from Baruch [5:1-9]

Take off the garment of your sorrow and affliction, O Jerusalem, and put on for ever the beauty of the glory from God. Put on the robe of the righteousness from God; put on your head the diadem of the glory of the Everlasting. For God will show your splendor everywhere under heaven. For your name will for ever be called by God, "Peace of righteousness and glory of godliness." Arise, O

Jerusalem, stand upon the height and look toward the east, and see your children gathered from west and east, at the word of the Holy One, rejoicing that God has remembered them. For they went forth from you on foot, led away by their enemies; but God will bring them back to you, carried in glory, as on a royal throne. For God has ordered that every high mountain and the everlasting hills be made low and the valleys filled up, to make level ground, so that Israel may walk safely in the glory of God. The woods and every fragrant tree have shaded Israel at God's command. For God will lead Israel with joy, in the light of his glory, with the mercy and righteousness that come from him.

Psalm 126 [page 782]

*A Reading (Lesson) from the Letter of Paul
to the Philippians* [1:1-11]

Paul and Timothy, servants of Christ Jesus, to all the saints in Christ Jesus who are at Philippi, with the bishops and deacons: Grace to you and peace from God our Father and the Lord Jesus Christ. I thank my God in all my remembrance of you, always in every prayer of mine for you all, making my prayer with joy, thankful for your partnership in the gospel from the first day until now. And I am sure that he who began a good work in you will bring it to completion at the day of Jesus Christ. It is right for me to feel thus about you all, because I hold you in my heart, for you are all partakers with me of grace, both in my imprisonment and in the defense and confirmation of the gospel. For God is my witness, how I yearn for you all with the affection of Christ Jesus. And it is my prayer that your love may abound more and more, with knowledge and all discernment, so that you may approve what is excellent, and may be pure and blameless for the day of Christ, filled with the fruits of righteousness which come through Jesus Christ, to the glory and praise of God.

✝ *The Holy Gospel of Our Lord Jesus Christ*
According to Luke [3:1-6]

In the fifteenth year of the reign of Tibe′ri-us Caesar,
Pontius Pilate being governor of Judea, and Herod being
tetrarch of Galilee, and his brother Philip tetrarch of the
region of Iturae′a and Trachoni′tis, and Lysa′ni-as tetrarch
of Abile′ne, in the high-priesthood of Annas and Ca′iaphas,
the word of God came to John the son of Zechari′ah in the
wilderness; and he went into all the region about the
Jordan, preaching a baptism of repentance for the
forgiveness of sins. As it is written in the book of the words
of Isaiah the prophet, "The voice of one crying in the
wilderness: Prepare the way of the Lord, make his paths
straight. Every valley shall be filled, and every mountain
and hill shall be brought low, and the crooked shall be
made straight, and the rough ways shall be made smooth;
and all flesh shall see the salvation of God."

Third Sunday of Advent

A Reading (Lesson) from the Book of Zephaniah [3:14-20]

Sing aloud, O daughter of Zion; shout, O Israel! Rejoice
and exult with all your heart, O daughter of Jerusalem!
The Lord has taken away the judgments against you, he
has cast out your enemies. The King of Israel, the Lord, is
in your midst; you shall fear evil no more. On that day it
shall be said to Jerusalem: "Do not fear, O Zion; let not
your hands grow weak. The Lord, your God, is in your
midst, a warrior who gives victory; he will rejoice over you
with gladness, he will renew you in his love; he will exult
over you with loud singing as on a day of festival.
I will remove disaster from you, so that you will not bear
reproach for it. Behold, at that time I will deal with all your
oppressors. And I will save the lame and gather the
outcast, and I will change their shame into praise and

renown in all the earth. At that time I will bring you home, at the time when I gather you together; yea, I will make you renowned and praised among all the peoples of the earth, when I restore your fortunes before your eyes," says the Lord.

Psalm 85 [page 708] or *85:7-13* [page 709] or
Ecce Deus, Canticle 9 [page 86]

*A Reading (Lesson) from the Letter of Paul
to the Philippians* [4:4-7 (8-9)]

Rejoice in the Lord always; again I will say, Rejoice. Let all men know your forbearance. The Lord is at hand. Have no anxiety about anything, but in everything by prayer and supplication with thanksgiving let your requests be made known to God. And the peace of God, which passes all understanding, will keep your hearts and your minds in Christ Jesus.

> Finally, brethren, whatever is true, whatever is honorable, whatever is just, whatever is pure, whatever is lovely, whatever is gracious, if there is any excellence, if there is anything worthy of praise, think about these things. What you have learned and received and heard and see in me, do; and the God of peace will be with you.

✝ *The Holy Gospel of Our Lord Jesus Christ
According to Luke* [3:7-18]

John the Baptist said to the multitudes that came out to be baptized by him, "You brood of vipers! Who warned you to flee from the wrath to come? Bear fruits that befit repentance, and do not begin to say to yourselves, 'We have Abraham as our father'; for I tell you, God is able from these stones to raise up children to Abraham. Even now the axe is laid to the root of the trees; every tree therefore that does not bear good fruit is cut down and thrown into the fire." And the multitudes asked him, "What then shall we do?" And he answered them, "He who has two coats, let him share with him who has none; and he who has food, let him do likewise." Tax collectors also came to be baptized, and said to him, "Teacher, what shall we do?" And he said to them, "Collect no more than is appointed you." Soldiers also asked him, "And we, what shall we do?" And he said to them, "Rob no one by violence or by false accusation, and be content with your wages." As the people were in expectation, and all men questioned in their hearts concerning John, whether perhaps he were the Christ, John answered them all, "I baptize you with water; but he who is mightier than I is coming, the thong of whose sandals I am not worthy to untie; he will baptize you with the Holy Spirit and with fire. His winnowing fork is in his hand, to clear his threshing floor, and to gather the wheat into his granary, but the chaff he will burn with unquenchable fire." So, with many other exhortations, he preached good news to the people.

Fourth Sunday of Advent

A Reading (Lesson) from the Book of Micah [5:2-4]

You, O Bethlehem Eph'rathah, who are little to be among the clans of Judah, from you shall come forth for me one who is to be ruler in Israel, whose origin is from of old, from ancient days. Therefore he shall give them up until the time when she who is in travail has brought forth; then the rest of his brethren shall return to the people of Israel . And he shall stand and feed his flock in the strength of the Lord, in the majesty of the name of the Lord his God. And they shall dwell secure, for now he shall be great to the ends of the earth.

Psalm 80 [page 702]   or   *80:1-7* [page 702]

A Reading (Lesson) from the Letter to the Hebrews [10:5-10]

When Christ came into the world, he said, "Sacrifices and offerings thou hast not desired, but a body hast thou prepared for me; in burnt offerings and sin offerings thou hast taken no pleasure. Then I said, 'Lo, I have come to do thy will, O God,' as it is written of me in the roll of the book." When he said above, "Thou hast neither desired nor taken pleasure in sacrifices and offerings and burnt offerings and sin offerings" (these are offered according to the law), then he added, "Lo, I have come to do thy will." He abolishes the first in order to establish the second. And by that will we have been sanctified through the offering of the body of Jesus Christ once for all.

✝ *The Holy Gospel of Our Lord Jesus Christ According to Luke* [1:39-49 (50-56)]

In those days Mary arose and went with haste into the hill country, to a city of Judah, and she entered the house of Zechari'ah and greeted Elizabeth. And when Elizabeth heard the greeting of Mary, the babe leaped in her womb; and Elizabeth was filled with the Holy Spirit and she exclaimed with a loud cry, "Blessed are you among women, and blessed is the fruit of your womb! And why is this granted me, that the mother of my Lord should come to me? For behold, when the voice of your greeting came to my ears, the babe in my womb leaped for joy. And blessed is she who believed that there would be a fulfillment of what was spoken to her from the Lord." And Mary said, "My soul magnifies the Lord, and my spirit rejoices in God my Savior, for he has regarded the low estate of his handmaiden. For behold, henceforth all generations will call me blessed; for he who is mighty has done great things for me, and holy is his name.

And his mercy is on those who fear him from generation to generation. He has shown strength with his arm, he has scattered the proud in the imagination of their hearts, he has put down the mighty from their thrones, and exalted those of low degree; he has filled the hungry with good things, and the rich he has sent empty away. He has helped his servant Israel, in remembrance of his mercy, as he spoke to our fathers, to Abraham and to his posterity for ever." And Mary remained with her about three months, and returned to her home.

The Nativity of Our Lord: Christmas Day I

A Reading (Lesson) from the Book of Isaiah [9:2-4, 6-7]

The people who walked in darkness have seen a great light; those who dwelt in a land of deep darkness, on them has light shined. Thou hast multiplied the nation, thou hast increased its joy; they rejoice before thee as with joy at the harvest, as men rejoice when they divide the spoil. For the yoke of his burden, and the staff for his shoulder, the rod of his oppressor, thou hast broken as on the day of Mid'ian. For to us a child is born, to us a son is given; and the government will be upon his shoulder, and his name will be called, "Wonderful Counselor, Mighty God, Everlasting Father, Prince of Peace." Of the increase of his government and of peace there will be no end, upon the throne of David, and over his kingdom, to establish it, and to uphold it with justice and with righteousness, from this time forth and for evermore. The zeal of the Lord of hosts will do this.

Psalm 96 [page 725]   or   *96:1-4, 11-12* [page 725]

A Reading (Lesson) from the Letter of Paul to Titus [2:11-14]

The grace of God has appeared for the salvation of all men,
training us to renounce irreligion and worldly passions,
and to live sober, upright, and godly lives in this world,
awaiting our blessed hope, the appearing of the glory of our
great God and Savior Jesus Christ, who gave himself for us
to redeem us from all iniquity and to purify for himself
a people of his own who are zealous for good deeds.

✝ *The Holy Gospel of Our Lord Jesus Christ
Accoding to Luke* [2:1-14 (15-20)]

In those days a decree went out from Caesar Augustus that
all the world should be enrolled. This was the first
enrollment, when Quirin'i-us was governor of Syria. And
all went to be enrolled, each to his own city. And Joseph
also went up from Galilee, from the city of Nazareth, to
Judea, to the city of David, which is called Bethlehem,
because he was of the house and lineage of David, to be
enrolled with Mary, his betrothed, who was with child.
And while they were there, the time came for her to be
delivered. And she gave birth to her first-born son and
wrapped him in swaddling cloths, and laid him in a
manger, because there was no place for them in the inn.
And in that region there were shepherds out in the field,
keeping watch over their flock by night. And an angel of
the Lord appeared to them and the glory of the Lord shone
around them and they were filled with fear. And the angel
said to them, "Be not afraid; for behold, I bring you good
news of a great joy which will come to all the people; for to
you is born this day in the city of David a Savior, who is
Christ the Lord. And this will be a sign for you: you will
find a babe wrapped in swaddling cloths and lying in a
manger." And suddenly there was with the angel a
multitude of the heavenly host praising God and
saying, "Glory to God in the highest, and on earth peace
among men with whom he is pleased!"

When the angels went away from them into heaven, the shepherds said to one another, "Let us go over to Bethlehem and see this thing that has happened, which the Lord has made known to us." And they went with haste, and found Mary and Joseph, and the babe lying in a manger. And when they saw it they made known the saying which had been told them concerning this child; and all who heard it wondered at what the shepherds told them. But Mary kept all these things, pondering them in her heart. And the shepherds returned, glorifying and praising God for all they had heard and seen, as it had been told them.

Christmas Day II

A Reading (Lesson) from the Book of Isaiah [62:6-7, 10-12]

Upon your walls, O Jerusalem, I have set watchmen; all the day and all the night they shall never be silent. You who put the Lord in remembrance, take no rest, and give him no rest until he establishes Jerusalem and makes it a praise in the earth. Go through, go through the gates, prepare the way for the people; build up, build up the highway, clear it of stones, lift up an ensign over the peoples. Behold, the Lord has proclaimed to the end of the earth: Say to the daughter of Zion, "Behold, your salvation comes; behold, his reward is with him, and his recompense before him." And they shall be called The holy people, The redeemed of the Lord; and you shall be called Sought out, a city not forsaken.

Psalm 97 [page 726]   or   *97:1-4, 11-12* [page 726]

A Reading (Lesson) from the Letter of Paul to Titus [3:4-7]

When the goodness and loving kindness of God our Savior appeared, he saved us, not because of deeds done by us in righteousness, but in virtue of his own mercy, by the washing of regeneration and renewal in the Holy Spirit, which he poured out upon us richly through Jesus Christ our Savior, so that we might be justified by his grace and become heirs in hope of eternal life.

✝ *The Holy Gospel of Our Lord Jesus Christ According to Luke* [2:(1-14)15-20]

In those days a decree went out from Caesar Augustus that all the world should be enrolled. This was the first enrollment, when Quirin'i-us was governor of Syria. And all went to be enrolled, each to his own city. And Joseph also went up from Galilee, from the city of Nazareth, to Judea, to the city of David, which is called Bethlehem, because he was of the house and lineage of David, to be enrolled with Mary, his betrothed, who was with child. And while they were there, the time came for her to be delivered. And she gave birth to her first-born son and wrapped him in swaddling cloths, and laid him in a manger, because there was no place for them in the inn. And in that region there were shepherds out in the field, keeping watch over their flock by night. And an angel of the Lord appeared to them, and the glory of the Lord shone around them, and they were filled with fear. And the angel said to them,"Be not afraid; for behold, I bring you good news of a great joy which will come to all the people; for to you is born this day in the city of David a Savior, who is Christ the Lord. And this will be a sign for you: You will find a babe wrapped in swaddling cloths and lying in a manger." And suddenly there was with the angel a multitude of the heavenly host praising God and saying,"Glory to God in the highest, and on earth peace among men with whom he is pleased!"

When the angels went away from them into heaven, the shepherds said to one another,"Let us go over to Bethlehem and see this thing that has happened, which the Lord has made known to us." And they went with haste, and found Mary and Joseph, and the babe lying in a manger. And when they saw it they made known the saying which had been told them concerning this child; and all who heard it wondered at what the shepherds told them. But Mary kept all these things, pondering them in her heart. And the shepherds returned, glorifying and praising God for all they had heard and seen, as it had been told them.

Christmas Day III

A Reading (Lesson) from the Book of Isaiah [52:7-10]

How beautiful upon the mountains are the feet of him who brings good tidings, who publishes peace, who brings good tidings of good, who publishes salvation, who says to Zion,"Your God reigns." Hark, your watchmen lift up their voice, together they sing for joy; for eye to eye they see the return of the Lord to Zion. Break forth together into singing, you waste places of Jerusalem; for the Lord has comforted his people, he has redeemed Jerusalem. The Lord has bared his holy arm before the eyes of all the nations; and all the ends of the earth shall see the salvation of our God.

Psalm 98 [page 727] or *98:1-6* [page 727]

A Reading (Lesson) from the Letter to the Hebrews [1:1-12]

In many and various ways God spoke of old to our fathers by the prophets; but in these last days he has spoken to us by a son, whom he appointed the heir of all things, through whom also he created the world. He reflects the glory of

God and bears the very stamp of his nature, upholding the universe by his word of power. When he had made purification for sins, he sat down at the right hand of the Majesty on high, having become as much superior to angels as the name he has obtained is more excellent than theirs. For to what angel did God ever say,"Thou art my Son, today I have begotten thee"? Or again,"I will be to him a father, and he shall be to me a son"? And again, when he brings the firstborn into the world, he says,"Let all God's angels worship him." Of the angels he says, "Who makes his angels winds, and his servants flames of fire."But of the Son he says,"Thy throne, O God, is for ever and ever, the righteous scepter is the scepter of thy kingdom. Thou hast loved righteousness and hated lawlessness; therefore God, thy God, has anointed thee with the oil of gladness beyond thy comrades." And, "Thou, Lord, didst found the earth in the beginning, and the heavens are the work of thy hands; they will perish, but thou remainest; they will all grow old like a garment, like a mantle thou wilt roll them up, and they will be changed. But thou art the same, and thy years will never end."

✝ *The Holy Gospel of Our Lord Jesus Christ*
According to John [1:1-14]

In the beginning was the Word, and the Word was with God, and the Word was God. He was in the beginning with God; all things were made through him, and without him was not anything made that was made. In him was life, and the life was the light of men. The light shines in the darkness, and the darkness has not overcome it. There was a man sent from God, whose name was John. He came for testimony, to bear witness to the light, that all might believe through him. He was not the light, but came to bear witness to the light. The true light that enlightens every man was coming into the world. He was in the world, and the world was made through him, yet the world knew him not. He came to his own home, and his own people received him not. But to all who received him, who believed in his name, he gave power to become children of God; who were born, not of blood nor of the will of the flesh nor of the will of man, but of God. And the Word became flesh and dwelt among us, full of grace and truth; we have beheld his glory, glory as of the only Son from the Father.

First Sunday after Christmas

A Reading (Lesson) from the Book of Isaiah [61:10—62:3]

I will greatly rejoice in the Lord, my soul shall exult in my God; for he has clothed me with the garments of salvation, he has covered me with the robe of righteousness, as a bridegroom decks himself with a garland, and as a bride adorns herself with her jewels. For as the earth brings forth its shoots, and as a garden causes what is sown in it to spring up, so the Lord God will cause righteousness and praise to spring forth before all the nations. For Zion's sake I will not keep silent, and for Jerusalem's sake I will not rest, until her vindication goes forth as brightness, and her salvation as a burning torch. The nations shall see your vindication, and all the kings your glory; and you shall be called by a new name which the mouth of the Lord will give. You shall be a crown of beauty in the hand of the Lord, and a royal diadem in the hand of your God.

Psalm 147 [page 804]   or   *147:13-21* [page 805]

A Reading (Lesson) from the Letter of Paul to the Galatians [3:23-25; 4:4-7]

Now before faith came, we were confined under the law, kept under restraint until faith should be revealed. So that the law was our custodian until Christ came, that we might be justified by faith. But now that faith has come, we are no longer under a custodian. But when the time had fully come, God sent forth his Son, born of woman, born under the law, to redeem those who were under the law, so that we might receive adoption as sons. And because you are sons, God has sent the Spirit of his Son into our hearts, crying, "Abba! Father!" So through God you are no longer a slave but a son, and if a son then an heir.

✝ *The Holy Gospel of Our Lord Jesus Christ According to John* [1:1-18]

In the beginning was the Word, and the Word was with God, and the Word was God. He was in the beginning with God; all things were made through him, and without him was not anything made that was made. In him was life, and the life was the light of men. The light shines in the darkness, and the darkness has not overcome it. There was a man sent from God, whose name was John. He came for testimony, to bear witness to the light, that all might believe through him. He was not the light, but came to bear witness to the light. The true light that enlightens every man was coming into the world. He was in the world, and the world was made through him, yet the world knew him not. He came to his own home, and his own people received him not. But to all who received him, who believed in his name, he gave power to become children of God; who were born, not of blood nor of the will of the flesh nor of the will of man, but of God. And the Word became flesh and dwelt among us, full of grace and truth; we have beheld his glory, glory as of the only Son from the Father. (John bore witness to him, and cried, "This was he of whom I said, 'He who comes after me ranks before me, for he was before me.'") And from his fullness have we all received, grace upon grace. For the law was given through Moses; grace and truth came through Jesus Christ. No one has ever seen God; the only Son, who is in the bosom of the Father, he has made him known.

The Holy Name of Our Lord Jesus Christ   *January 1*

A Reading (Lesson) from the Book of Exodus [34:1-8]

The Lord said to Moses,"Cut two tables of stone like the
first; and I will write upon the tables the words that were
on the first tables, which you broke. Be ready in the
morning, and come up in the morning to Mount Sinai, and
present yourself there to me on the top of the mountain.
No man shall come up with you, and let no man be seen
throughout all the mountain; let no flocks or herds feed
before the mountain." So Moses cut two tables of stone
like the first; and he rose early in the morning and went up
on Mount Sinai, as the Lord had commanded him, and
took in his hand two tables of stone. And the Lord
descended in the cloud and stood with him there, and
proclaimed the name of the Lord. The Lord passed before
him, and proclaimed,"The Lord, the Lord, a God merciful
and gracious, slow to anger, and abounding in steadfast
love and faithfulness, keeping steadfast love for thousands,
forgiving iniquity and transgression and sin, but who will
by no means clear the guilty, visiting the iniquity of the
fathers upon the children and the children's children, to the
third and the fourth generation." And Moses made haste to
bow his head toward the earth, and worshiped.

Psalm 8 [page 592]

*A Reading (Lesson) from the Letter of Paul
to the Romans* [1:1-7]

Paul, a servant of Jesus Christ, called to be an apostle, set
apart for the gospel of God which he promised beforehand
through his prophets in the holy scriptures, the gospel
concerning his Son, who was descended from David
according to the flesh, and designated Son of God in power
according to the Spirit of holiness by his resurrection from
the dead, Jesus Christ our Lord, through whom we have

received grace and apostleship to bring about the obedience of faith for the sake of his name among all the nations, including yourselves who are called to belong to Jesus Christ; to all God's beloved in Rome, who are called to be saints: Grace to you and peace from God our Father and the Lord Jesus Christ.

✝ *The Holy Gospel of Our Lord Jesus Christ According to Luke* [2:15-21]

When the angels went away from them into heaven, the shepherds said to one another,"Let us go over to Bethlehem and see this thing that has happened, which the Lord has made known to us." And they went with haste, and found Mary and Joseph, and the babe lying in a manger. And when they saw it they made known the saying which had been told them concerning this child; and all who heard it wondered at what the shepherds told them. But Mary kept all these things, pondering them in her heart. And the shepherds returned, glorifying and praising God for all they had heard and seen, as it had been told them. And at the end of eight days, when he was circumcised, he was called Jesus, the name given by the angel before he was conceived in the womb.

Second Sunday after Christmas Day

A Reading (Lesson) from the Book of Jeremiah [31:7-14]

Thus says the Lord: "Sing aloud with gladness for Jacob, and raise shouts for the chief of the nations; proclaim, give praise, and say,'The Lord has saved his people, the remnant of Israel.'Behold, I will bring them from the north country, and gather them from the farthest parts of the earth, among them the blind and the lame, the woman with child and her who is in travail, together; a great company, they shall return here. With weeping they shall come, and with consolations I will lead them back, I will make them walk by brooks of water, in a straight path in which they shall not stumble; for I am a father to Israel, and E'phraim is my first-born. Hear the word of the Lord, O nations, and declare it in the coastlands afar off; say,'He who scattered Israel will gather him, and will keep him as a shepherd keeps his flock.' For the Lord has ransomed Jacob, and has redeemed him from hands too strong for him. They shall come and sing aloud on the height of Zion, and they shall be radiant over the goodness of the Lord, over the grain, the wine, and the oil, and over the young of the flock and the herd; their life shall be like a watered garden, and they shall languish no more. Then shall the maidens rejoice in the dance, and the young men and the old shall be merry. I will turn their mourning into joy, I will feast the soul of the priests with abundance, and my people shall be satisfied with my goodness, says the Lord."

Psalm 84 [page 707]   or   *84:1-8* [page 707]

A Reading (Lesson) from the Letter of Paul to the Ephesians [1:3-6, 15-19a]

Blessed be the God and Father of our Lord Jesus Christ, who has blessed us in Christ with every spiritual blessing in the heavenly places, even as he chose us in him before the foundation of the world, that we should be holy and blameless before him. He destined us in love to be his sons through Jesus Christ, according to the purpose of his will, to the praise of his glorious grace which he freely bestowed on us in the Beloved. For this reason, because I have heard of your faith in the Lord Jesus and your love toward all the saints, I do not cease to give thanks for you, remembering you in my prayers, that the God of our Lord Jesus Christ, the Father of glory, may give you a spirit of wisdom and revelation in the knowledge of him, having the eyes of your hearts enlightened, that you may know what is the hope to which he has called you, what are the riches of his glorious inheritance in the saints, and what is the immeasurable greatness of his power in us who believe.

✝ *The Holy Gospel of Our Lord Jesus Christ According to Matthew* [2:13-15, 19-23]

Now when the wise men had departed, behold, an angel of the Lord appeared to Joseph in a dream and said,"Rise, take the child and his mother, and flee to Egypt, and remain there till I tell you; for Herod is about to search for the child, to destroy him." And he rose and took the child and his mother by night, and departed to Egypt, and remained there until the death of Herod. This was to fulfill what the Lord had spoken by the prophet,"Out of Egypt have I called my son."But when Herod died, behold, an angel of the Lord appeared in a dream to Joseph in Egypt, saying,"Rise, take the child and his mother, and go to the land of Israel, for those who sought the child's life are dead."And he rose and took the child and his mother, and went to the land of Israel. But when he heard that Archela'us reigned over Judea in place of his father Herod, he was afraid to go there, and being warned in a dream he withdrew to the district of Galilee. And he went and dwelt in a city called Nazareth, that what was spoken by the prophets might be fulfilled,"He shall be called a Nazarene."

or this

✝ *The Holy Gospel of Our Lord Jesus Christ According to Luke* [2:41-52]

Now the parents of Jesus went to Jerusalem every year at the feast of the Passover. And when he was twelve years old, they went up according to custom; and when the feast was ended, as they were returning, the boy Jesus stayed behind in Jerusalem. His parents did not know it, but supposing him to be in the company they went a day's journey, and they sought him among their kinsfolk and acquaintances; and when they did not find him, they returned to Jerusalem, seeking him. After three days they found him in the temple, sitting among the teachers, listening to them and asking them questions; and all who heard him were amazed at his understanding and his answers. And when they saw him they were astonished; and his mother said to him, "Son, why have you treated us so? Behold, your father and I have been looking for you anxiously." And he said to them, "How is it that you sought me? Did you not know that I must be in my Father's house?" And they did not understand the saying which he spoke to them. And he went down with them and came to Nazareth, and was obedient to them; and his mother kept all these things in her heart. And Jesus increased in wisdom and in stature, and in favor with God and man.

or this

Matthew 2:1-12 [page 26 below]

The Epiphany   *January 6*

A Reading (Lesson) from the Book of Isaiah [60:1-6,9]

Arise, shine; for your light has come, and the glory of the Lord has risen upon you. For behold, darkness shall cover the earth, and thick darkness the peoples; but the Lord will arise upon you, and his glory will be seen upon you. And nations shall come to your light, and kings to the brightness of your rising. Lift up your eyes round about, and see; they all gather together, they come to you; your sons shall come from far, and your daughters shall be carried in the arms. Then you shall see and be radiant, your heart shall thrill and rejoice; because the abundance of the sea shall be turned to you, the wealth of the nations shall come to you. A multitude of camels shall cover you, the young camels of Mid'ian and Ephah; all those from Sheba shall come. They shall bring gold and frankincense, and shall proclaim the praise of the Lord. For the coastlands shall wait for me, the ships of Tarshish first, to bring your sons from far, their silver and gold with them, for the name of the Lord your God, and for the Holy One of Israel, because he has glorified you.

Psalm 72 [page 685] or *72:1-2, 10-17* [page 685]

A Reading (Lesson) from the Letter of Paul to the Ephesians [3:1-12]

I, Paul, a prisoner for Christ Jesus on behalf of you Gentiles, assume that you have heard of the stewardship of God's grace that was given to me for you, how the mystery was made known to me by revelation, as I have written briefly. When you read this you can perceive my insight into the mystery of Christ, which was not made known to the sons of men in other generations as it has now been revealed to his holy apostles and prophets by the Spirit; that is, how the Gentiles are fellow heirs, members of the same body, and partakers of the promise in Christ Jesus through the gospel. Of this gospel I was made a minister according to the gift of God's grace which was given me by the working of his power. To me, though I am the very least of all the saints, this grace was given, to preach to the Gentiles the unsearchable riches of Christ, and to make all men see what is the plan of the mystery hidden for ages in God who created all things; that through the church the manifold wisdom of God might now be made known to the principalities and powers in the heavenly places. This was according to the eternal purpose which he has realized in Christ Jesus our Lord, in whom we have boldness and confidence of access through our faith in him.

✝ *The Holy Gospel of Our Lord Jesus Christ*
According to Matthew [2:1-12]

Now when Jesus was born in Bethlehem of Judea in the days of Herod the king, behold, wise men from the East came to Jerusalem, saying, "Where is he who has been born king of the Jews? For we have seen his star in the East, and have come to worship him." When Herod the king heard this, he was troubled, and all Jerusalem with him; and assembling all the chief priests and scribes of the people, he inquired of them where the Christ was to be born. They told him, "In Bethlehem of Judea; for so it is written by the prophet: 'And you, O Bethlehem, in the land of Judah, are by no means least among the rulers of Judah; for from you shall come a ruler who will govern my people Israel.'" Then Herod summoned the wise men secretly and ascertained from them what time the star appeared; and he sent them to Bethlehem, saying, "Go and search diligently for the child, and when you have found him bring me word, that I too may come and worship him." When they had heard the king they went their way; and lo, the star which they had seen in the East went before them till it came to rest over the place where the child was. When they saw the star, they rejoiced exceedingly with great joy; and going into the house they saw the child with Mary his mother, and they fell down and worshiped him. Then, opening their treasures, they offered him gifts, gold and frankincense and myrrh. And being warned in a dream not to return to Herod, they departed to their own country by another way.

First Sunday after the Epiphany

A Reading (Lesson) from the Book of Isaiah [42:1-9]

Behold my servant, whom I uphold, my chosen, in whom my soul delights; I have put my Spirit upon him, he will bring forth justice to the nations. He will not cry or lift up his voice, or make it heard in the street; a bruised reed he will not break, and a dimly burning wick he will not quench; he will faithfully bring forth justice. He will not fail or be discouraged till he has established justice in the earth; and the coastlands wait for his law. Thus says God, the Lord, who created the heavens and stretched them out, who spread forth the earth and what comes from it, who gives breath to the people upon it and spirit to those who walk in it: "I am the Lord, I have called you in righteousness, I have taken you by the hand and kept you; I have given you as a covenant to the people, a light to the nations, to open the eyes that are blind, to bring out the prisoners from the dungeon, from the prison those who sit in darkness. I am the Lord, that is my name; my glory I give to no other, nor my praise to graven images. Behold, the former things have come to pass, and new things I now declare; before they spring forth, I tell you of them."

Psalm 89:1-29 [page 713]   or   *89:20-29* [page 715]

A Reading (Lesson) from the Acts of the Apostles [10:34-38]

Peter opened his mouth and said: "Truly I perceive that God shows no partiality, but in every nation any one who fears him and does what is right is acceptable to him. You know the word which he sent to Israel, preaching good news of peace by Jesus Christ (he is Lord of all), the word which was proclaimed throughout all Judea, beginning from Galilee after the baptism which John preached: how God anointed Jesus of Nazareth with the Holy Spirit and with power; how he went about doing good and healing all that were oppressed by the devil, for God was with him."

✝ *The Holy Gospel of Our Lord Jesus Christ*
According to Luke [3:15-16, 21-22]

As the people were in expectation, and all men questioned in their hearts concerning John, whether perhaps he were the Christ, John answered them all, "I baptize you with water; but he who is mightier than I is coming, the thong of whose sandals I am not worthy to untie; he will baptize you with the Holy Spirit and with fire." Now when all the people were baptized, and when Jesus also had been baptized and was praying, the heaven was opened, and the Holy Spirit descended upon him in bodily form, as a dove, and a voice came from heaven, "Thou art my beloved Son; with thee I am well pleased."

Second Sunday after the Epiphany

A Reading (Lesson) from the Book of Isaiah [62:1-5]

For Zion's sake I will not keep silent, and for Jerusalem's sake I will not rest, until her vindication goes forth as brightness, and her salvation as a burning torch. The nations shall see your vindication, and all the kings your glory; and you shall be called by a new name which the mouth of the Lord will give. You shall be a crown of beauty in the hand of the Lord, and a royal diadem in the hand of your God. You shall no more be termed "Forsaken," and your land shall no more be termed "Desolate"; but you shall be called "My delight is in her," and your land "Married"; for the Lord delights in you, and your land shall be married. For as a young man marries a virgin, so shall your sons marry you, and as the bridegroom rejoices over the bride, so shall your God rejoice over you.

Psalm 96 [page 725]   or   *96:1-10* [page 725]

*A Reading (Lesson) from the First Letter of Paul
to the Corinthians* [12:1-11]

Now concerning spiritual gifts, brethren, I do not want
you to be uninformed. You know that when you were
heathen, you were led astray to dumb idols, however you
may have been moved. Therefore I want you to understand
that no one speaking by the Spirit of God ever says "Jesus
be cursed!" and no one can say "Jesus is Lord" except by
the Holy Spirit. Now there are varieties of gifts, but the
same Spirit; and there are varieties of service, but the same
Lord; and there are varieties of working, but it is the same
God who inspires them all in every one. To each is given
the manifestation of the Spirit for the common good. To
one is given through the Spirit the utterance of wisdom,
and to another the utterance of knowledge according to
the same Spirit, to another faith by the same Spirit, to
another gifts of healing by the one Spirit, to another the
working of miracles, to another prophecy, to another the
ability to distinguish between spirits, to another various
kinds of tongues, to another the interpretation of tongues.
All these are inspired by one and the same Spirit, who
apportions to each one individually as he wills.

✝ *The Holy Gospel of Our Lord Jesus Christ
According to John* [2:1-11]

On the third day there was a marriage at Cana in Galilee,
and the mother of Jesus was there; Jesus also was invited to
the marriage, with his disciples. When the wine gave out,
the mother of Jesus said to him,"They have no wine." And
Jesus said to her,"O woman, what have you to do with
me? My hour has not yet come." His mother said to the
servants,"Do whatever he tells you." Now six stone jars
were standing there, for the Jewish rites of purification,
each holding twenty or thirty gallons. Jesus said to
them,"Fill the jars with water." And they filled them up to

the brim. He said to them,"Now draw some out, and take it to the steward of the feast." So they took it. When the steward of the feast tasted the water now become wine, and did not know where it came from (though the servants who had drawn the water knew), the steward of the feast called the bridegroom and said to him,"Every man serves the good wine first; and when men have drunk freely, then the poor wine; but you have kept the good wine until now." This, the first of his signs, Jesus did at Cana in Galilee, and manifested his glory; and his disciples believed in him.

Third Sunday after the Epiphany

A Reading (Lesson) from the Book of Nehemiah [8:2-10]

Ezra the priest brought the law before the assembly, both men and women and all who could hear with understanding, on the first day of the seventh month. And he read from it facing the square before the Water Gate from early morning until midday, in the presence of the men and the women and those who could understand; and the ears of all the people were attentive to the book of the law. And Ezra the scribe stood on a wooden pulpit which they had made for the purpose; and beside him stood six elders [*Mattithi'ah, Shema, Anai'ah, Uri'ah, Hilki'ah, and Maasei'ah*] on his right hand; and seven others [*Peda'iah, Mish'a-el, Malchi'jah, Hashum, Hashbad'danah, Zechari'ah, and Meshul' lam*] on his left hand. And Ezra opened the book in the sight of all the people, for he was above all the people; and when he opened it all the people stood. And Ezra blessed the Lord, the great God; and all the people answered, "Amen, Amen," lifting up their hands; and they bowed their heads and worshiped the Lord with their faces to the ground. Also [*Jeshua, Bani, Sherebi'ah, Jamin, Akkub, Shab'bethai, Hodi'ah, Ma-asei'ah, Keli'ta,*

Azari'ah, Jo'zabad, Hanan, Pelai'ah] the Levites helped the people to understand the law, while the people remained in their places. And they read from the book, from the law of God, clearly; and they gave the sense, so that the people understood the reading. And Nehemi'ah, who was the governor, and Ezra the priest and scribe, and the Levites who taught the people said to all the people, "This day is holy to the Lord your God; do not mourn or weep." For all the people wept when they heard the words of the law. Then he said to them, "Go your way, eat the fat and drink sweet wine and send portions to him for whom nothing is prepared; for this day is holy to our Lord; and do not be grieved, for the joy of the Lord is your strength."

Psalm 113 [page 756]

A Reading (Lesson) from the First Letter of Paul to the Corinthians [12:12-27]

Just as the body is one and has many members, and all the members of the body, though many, are one body, so it is with Christ. For by one Spirit we were all baptized into one body—Jews or Greeks, slaves or free—and all were made to drink of one Spirit. For the body does not consist of one member but of many. If the foot should say, "Because I am not a hand, I do not belong to the body," that would not make it any less a part of the body. And if the ear should say, "Because I am not an eye, I do not belong to the body," that would not make it any less a part of the body. If the whole body were an eye, where would be the hearing? If the whole body were an ear, where would be the sense of smell? But as it is, God arranged the organs in the body, each one of them, as he chose. If all were a single organ, where would the body be? As it is, there are many parts, yet one body. The eye cannot say to the hand, "I have no need of you," nor again the head to the feet, "I have no need of you." On the contrary, the parts of the body which seem to be weaker are indispensable, and those parts of the body which we think less honorable we invest with the greater honor, and our unpresentable parts are treated with greater modesty, which our more presentable parts do not require. But God has so composed the body, giving the greater honor to the inferior part, that there may be no discord in the body, but that the members may have the same care for one another. If one member suffers, all suffer together; if one member is honored, all rejoice together. Now you are the body of Christ and individually members of it.

✠ *The Holy Gospel of Our Lord Jesus Christ According to Luke* [4:14-21]

Jesus returned in the power of the Spirit into Galilee, and a report concerning him went out through all the surrounding country. And he taught in their synagogues, being glorified by all. And he came to Nazareth, where he had been brought up; and he went to the synagogue, as his custom was, on the sabbath day. And he stood up to read; and there was given to him the book of the prophet Isaiah. He opened the book and found the place where it was written,"The Spirit of the Lord is upon me, because he has anointed me to preach good news to the poor. He has sent me to proclaim release to the captives and recovering of sight to the blind, to set at liberty those who are oppressed, to proclaim the acceptable year of the Lord." And he closed the book, and gave it back to the attendant, and sat down; and the eyes of all in the synagogue were fixed on him. And he began to say to them,"Today this scripture has been fulfilled in your hearing."

Fourth Sunday after the Epiphany

A Reading (Lesson) from the Book of Jeremiah [1:4-10]

The word of the Lord came to me, saying, "Before I formed you in the womb I knew you, and before you were born I consecrated you; I appointed you a prophet to the nations." Then I said, "Ah, Lord God! Behold, I do not know how to speak, for I am only a youth." But the Lord said to me, "Do not say, 'I am only a youth'; for to all to whom I send you you shall go, and whatever I command you you shall speak. Be not afraid of them, for I am with you to deliver you, says the Lord." Then the Lord put forth his hand and touched my mouth; and the Lord said to me, "Behold, I have put my words in your mouth. See, I have set you this day over nations and over kingdoms, to pluck up and to break down, to destroy and to overthrow, to build and to plant."

Psalm 71:1-17 [page 683]   or   *71:1-6, 15-17* [page 683]

A Reading (Lesson) from the First Letter of Paul to the Corinthians [14:12b-20]

Since you are eager for manifestations of the Spirit, strive to excel in building up the church. Therefore, he who speaks in a tongue should pray for the power to interpret. For if I pray in a tongue, my spirit prays but my mind is unfruitful. What am I to do? I will pray with the spirit and I will pray with the mind also; I will sing with the spirit and I will sing with the mind also. Otherwise, if you bless with the spirit, how can any one in the position of an outsider say the "Amen" to your thanksgiving when he does not know what you are saying? For you may give thanks well enough, but the other man is not edified. I thank God that I speak in tongues more than you all; nevertheless, in church I would rather speak five words with my mind, in order to instruct others, than ten thousand words in a tongue. Brethren, do not be children in your thinking; be babes in evil, but in thinking be mature.

✝ *The Holy Gospel of Our Lord Jesus Christ According to Luke* [4:21-32]

In the synagogue at Nazareth, Jesus read from the book of the prophet Isaiah, and began to say, "Today this scripture has been fulfilled in your hearing." And all spoke well of him, and wondered at the gracious words which proceeded out of his mouth; and they said, "Is not this Joseph's son?" And he said to them, "Doubtless you will quote to me this proverb, 'Physician, heal yourself; what we have heard you did at Caper'na-um, do here also in your own country.'" And he said, "Truly, I say to you, no prophet is acceptable in his own country. But in truth, I tell you, there were many widows in Israel in the days of Eli'jah, when the heaven was shut up three years and six months, when there came a great famine over all the land; and Eli'jah was sent to none of them but only to Zar'ephath, in the land of Sidon, to a woman who was a widow. And there were many lepers in Israel in the time of the prophet Eli'sha; and none of them was cleansed, but only Na'aman the Syrian." When they heard this, all in the synagogue were filled with wrath. And they rose up and put him out of the city, and led him to the brow of the hill on which their city was built, that they might throw him down headlong. But passing through the midst of them he went away. And he went down to Caper'na-um, a city of Galilee. And he was teaching them on the sabbath; and they were astonished at his teaching, for his word was with authority.

Fifth Sunday after the Epiphany

A Reading (Lesson) from the Book of Judges [6:11-24a]

The angel of the Lord came and sat under the oak at
Ophrah, which belonged to Jo'ash the Abiez'rite, as his son
Gideon was beating out wheat in the wine press, to hide it
from the Mid'ianites. And the angel of the Lord appeared
to him and said to him, "The Lord is with you, you mighty
man of valor." And Gideon said to him, "Pray, sir, if the
Lord is with us, why then has all this befallen us? And
where are all his wonderful deeds which our fathers
recounted to us, saying, 'Did not the Lord bring us up from
Egypt?' But now the Lord has cast us off, and given us into
the hand of Mid'ian." And the Lord turned to him and
said, "Go in this might of yours and deliver Israel from the
hand of Mid'ian; do not I send you?" And he said to
him, "Pray, Lord, how can I deliver Israel? Behold, my clan
is the weakest in Manas'seh, and I am the least in my
family." And the Lord said to him, "But I will be with you,
and you shall smite the Mid'ianites as one man." And he
said to him, "If now I have found favor with thee, then
show me a sign that it is thou who speakest with me. Do
not depart from here, I pray thee, until I come to thee, and
bring out my present, and set it before thee." And he
said, "I will stay till you return." So Gideon went into his
house and prepared a kid, and unleavened cakes from an
ephah of flour; the meat he put in a basket, and the broth
he put in a pot, and brought them to him under the oak
and presented them. And the angel of God said to
him, "Take the meat and the unleavened cakes, and put
them on this rock, and pour the broth over them." And he
did so. Then the angel of the Lord reached out the tip of the
staff that was in his hand, and touched the meat and the
unleavened cakes; and there sprang up fire from the rock
and consumed the flesh and the unleavened cakes; and the
angel of the Lord vanished from his sight. Then Gideon

perceived that he was the angel of the Lord; and Gideon said,"Alas, O Lord God! For now I have seen the angel of the Lord face to face."But the Lord said to him,"Peace be to you; do not fear, you shall not die."Then Gideon built an altar there to the Lord, and called it, The Lord is peace.

Psalm 85 [page 708] or *85:7-13* [page 709]

A Reading (Lesson) from the First Letter of Paul to the Corinthians [15:1-11]

I would remind you, brethren, in what terms I preached to you the gospel, which you received, in which you stand, by which you are saved, if you hold it fast—unless you believed in vain. For I delivered to you as of first importance what I also received, that Christ died for our sins in accordance with the scriptures, that he was buried, that he was raised on the third day in accordance with the scriptures, and that he appeared to Cephas, then to the twelve. Then he appeared to more than five hundred brethren at one time, most of whom are still alive, though some have fallen asleep. Then he appeared to James, then to all the apostles. Last of all, as to one untimely born, he appeared also to me. For I am the least of the apostles, unfit to be called an apostle, because I persecuted the church of God. But by the grace of God I am what I am, and his grace toward me was not in vain. On the contrary, I worked harder than any of them, though it was not I, but the grace of God which is with me. Whether then it was I or they, so we preach and so you believed.

✝ *The Holy Gospel of Our Lord Jesus Christ According to Luke* [5:1-11]

While the people pressed upon Jesus to hear the word of God, he was standing by the lake of Gennes'aret. And he saw two boats by the lake; but the fishermen had gone out of them and were washing their nets. Getting into one of the boats, which was Simon's, he asked him to put out a little from the land. And he sat down and taught the people from the boat. And when he had ceased speaking, he said to Simon, "Put out into the deep and let down your nets for a catch." And Simon answered, "Master, we toiled all night and took nothing! But at your word I will let down the nets." And when they had done this, they enclosed a great shoal of fish; and as their nets were breaking, they beckoned to their partners in the other boat to come and help them. And they came and filled both the boats, so that they began to sink. But when Simon Peter saw it, he fell down at Jesus' knees, saying, "Depart from me, for I am a sinful man, O Lord." For he was astonished, and all that were with him, at the catch of fish which they had taken; and so also were James and John, sons of Zeb'edee, who were partners with Simon. And Jesus said to Simon, "Do not be afraid; henceforth you will be catching men." And when they had brought their boats to land, they left everything and followed him.

Sixth Sunday after the Epiphany

A Reading (Lesson) from the Book of Jeremiah [17:5-10]

Thus says the Lord: "Cursed is the man who trusts in man and makes flesh his arm, whose heart turns away from the Lord. He is like a shrub in the desert, and shall not see any good come. He shall dwell in the parched places of the wilderness, in an uninhabited salt land. Blessed is the man who trusts in the Lord, whose trust is the Lord. He is like a tree planted by water, that sends out its roots by the stream, and does not fear when heat comes, for its leaves remain green, and is not anxious in the year of drought, for it does not cease to bear fruit." The heart is deceitful above all things, and desperately corrupt; who can understand it?

"I the Lord search the mind and try the heart, to give to every man according to his ways, according to the fruit of his doings."

Psalm 1 [page 585]

A Reading (Lesson) from the First Letter of Paul to the Corinthians [15:12-20]

Now if Christ is preached as raised from the dead, how can some of you say that there is no resurrection of the dead? But if there is no resurrection of the dead, then Christ has not been raised; if Christ has not been raised, then our preaching is in vain and your faith is in vain. We are even found to be misrepresenting God, because we testified of God that he raised Christ, whom he did not raise if it is true that the dead are not raised. For if the dead are not raised, then Christ has not been raised. If Christ has not been raised, your faith is futile and you are still in your sins. Then those also who have fallen asleep in Christ have perished. If for this life only we have hoped in Christ, we are of all men most to be pitied. But in fact Christ has been raised from the dead, the first fruits of those who have fallen asleep.

✝ *The Holy Gospel of Our Lord Jesus Christ According to Luke* [6:17-26]

Jesus came down with the twelve apostles, and stood on a level place, with a great crowd of his disciples and a great multitude of people from all Judea and Jerusalem and the seacoast of Tyre and Sidon, who came to hear him and to be healed of their diseases; and those who were troubled with unclean spirits were cured. And all the crowd sought to touch him, for power came forth from him and healed them all. And he lifted up his eyes on his disciples, and said: "Blessed are you poor, for yours is the kingdom of God.

Blessed are you that hunger now, for you shall be satisfied. Blessed are you that weep now, for you shall laugh. Blessed are you when men hate you, and when they exclude you and revile you, and cast out your name as evil, on account of the Son of man! Rejoice in that day, and leap for joy, for behold, your reward is great in heaven; for so their fathers did to the prophets. But woe to you that are rich, for you have received your consolation. Woe to you that are full now, for you shall hunger. Woe to you that laugh now, for you shall mourn and weep. Woe to you, when all men speak well of you, for so their fathers did to the false prophets."

Seventh Sunday after the Epiphany

A Reading (Lesson) from the Book of Genesis
[45:3-11, 21-28]

And Joseph said to his brothers, "I am Joseph; is my father still alive?" But his brothers could not answer him, for they were dismayed at his presence. So Joseph said to his brothers, "Come near to me, I pray you." And they came near. And he said, "I am your brother, Joseph, whom you sold into Egypt. And now do not be distressed, or angry with yourselves, because you sold me here; for God sent me before you to preserve life. For the famine has been in the land these two years; and there are yet five years in which there will be neither plowing nor harvest. And God sent me before you to preserve for you a remnant on earth, and to keep alive for you many survivors. So it was not you who sent me here, but God; and he has made me a father to Pharaoh, and lord of all his house and ruler over all the land of Egypt. Make haste and go up to my father and say to him, 'Thus says your son Joseph, God has made me lord of all Egypt; come down to me, do not tarry; you shall dwell in the land of Goshen, and you shall be near me, you

and your children and your children's children, and your
flocks, your herds, and all that you have; and there I will
provide for you, for there are yet five years of famine to
come; lest you and your household, and all that you have,
come to poverty.'" The sons of Israel did so; and Joseph
gave them wagons, according to the command of Pharaoh,
and gave them provisions for the journey. To each and all
of them he gave festal garments; but to Benjamin he gave
three hundred shekels of silver and five festal garments. To
his father he sent as follows: ten asses loaded with the good
things of Egypt, and ten she-asses loaded with grain, bread,
and provision for his father on the journey. Then he sent
his brothers away, and as they departed, he said to them,
"Do not quarrel on the way." So they went up out of
Egypt, and came to the land of Canaan to their father
Jacob. And they told him,"Joseph is still alive, and he is
ruler over all the land of Egypt." And his heart fainted, for
he did not believe them. But when they told him all the
words of Joseph, which he had said to them, and when he
saw the wagons which Joseph had sent to carry him, the
spirit of their father Jacob revived; and Israel said,"It is
enough; Joseph my son is still alive; I will go and see him
before I die."

Psalm 37:1-18 [page 633]   or   *37:3-10* [page 633]

*A Reading (Lesson) from the First Letter of Paul
to the Corinthians* [15:35-38, 42-50]

But some one will ask,"How are the dead raised? With
what kind of body do they come?" You foolish man! What
you sow does not come to life unless it dies. And what you
sow is not the body which is to be, but a bare kernel,
perhaps of wheat or of some other grain. But God gives it
a body as he has chosen, and to each kind of seed its own
body. So is it with the resurrection of the dead. What is
sown is perishable, what is raised is imperishable. It is

sown in dishonor, it is raised in glory. It is sown in weakness, it is raised in power. It is sown a physical body, it is raised a spiritual body. If there is a physical body, there is also a spiritual body. Thus it is written, "The first man Adam became a living being"; the last Adam became a life-giving spirit. But it is not the spiritual which is first but the physical, and then the spiritual. The first man was from the earth, a man of dust; the second man is from heaven. As was the man of dust, so are those who are of the dust; and as is the man of heaven, so are those who are of heaven. Just as we have borne the image of the man of dust, we shall also bear the image of the man of heaven. I tell you this, brethren: flesh and blood cannot inherit the kingdom of God, nor does the perishable inherit the imperishable.

✝ *The Holy Gospel of Our Lord Jesus Christ According to Luke* [6:27-38]

Jesus said, "I say to you that hear, Love your enemies, do good to those who hate you, bless those who curse you, pray for those who abuse you. To him who strikes you on the cheek, offer the other also; and from him who takes away your coat do not withhold even your shirt. Give to every one who begs from you; and of him who takes away your goods do not ask them again. And as you wish that men would do to you, do so to them. If you love those who love you, what credit is that to you? For even sinners love those who love them. And if you do good to those who do good to you, what credit is that to you? For even sinners do the same. And if you lend to those from whom you hope to receive, what credit is that to you? Even sinners lend to sinners, to receive as much again. But love your enemies, and do good, and lend, expecting nothing in return; and your reward will be great, and you will be sons of the Most High; for he is kind to the ungrateful and the selfish. Be merciful, even as your Father is merciful. Judge not, and you will not be judged; condemn not, and you will not be condemned; forgive, and you will be forgiven; give, and it will be given to you; good measure, pressed down, shaken together, running over, will be put into your lap. For the measure you give will be the measure you get back."

Eighth Sunday after the Epiphany

A Reading (Lesson) from the Book of Jeremiah [7:1-7(8-15)]

The word that came to Jeremiah from the Lord: "Stand in the gate of the Lord's house, and proclaim there this word, and say, Hear the word of the Lord, all you men of Judah who enter these gates to worship the Lord. Thus says the Lord of hosts, the God of Israel, Amend your ways and your doings, and I will let you dwell in this place. Do not trust in these deceptive words: 'This is the temple of the Lord, the temple of the Lord, the temple of the Lord.' For if you truly amend your ways and your doings, if you truly execute justice one with another, if you do not oppress the alien, the fatherless or the widow, or shed innocent blood in this place, and if you do not go after other gods to your own hurt, then I will let you dwell in this place, in the land that I gave of old to your fathers for ever."

"Behold, you trust in deceptive words to no avail. Will you steal, murder, commit adultery, swear falsely, burn incense to Ba'al, and go after other gods that you have not known, and then come and stand before me in this house, which is called by my name, and say, 'We are delivered!'—only to go on doing all these abominations? Has this house, which is called by my name, become a den of robbers in your eyes? Behold, I myself have seen it, says the Lord. Go now to my place that was in Shiloh, where I made my name dwell at first, and see what I did to it for the wickedness of my people Israel. And now, because you have done all these things, says the Lord, and when I spoke to you persistently you did not listen, and when I called you, you did not answer, therefore I will do to the house which is called by my name, and in which you trust, and to the place which I gave to you and to your fathers, as I did to Shiloh. And I will cast you out of my sight, as I cast out all your kinsmen, all the offspring of E'phraim."

Psalm 92 [page 720] or *92:1-5, 11-14* [page 720]

A Reading (Lesson) from the First Letter of Paul to the Corinthians [15:50-58]

I tell you this, brethren: flesh and blood cannot inherit the kingdom of God, nor does the perishable inherit the imperishable. Lo! I tell you a mystery. We shall not all sleep, but we shall all be changed, in a moment, in the twinkling of an eye, at the last trumpet. For the trumpet will sound, and the dead will be raised imperishable, and we shall be changed. For this perishable nature must put on the imperishable, and this mortal nature must put on immortality. When the perishable puts on the imperishable, and the mortal puts on immortality, then shall come to pass the saying that is written: "Death is swallowed up in victory." "O death, where is thy victory? O death, where is thy sting?" The sting of death is sin, and the power of sin is the law. But thanks be to God, who gives us the victory through our Lord Jesus Christ. Therefore, my beloved brethren, be steadfast, immovable, always abounding in the work of the Lord, knowing that in the Lord your labor is not in vain.

✝ *The Holy Gospel of Our Lord Jesus Christ According to Luke* [6:39-49]

Jesus told the people a parable: "Can a blind man lead a blind man? Will they not both fall into a pit? A disciple is not above his teacher, but every one when he is fully taught will be like his teacher. Why do you see the speck that is in your brother's eye, but do not notice the log that is in your own eye? Or how can you say to your brother, 'Brother, let me take out the speck that is in your eye,' when you yourself do not see the log that is in your own eye? You hypocrite, first take the log out of your own eye, and then you will see clearly to take out the speck that is in your brother's eye. For no good tree bears bad fruit, nor again does a bad tree bear good fruit; for each tree is known by its own fruit. For figs are not gathered from thorns, nor are grapes picked from a bramble bush. The good man out of the good treasure of his heart produces good, and the evil man out of his evil treasure produces evil; for out of the abundance of the heart his mouth speaks. Why do you call me 'Lord, Lord,' and not do what I tell you? Every one who comes to me and hears my words and does them, I will show you what he is like: he is like a man building a house, who dug deep, and laid the foundation upon rock; and when a flood arose, the stream broke against that house, and could not shake it, because it had been well built. But he who hears and does not do them is like a man who built a house on the ground without a foundation; against which the stream broke, and immediately it fell, and the ruin of that house was great."

Last Sunday after the Epiphany

A Reading (Lesson) from the Book of Exodus [34:29-35]

When Moses came down from Mount Sinai, with the two tables of the testimony in his hand as he came down from the mountain, Moses did not know that the skin of his face shone because he had been talking with God. And when Aaron and all the people of Israel saw Moses, behold, the skin of his face shone, and they were afraid to come near him. But Moses called to them; and Aaron and all the leaders of the congregation returned to him, and Moses talked with them. And afterward all the people of Israel came near, and he gave them in commandment all that the Lord had spoken with him in Mount Sinai. And when Moses had finished speaking with them, he put a veil on his face; but whenever Moses went in before the Lord to speak with him, he took the veil off, until he came out; and when he came out, and told the people of Israel what he was commanded, the people of Israel saw the face of Moses, that the skin of Moses' face shone; and Moses would put the veil upon his face again, until he went in to speak with him.

Psalm 99 [page 728]

A Reading (Lesson) from the First Letter of Paul to the Corinthians [12:27—13:13]

Now you are the body of Christ and individually members of it. And God has appointed in the church first apostles, second prophets, third teachers, then workers of miracles, then healers, helpers, administrators, speakers in various kinds of tongues. Are all apostles? Are all prophets? Are all teachers? Do all work miracles? Do all possess gifts of healing? Do all speak with tongues? Do all interpret? But earnestly desire the higher gifts. And I will show you a still more excellent way. If I speak in the tongues of men and of angels, but have not love, I am a noisy gong or a clanging cymbal. And if I have prophetic powers, and understand all mysteries and all knowledge, and if I have all faith, so as to remove mountains, but have not love, I am nothing. If I give away all I have, and if I deliver my body to be burned, but have not love, I gain nothing. Love is patient and kind; love is not jealous or boastful; it is not arrogant or rude. Love does not insist on its own way; it is not irritable or resentful; it does not rejoice at wrong, but rejoices in the right. Love bears all things, believes all things, hopes all things, endures all things. Love never ends; as for prophecies, they will pass away; as for tongues, they will cease; as for knowledge, it will pass away. For our knowledge is imperfect and our prophecy is imperfect; but when the perfect comes, the imperfect will pass away. When I was a child, I spoke like a child, I thought like a child, I reasoned like a child; when I became a man, I gave up childish ways. For now we see in a mirror dimly, but then face to face. Now I know in part; then I shall understand fully, even as I have been fully understood. So faith, hope, love abide, these three; but the greatest of these is love.

✝ *The Holy Gospel of Our Lord Jesus Christ According to Luke* [9:28-36]

About eight days after Peter had acknowledged Jesus as the Christ of God, Jesus took with him Peter and John and James, and went up on the mountain to pray. And as he was praying, the appearance of his countenance was altered, and his raiment became dazzling white. And behold, two men talked with him, Moses and Eli'jah, who appeared in glory and spoke of his departure, which he was to accomplish at Jerusalem. Now Peter and those who were with him were heavy with sleep, and when they wakened they saw his glory and the two men who stood with him. And as the men were parting from him, Peter said to Jesus, "Master, it is well that we are here; let us make three booths, one for you and one for Moses and one for Eli'jah"—not knowing what he said. As he said this, a cloud came and overshadowed them; and they were afraid as they entered the cloud. And a voice came out of the cloud, saying, "This is my Son, my Chosen; listen to him!" And when the voice had spoken, Jesus was found alone. And they kept silence and told no one in those days anything of what they had seen.

Ash Wednesday

A Reading (Lesson) from the Book of Joel [2:1-2,12-17]

Blow the trumpet in Zion; sound the alarm on my holy mountain! Let all the inhabitants of the land tremble, for the day of the Lord is coming, it is near, a day of darkness and gloom, a day of clouds and thick darkness! Like blackness there is spread upon the mountains a great and powerful people; their like has never been from of old, nor will be again after them through the years of all generations. "Yet even now," says the Lord, "return to me with all your heart, with fasting, with weeping, and with mourning; and rend your hearts and not your garments." Return to the Lord, your God, for he is gracious and merciful, slow to anger, and abounding in steadfast love, and repents of evil. Who knows whether he will not turn and repent, and leave a blessing behind him, a cereal offering and a drink offering for the Lord, your God? Blow the trumpet in Zion; sanctify a fast; call a solemn assembly; gather the people. Sanctify the congregation; assemble the elders; gather the children, even nursing infants. Let the bridegroom leave his room, and the bride her chamber. Between the vestibule and the altar let the priests, the ministers of the Lord, weep and say, "Spare thy people, O Lord, and make not thy heritage a reproach, a byword among the nations. Why should they say among the peoples, 'Where is their God?'"

or this

A Reading (Lesson) from the Book of Isaiah [58:1-12]

Thus says the high and lofty One who inhabits eternity, whose name is Holy: "Cry aloud, spare not, lift up your voice like a trumpet; declare to my people their transgression, to the house of Jacob their sins. Yet they seek me daily, and delight to know my ways, as if they were a nation that did righteousness and did not forsake the ordinance of their God; they ask of me righteous judgments, they delight to draw near to God. 'Why have we fasted, and thou seest it not? Why have we humbled ourselves, and thou takest no knowledge of it?' Behold, in the day of your fast you seek your own pleasure, and oppress all your workers. Behold, you fast only to quarrel and to fight and to hit with wicked fist. Fasting like yours this day will not make your voice to be heard on high. Is such the fast that I choose, a day for a man to humble himself? Is it to bow down his head like a rush, and to spread sackcloth and ashes under him? Will you call this a fast, and a day acceptable to the Lord? Is not this the fast that I choose: to loose the bonds of wickedness, to undo the thongs of the yoke, to let the oppressed go free, and to break every yoke? Is it not to share your bread with the hungry, and bring the homeless poor into your house; when you see the naked, to cover him, and not to hide yourself from your own flesh? Then shall your light break forth like the dawn, and your healing shall spring up speedily; your righteousness shall go before you, the glory of the Lord shall be your rear guard. Then you shall call, and the Lord will answer; you shall cry, and he will say, Here I am. If you take away from the midst of you the yoke, the pointing of the finger, and speaking wickedness, if you pour yourself out for the hungry and satisfy the desire of the afflicted, then shall your light rise in the darkness and your gloom be as the noonday. And the Lord will guide you continually, and satisfy your desire with good things, and make your bones strong; and you shall be like a watered garden, like a spring of water, whose waters fail not. And your ancient ruins shall be rebuilt; you shall raise up the foundations of many generations; you shall be called the repairer of the breach, the restorer of streets to dwell in."

Psalm 103 [page 733] or *103:8-14* [page 733]

*A Reading (Lesson) from the Second Letter of Paul
to the Corinthians* [5:20b—6:10]

We beseech you on behalf of Christ, be reconciled to God.
For our sake he made him to be sin who knew no sin, so
that in him we might become the righteousness of God.
Working together with him, then, we entreat you not to
accept the grace of God in vain. For he says, "At the
acceptable time I have listened to you, and helped you on
the day of salvation." Behold, now is the acceptable time;
behold, now is the day of salvation. We put no obstacle in
any one's way, so that no fault may be found with our
ministry, but as servants of God we commend ourselves in
every way: through great endurance, in afflictions,
hardships, calamities, beatings, imprisonments, tumults,
labors, watching, hunger; by purity, knowledge,
forbearance, kindness, the Holy Spirit, genuine love,
truthful speech, and the power of God; with the weapons
of righteousness for the right hand and for the left; in
honor and dishonor, in ill repute and good repute. We are
treated as impostors, and yet are true; as unknown, and yet
well known; as dying, and behold we live; as punished,
and yet not killed; as sorrowful, yet always rejoicing; as
poor, yet making many rich; as having nothing, and yet
possessing everything.

✝ *The Holy Gospel of Our Lord Jesus Christ
According to Matthew* [6:1-6,16-21]

Jesus said, "Beware of practicing your piety before men in
order to be seen by them; for then you will have no reward
from your Father who is in heaven. Thus, when you give
alms, sound no trumpet before you, as the hypocrites do in
the synagogues and in the streets, that they may be praised
by men. Truly, I say to you, they have received their

reward. But when you give alms, do not let your left hand know what your right hand is doing, so that your alms may be in secret; and your Father who sees in secret will reward you. And when you pray, you must not be like the hypocrites; for they love to stand and pray in the synagogues and at the street corners, that they may be seen by men. Truly, I say to you, they have received their reward. But when you pray, go into your room and shut the door and pray to your Father who is in secret; and your Father who sees in secret will reward you. And when you fast, do not look dismal, like the hypocrites, for they disfigure their faces that their fasting may be seen by men. Truly, I say to you, they have received their reward. But when you fast, anoint your head and wash your face, that your fasting may not be seen by men but by your Father who is in secret; and your Father who sees in secret will reward you. Do not lay up for yourselves treasures on earth, where moth and rust consume and where thieves break in and steal, but lay up for yourselves treasure in heaven, where neither moth nor rust consumes and where thieves do not break in and steal. For where your treasure is, there will your heart be also."

First Sunday in Lent

A Reading (Lesson) from the Book of Deuteronomy
[26:(1-4) 5-11]

These are the words that Moses spoke to all Israel: "When you come into the land which the Lord your God gives you for an inheritance, and have taken possession of it, and live in it, you shall take some of the first of all the fruit of the ground, which you harvest from your land that the Lord your God gives you, and you shall put it in a basket, and you shall go to the place which the Lord your God will choose, to make his name to dwell there. And you shall go to the priest who is in office at that time, and say to him, 'I declare this day to the Lord your God that I have come into the land which the Lord swore to our fathers to give us.' Then the priest shall take the basket from your hand, and set it down before the altar of the Lord your God. And you shall make response before the Lord your God,

[*Moses said these words to all Israel: "Thus you shall say. when you present the first-fruits to the Lord your God:*]
'A wandering Aramean was my father; and he went down into Egypt and sojourned there, few in number; and there he became a nation, great, mighty, and populous. And the Egyptians treated us harshly, and afflicted us, and laid upon us hard bondage. Then we cried to the Lord the God of our fathers, and the Lord heard our voice, and saw our affliction, our toil, and our oppression; and the Lord brought us out of Egypt with a mighty hand and an outstretched arm, with great terror, with signs and wonders; and he brought us into this place and gave us this land, a land flowing with milk and honey. And behold, now I bring the first of the fruit of the ground, which thou, O Lord, hast given me.' And you shall set it down before the Lord your God, and worship before the Lord your God; and you shall rejoice in all the good which the Lord your God has given to you and to your house, you, and the Levite, and the sojourner who is among you."

Psalm 91 [page 719]   or   *91:9-15* [page 720]

A Reading (Lesson) from the Letter of Paul to the Romans [10:(5-8a)8b-13]

Moses writes that the man who practices the righteousness which is based on the law shall live by it. But the righteousness based on faith says, Do not say in your heart, "Who will ascend into heaven?" (that is, to bring Christ down), or "Who will descend into the abyss?" (that is, to bring Christ up from the dead). But what does it say?

The word is near you, on your lips and in your heart (that is, the word of faith which we preach); because, if you confess with your lips that Jesus is Lord and believe in your heart that God raised him from the dead, you will be saved. For man believes with his heart and so is justified, and he confesses with his lips and so is saved. The scripture says, "No one who believes in him will be put to shame." For there is no distinction between Jew and Greek; the same Lord is Lord of all and bestows his riches upon all who call upon him. For, "Every one who calls upon the name of the Lord will be saved."

✝ *The Holy Gospel of Our Lord Jesus Christ*
According to Luke [4:1-13]

After his baptism, Jesus, full of the Holy Spirit, returned from the Jordan, and was led by the Spirit for forty days in the wilderness, tempted by the devil. And he ate nothing in those days; and when they were ended, he was hungry. The devil said to him, "If you are the Son of God, command this stone to become bread." And Jesus answered him, "It is written, 'Man shall not live by bread alone.'" And the devil took him up, and showed him all the kingdoms of the world in a moment of time, and said to him, "To you I will give all this authority and their glory; for it has been delivered to me, and I give it to whom I will. If you, then, will worship me, it shall all be yours." And Jesus answered him, "It is written, 'You shall worship the Lord your God, and him only shall you serve.'" And he took him to Jerusalem, and set him on the pinnacle of the temple, and said to him, "If you are the Son of God, throw yourself down from here; for it is written, 'He will give his angels charge of you, to guard you,' and 'On their hands they will

bear you up, lest you strike your foot against a stone.'"
And Jesus answered him, "It is said, 'You shall not tempt
the Lord your God.'" And when the devil had ended every
temptation, he departed from him until an opportune time.

Second Sunday in Lent

A Reading (Lesson) from the Book of Genesis [15:1-12, 17-18]

The word of the Lord came to Abram in a vision, "Fear not,
Abram, I am your shield; your reward shall be very great."
But Abram said, "O Lord God, what wilt thou give me, for
I continue childless, and the heir of my house is Elie'zer of
Damascus?" And Abram said, "Behold, thou hast given me
no offspring; and a slave born in my house will be my
heir." And behold, the word of the Lord came to him, "This
man shall not be your heir; your own son shall be your
heir." And he brought him outside and said, "Look toward
heaven, and number the stars, if you are able to number
them." Then he said to him, "So shall your descendants
be." And he believed the Lord and he reckoned it to him as
righteousness. And he said to him, "I am the Lord who
brought you from Ur of the Chalde'ans, to give you this
land to possess." But he said, "O Lord God, how am I to
know that I shall possess it?" He said to him, "Bring me a
heifer three years old, a she-goat three years old, a ram
three years old, a turtledove, and a young pigeon." And he
brought him all these, cut them in two, and laid each half
over against the other; but he did not cut the birds in two.
And when birds of prey came down upon the carcasses,
Abram drove them away. As the sun was going down, a
deep sleep fell on Abram; and lo, a dread and great
darkness fell upon him. When the sun had gone down and
it was dark, behold, a smoking fire pot and a flaming torch
passed between these pieces. On that day the Lord made a
covenant with Abram, saying, "To your descendants I give

this land, from the river of Egypt to the great river, the river Eu-phra'tes."

Psalm 27 [page 617]   or   *27:10-18* [page 618]

A Reading (Lesson) from the Letter of Paul to the Philippians [3:17—4:1]

Brethren, join in imitating me, and mark those who so live as you have an example in us. For many, of whom I have often told you and now tell you even with tears, live as enemies of the cross of Christ. Their end is destruction, their god is the belly, and they glory in their shame, with minds set on earthly things. But our commonwealth is in heaven, and from it we await a Savior, the Lord Jesus Christ, who will change our lowly body to be like his glorious body, by the power which enables him even to subject all things to himself. Therefore, my brethren, whom I love and long for, my joy and crown, stand firm thus in the Lord, my beloved.

✝ *The Holy Gospel of Our Lord Jesus Christ According to Luke* [13:(22-30)31-35]

Jesus went on his way through towns and villages, teaching, and journeying toward Jerusalem. And some one said to him, "Lord, will those who are saved be few?" And he said to them, "Strive to enter by the narrow door; for many, I tell you, will seek to enter and will not be able. When once the householder has risen up and shut the door, you will begin to stand outside and to knock at the door, saying, 'Lord, open to us.' He will answer you, 'I do not know where you come from.' Then you will begin to say, 'We ate and drank in your presence, and you taught in our streets.' But he will say, 'I tell you, I do not know where you come from; depart from me, all you workers of iniquity!' There you will weep and gnash your teeth, when you see Abraham and Isaac and Jacob and all the prophets in the kingdom of God and you yourselves thrust out. And men will come from east and west, and from north and south, and sit at table in the kingdom of God. And behold, some are last who will be first, and some are first who will be last." At that very hour,

Some Pharisees came, and said to Jesus, "Get away from here, for Herod wants to kill you." And he said to them, "Go and tell that fox, 'Behold, I cast out demons and perform cures today and tomorrow, and the third day I finish my course. Nevertheless I must go on my way today and tomorrow and the day following; for it cannot be that a prophet should perish away from Jerusalem.' O Jerusalem, Jerusalem, killing the prophets and stoning those who are sent to you! How often would I have gathered your children together as a hen gathers her brood under her wings, and you would not! Behold, your house is forsaken. And I tell you, you will not see me until you say, 'Blessed is he who comes in the name of the Lord!' "

Third Sunday in Lent

A Reading (Lesson) from the Book of Exodus [3:1-15]

Now Moses was keeping the flock of his father-in-law, Jethro, the priest of Mid'ian; and he led his flock to the west side of the wilderness, and came to Horeb, the mountain of God. And the angel of the Lord appeared to him in a flame of fire out of the midst of a bush; and he looked, and lo, the bush was burning, yet it was not consumed. And Moses said, "I will turn aside and see this great sight, why the bush is not burnt." When the Lord saw that he turned aside to see, God called to him out of the bush, "Moses, Moses!" And he said, "Here am I." Then he said, "Do not come near; put off your shoes from your feet, for the place on which you are standing is holy ground." And he said, "I am the God of your father, the God of Abraham, the God of Isaac, and the God of Jacob." And Moses hid his face, for he was afraid to look at God. Then the Lord said, "I have seen the affliction of my people who are in Egypt, and have heard their cry because of their taskmasters; I know their sufferings, and I have come down to deliver them out of the hand of the Egyptians, and to bring them up out of that land to a good and broad land, a land flowing with milk and honey, to the place of the Canaanites, the Hittites, the Amorites, the Per'izzites, the Hivites, and the Jeb'usites. And now, behold, the cry of the people of Israel has come to me, and I have seen the oppression with which the Egyptians oppress them. Come, I will send you to Pharaoh that you may bring forth my people, the sons of Israel, out of Egypt." But Moses said to God, "Who am I that I should go to Pharaoh, and bring the sons of Israel out of Egypt?" He said, "But I will be with you; and this shall be the sign for you, that I have sent you: when you have brought forth the people out of Egypt, you shall serve God upon this mountain." Then Moses said to God, "If I come to the people of Israel and say to them, 'The God of your fathers has sent me to you,' and they ask me, 'What is his name?' what shall I say to them?" God said to Moses, "I AM WHO I AM." And he said, "Say this to the people of Israel, 'I AM has sent me to you.'" God also said to Moses, "Say this to the people of Israel, 'The Lord, the God of your fathers, the God of Abraham, the God of Isaac, and the God of Jacob, has sent me to you': this is my name for ever, and thus I am to be remembered throughout all generations."

Psalm 103 [page 733]   or   *103:1-11* [page 733]

A Reading (Lesson) from the First Letter of Paul to the Corinthians [10:1-13]

I want you to know, brethren, that our fathers were all under the cloud, and all passed through the sea, and all were baptized into Moses in the cloud and in the sea, and all ate the same supernatural food, and all drank the same supernatural drink. For they drank from the supernatural Rock which followed them, and the Rock was Christ. Nevertheless with most of them God was not pleased; for they were overthrown in the wilderness. Now these things are warnings for us, not to desire evil as they did. Do not be idolaters as some of them were; as it is written, "The people sat down to eat and drink and rose up to dance." We must not indulge in immorality as some of them did, and twenty-three thousand fell in a single day. We must not put the Lord to the test, as some of them did and were destroyed by serpents; nor grumble, as some of them did and were destroyed by the Destroyer. Now these things happened to them as a warning, but they were written down for our instruction, upon whom the end of the ages has come. Therefore let any one who thinks that he stands take heed lest he fall. No temptation has overtaken you that is not common to man. God is faithful, and he will not let you be tempted beyond your strength, but with the temptation will also provide the way of escape, that you may be able to endure it.

✝ *The Holy Gospel of Our Lord Jesus Christ According to Luke* [13:1-9]

There were some who told Jesus of the Galileans whose blood Pilate had mingled with their sacrifices. And he answered them, "Do you think that these Galileans were worse sinners than all the other Galileans, because they suffered thus? I tell you, No; but unless you repent you will all likewise perish. Or those eighteen upon whom the tower of Silo'am fell and killed them, do you think that they were worse offenders than all the others who dwelt in Jerusalem? I tell you, No; but unless you repent you will all likewise perish." And he told this parable: "A man had a fig tree planted in his vineyard; and he came seeking fruit on it and found none. And he said to the vinedresser, 'Lo, these three years I have come seeking fruit on this fig tree, and I find none. Cut it down; why should it use up the ground?' And he answered him, 'Let it alone, sir, this year also, till I dig about it and put on manure. And if it bears fruit next year, well and good; but if not, you can cut it down.'"

Fourth Sunday in Lent

A Reading (Lesson) from the Book of Joshua
[(4:19-24); 5:9-12]

> The people came up out of the Jordan on the tenth day of the first month, and they encamped in Gilgal on the east border of Jericho. And those twelve stones, which they took out of the Jordan, Joshua set up in Gilgal. And he said to the people of Israel, "When your children ask their fathers in time to come, 'What do these stones mean?' then you shall let your children know, 'Israel passed over this Jordan on dry ground.' For the Lord your God dried up the waters of the Jordan for you until you passed over, as the Lord your God did to the Red Sea, which he dried up for us until we passed over, so that all the peoples of the earth may know that the hand of the Lord is mighty; that you may fear the Lord your God for ever."

[*And*] The Lord said to Joshua, "This day I have rolled away the reproach of Egypt from you." And so the name of that place is called Gilgal to this day. While the people of Israel were encamped in Gilgal they kept the passover on the fourteenth day of the month at evening in the plains of Jericho. And on the morrow after the passover, on that very day, they ate of the produce of the land, unleavened cakes and parched grain. And the manna ceased on the morrow, when they ate of the produce of the land; and the people of Israel had manna no more, but ate of the fruit of the land of Canaan that year.

Psalm 34 [page 627] or *34:1-8* [page 627]

A Reading (Lesson) from the Second Letter of Paul to the Corinthians [5:17-21]

If any one is in Christ, he is a new creation; the old has passed away, behold, the new has come. All this is from God, who through Christ reconciled us to himself and gave us the ministry of reconciliation; that is, in Christ God was reconciling the world to himself, not counting their trespasses against them, and entrusting to us the message of reconciliation. So we are ambassadors for Christ, God making his appeal through us. We beseech you on behalf of Christ, be reconciled to God. For our sake he made him to be sin who knew no sin, so that in him we might become the righteousness of God.

✝ *The Holy Gospel of Our Lord Jesus Christ According to Luke* [15:11-32]

Jesus said,"There was a man who had two sons; and the younger of them said to his father,'Father, give me the share of property that falls to me.' And he divided his living between them. Not many days later, the younger son gathered all he had and took his journey into a far country and there he squandered his property in loose living. And when he had spent everything, a great famine arose in that country, and he began to be in want. So he went and joined himself to one of the citizens of that country, who sent him

into his fields to feed swine. And he would gladly have fed
on the pods that the swine ate; and no one gave him
anything. But when he came to himself he said, 'How many
of my father's hired servants have bread enough and to
spare, but I perish here with hunger! I will arise and go to
my father, and I will say to him, Father, I have sinned
against heaven and before you; I am no longer worthy to
be called your son; treat me as one of your hired servants.'
And he arose and came to his father. But while he was yet
at a distance, his father saw him and had compassion, and
ran and embraced him and kissed him. And the son said to
him, 'Father, I have sinned against heaven and before you; I
am no longer worthy to be called your son.' But the father
said to his servants, 'Bring quickly the best robe, and put it
on him; and put a ring on his hand, and shoes on his feet;
and bring the fatted calf and kill it, and let us eat and make
merry; for this my son was dead, and is alive again; he was
lost, and is found.' And they began to make merry. Now his
elder son was in the field; and as he came and drew near to
the house, he heard music and dancing. And he called one
of the servants and asked what this meant. And he said to
him, 'Your brother has come, and your father has killed the
fatted calf, because he has received him safe and sound.'
But he was angry and refused to go in. His father came out
and entreated him, but he answered his father, 'Lo, these
many years I have served you, and I never disobeyed your
command; yet you never gave me a kid, that I might make
merry with my friends. But when this son of yours came,
who has devoured your living with harlots, you killed for
him the fatted calf!' And he said to him, 'Son, you are
always with me, and all that is mine is yours. It was fitting
to make merry and be glad, for this your brother was dead
and is alive; he was lost, and is found.' "

Fifth Sunday in Lent

A Reading (Lesson) from the Book of Isaiah [43:16-21]

Thus says the Lord, who makes a way in the sea, a path in the mighty waters, who brings forth chariot and horse, army and warrior; they lie down, they cannot rise, they are extinguished, quenched like a wick: "Remember not the former things nor consider the things of old. Behold, I am doing a new thing; now it springs forth, do you not perceive it? I will make a way in the wilderness and rivers in the desert. The wild beasts will honor me, the jackals and the ostriches; for I give water in the wilderness, rivers in the desert, to give drink to my chosen people, the people whom I formed for myself that they might declare my praise."

Psalm 126 [page 782]

A Reading (Lesson) from the Letter of Paul to the Philippians [3:8-14]

I count everything as loss because of the surpassing worth of knowing Christ Jesus my Lord. For his sake I have suffered the loss of all things, and count them as refuse, in order that I may gain Christ and be found in him, not having a righteousness of my own, based on law, but that which is through faith in Christ, the righteousness from God that depends on faith; that I may know him and the power of his resurrection, and may share his sufferings, becoming like him in his death, that if possible I may attain the resurrection from the dead. Not that I have already obtained this or am already perfect; but I press on to make it my own, because Christ Jesus has made me his own. Brethren, I do not consider that I have made it my own; but one thing I do, forgetting what lies behind and straining forward to what lies ahead, I press on toward the goal for the prize of the upward call of God in Christ Jesus.

✝ *The Holy Gospel of Our Lord Jesus Christ According to Luke* [20:9-19]

Jesus began to tell the people this parable: "A man planted a vineyard, and let it out to tenants, and went into another country for a long while. When the time came, he sent a servant to the tenants, that they should give him some of the fruit of the vineyard; but the tenants beat him, and sent him away empty-handed. And he sent another servant; him also they beat and treated shamefully, and sent him away empty-handed. And he sent yet a third; this one they wounded and cast out. Then the owner of the vineyard said, 'What shall I do? I will send my beloved son; it may be they will respect him.' But when the tenants saw him, they said to themselves, 'This is the heir; let us kill him, that the inheritance may be ours.' And they cast him out of the vineyard and killed him. What then will the owner of the vineyard do to them? He will come and destroy those tenants, and give the vineyard to others." When they heard this, they said, "God forbid!" But he looked at them and said, "What then is this that is written: 'The very stone which the builders rejected has become the head of the corner'? Everyone who falls on that stone will be broken to pieces; but when it falls on any one it will crush him." The scribes and the chief priests tried to lay hands on him at that very hour, but they feared the people; for they perceived that he had told this parable against them.

The Sunday of the Passion: Palm Sunday

At the Liturgy of the Palms

✝ *The Holy Gospel of Our Lord Jesus Christ*
According to Luke [19:29-40]

When Jesus drew near to Beth'phage and Bethany, at the
mount that is called Olivet, he sent two of the disciples,
saying, "Go into the village opposite, where on entering
you will find a colt tied, on which no one has ever yet sat;
untie it and bring it here. If any one asks you, 'Why are you
untying it?' you shall say this, 'The Lord has need of it.'" So
those who were sent went away and found it as he had told
them. And as they were untying the colt, its owners said to
them, "Why are you untying the colt?" And they said,
"The Lord has need of it." And they brought it to Jesus, and
throwing their garments on the colt they set Jesus upon it.
And as he rode along, they spread their garments on the
road. As he was now drawing near, at the descent of the
Mount of Olives, the whole multitude of the disciples
began to rejoice and praise God with a loud voice for all
the mighty works that they had seen, saying, "Blessed is the
King who comes in the name of the Lord! Peace in heaven
and glory in the highest!" And some of the Pharisees in the
multitude said to him, "Teacher, rebuke your disciples."
He answered, "I tell you, if these were silent, the very
stones would cry out."

The Blessing over the Branches follows
[page 271 of the Prayer Book]

Processional Psalm 118:19-29 [page 762]

At the Liturgy of the Word

A Reading (Lesson) from the Book of Isaiah [45:21-25]

Thus says the Lord,"Declare and present your case; let them take counsel together! Who told this long ago? Who declared it of old? Was it not I, the Lord? And there is no other god besides me, a righteous God and a Savior; there is none besides me. Turn to me and be saved, all the ends of the earth! For I am God, and there is no other. By myself I have sworn, from my mouth has gone forth in righteousness a word that shall not return: 'To me every knee shall bow, every tongue shall swear.' Only in the Lord, it shall be said of me, are righteousness and strength; to him shall come and be ashamed all who were incensed against him. In the Lord all the offspring of Israel shall triumph and glory."

or this

Isaiah 52:13 — 53:12 [page 85 below]

Psalm 22:1-21 [page 610] or *22:1-11* [page 610]

A Reading (Lesson) from the Letter of Paul to the Philippians [2:5-11]

Have this mind among yourselves, which is yours in Christ Jesus, who, though he was in the form of God, did not count equality with God a thing to be grasped, but emptied himself, taking the form of a servant, being born in the likeness of men. And being found in human form he humbled himself and became obedient unto death, even death on a cross. Therefore God has highly exalted him and bestowed on him the name which is above every name, that at the name of Jesus every knee should bow, in heaven and on earth and under the earth, and every tongue confess that Jesus Christ is Lord, to the glory of God the Father.

The Passion of Our Lord Jesus Christ According to Luke
[22:39—23:49(50-56)]   or   [23:1-49(50-56)]

> *The customary responses before and after the Gospel are
> omitted.*
>
> *The shorter form of the Passion [Luke 23:1-49(50-56)]
> begins on page 68.*
>
> *The Passion may be read by one or more persons.*
>
> *The congregation may be seated for the first part of the
> Passion. At the verse which mentions the arrival at
> Golgotha [Luke 23:33], page 70, all stand.*

Narrator And Jesus came out, and went, as was his custom,
to the Mount of Olives; and the disciples
followed him. And when he came to the place he
said to them,

Jesus Pray that you may not enter into temptation.

Narrator And he withdrew from them about a stone's
throw, and knelt down and prayed,

Jesus Father, if thou art willing, remove this cup from
me; nevertheless not my will, but thine be done.

Narrator And when he rose from prayer, he came to the
disciples and found them sleeping for sorrow, and
he said to them,

Jesus Why do you sleep? Rise and pray that you may
not enter into temptation.

Narrator While he was still speaking, there came a crowd,
and the man called Judas, one of the twelve, was
leading them. He drew near to Jesus to kiss him;
but Jesus said to him,

Jesus Judas, would you betray the Son of man with a
kiss?

Narrator And when those who were about him saw what would follow, they said,

Reader(s) Lord, shall we strike with the sword?

Narrator And one of them struck the slave of the high priest and cut off his right ear. But Jesus said,

Jesus No more of this!

Narrator And he touched his ear and healed him. Then Jesus said to the chief priests and officers of the temple and elders, who had come out against him,

Jesus Have you come out as against a robber, with swords and clubs? When I was with you day after day in the temple, you did not lay hands on me. But this is your hour, and the power of darkness.

Narrator Then they seized him and led him away, bringing him into the high priest's house. Peter followed at a distance; and when they had kindled a fire in the middle of the courtyard and sat down together, Peter sat among them. Then a maid, seeing him as he sat in the light and gazing at him, said,

Reader This man also was with him.

Narrator But he denied it, saying,

Reader Woman, I do not know him.

Narrator And a little later someone else saw him and said,

Reader You also are one of them.

Narrator But Peter said,

Reader Man, I am not.

Narrator And after an interval of about an hour still another insisted, saying,

Reader Certainly, this man also was with him; for he is a Galilean.

Narrator   But Peter said,

Reader   Man, I do not know what you are saying.

Narrator   And immediately, while he was still speaking, the cock crowed. And the Lord turned and looked at Peter. And Peter remembered the word of the Lord, how he had said to him, "Before the cock crows today, you will deny me three times." And he went out and wept bitterly. Now the men who were holding Jesus mocked him and beat him; they also blindfolded him and asked him,

Reader(s)   Prophesy! Who is it that struck you?

Narrator   And they spoke many other words against him, reviling him. When day came, the assembly of the elders of the people gathered together, both chief priests and scribes; and they led him away to their council, and they said,

Reader(s)   If you are the Christ, tell us.

Narrator   But he said to them,

Jesus   If I tell you, you will not believe; and if I ask you, you will not answer. But from now on the Son of man shall be seated at the right hand of the power of God.

Narrator   And they all said,

Reader(s)   Are you the Son of God, then?

Narrator   And he said to them,

Jesus   You say that I am.

Narrator   And they said,

Reader(s)   What further testimony do we need? We have heard it ourselves from his own lips.

The shorter form of the Passion begins here
[Luke 23:1-49(50-56)]

Narrator Then the whole company of them arose, and brought him before Pilate. And they began to accuse him, saying,

Reader(s) We found this man perverting our nation, and forbidding us to give tribute to Caesar, and saying that he himself is Christ a king.

Narrator And Pilate asked him,

Reader Are you the King of the Jews?

Narrator And he answered him,

Jesus You have said so.

Narrator And Pilate said to the chief priests and the multitudes,

Reader I find no crime in this man.

Narrator But they were urgent, saying,

Reader(s) He stirs up the people, teaching throughout all Judea, from Galilee even to this place.

Narrator When Pilate heard this, he asked whether the man was a Galilean. And when he learned that he belonged to Herod's jurisdiction, he sent him over to Herod, who was himself in Jerusalem at that time. When Herod saw Jesus, he was very glad, for he had long desired to see him, because he had heard about him, and he was hoping to see some sign done by him. So he questioned him at some length; but he made no answer. The chief priests and the scribes stood by, vehemently accusing him. And Herod with his soldiers treated him with contempt and mocked him; then, arraying him in gorgeous apparel, he sent him back to Pilate. And Herod and Pilate became friends with each other that very day, for before this they had been at enmity with each other. Pilate then called together the chief priests and the rulers and the people, and said to them,

Reader   You brought me this man as one who was perverting the people; and after examining him before you, behold, I did not find this man guilty of any of your charges against him; neither did Herod, for he sent him back to us. Behold, nothing deserving death has been done by him; I will therefore chastise him and release him.

Narrator   But they all cried out together,

Reader(s)   Away with this man, and release to us Barab'bas—

Narrator   A man who had been thrown into prison for an insurrection started in the city, and for murder. Pilate addressed them once more, desiring to release Jesus; but they shouted out,

Crowd   Crucify, crucify him!

Narrator   A third time he said to them,

Reader   Why, what evil has he done? I have found in him no crime deserving death; I will therefore chastise him and release him.

Narrator   But they were urgent, demanding with loud cries that he should be crucified. And their voices prevailed. So Pilate gave sentence that their demand should be granted. He released the man who had been thrown into prison for insurrection and murder, whom they asked for; but Jesus he delivered up to their will. And as they led him away, they seized one Simon of Cyre'ne, who was coming in from the country, and laid on him the cross, to carry it behind Jesus. And there followed him a great multitude of people, and of women who bewailed and lamented him. But Jesus turning to them said,

Jesus Daughters of Jerusalem, do not weep for me, but weep for yourselves and for your children. For behold, the days are coming when they will say, "Blessed are the barren, and the wombs that never bore, and the breasts that never gave suck!" Then they will begin to say to the mountains, "Fall on us"; and to the hills, "Cover us." For if they do this when the wood is green, what will happen when it is dry?

Narrator Two others also, who were criminals, were led away to be put to death with him.

All stand.

Narrator And when they came to the place which is called The Skull, there they crucified him, and the criminals, one on the right and one on the left. And Jesus said,

Jesus Father, forgive them; for they know not what they do.

Narrator And they cast lots to divide his garments. And the people stood by, watching; but the rulers scoffed at him, saying,

Reader(s) He saved others; let him save himself, if he is the Christ of God, his Chosen One!

Narrator The soldiers also mocked him, coming up and offering him vinegar, and saying,

Reader(s) If you are the King of the Jews, save yourself!

Narrator There was also an inscription over him, "This is the King of the Jews." One of the criminals who were hanged railed at him, saying,

Reader Are you not the Christ? Save yourself and us!

Narrator But the other rebuked him, saying,

Reader Do you not fear God, since you are under the same sentence of condemnation? And we indeed justly; for we are receiving the due reward of our deeds; but this man has done nothing wrong.

Narrator And he said,

Reader Jesus, remember me when you come into your kingdom.

Narrator And he said to him,

Jesus Truly, I say to you, today you will be with me in Paradise.

Narrator It was now about the sixth hour, and there was darkness over the whole land until the ninth hour, while the sun's light failed; and the curtain of the temple was torn in two. Then Jesus, crying with a loud voice, said,

Jesus Father, into thy hands I commit my spirit!

Narrator And having said this he breathed his last.

Silence may be kept.

Narrator Now when the centurion saw what had taken place, he praised God, and said,

Reader Certainly this man was innocent!

Narrator And all the multitudes who assembled to see the sight, when they saw what had taken place, returned home beating their breasts. And all his acquaintances and the women who had followed him from Galilee stood at a distance and saw these things.

The following passage may be added [Luke 23:50-56]

Narrator   Now there was a man named Joseph from the Jewish town of Arimathe'a. He was a member of the council, a good and righteous man, who had not consented to their purpose and deed, and he was looking for the kingdom of God. This man went to Pilate and asked for the body of Jesus. Then he took it down and wrapped it in a linen shroud, and laid him in a rock-hewn tomb, where no one had ever yet been laid. It was the day of Preparation, and the sabbath was beginning. The women who had come with him from Galilee followed, and saw the tomb, and how his body was laid; then they returned and prepared spices and ointments. On the sabbath they rested according to the commandment.

Monday in Holy Week

A Reading (Lesson) from the Book of Isaiah [42:1-9]

Behold my servant, whom I uphold, my chosen, in whom my soul delights; I have put my Spirit upon him, he will bring forth justice to the nations. He will not cry or lift up his voice, or make it heard in the street; a bruised reed he will not break, and a dimly burning wick he will not quench; he will faithfully bring forth justice. He will not fail or be discouraged till he has established justice in the earth; and the coastlands wait for his law. Thus says God, the Lord, who created the heavens and stretched them out, who spread forth the earth and what comes from it, who gives breath to the people upon it and spirit to those who walk in it: "I am the Lord, I have called you in righteousness, I have taken you by the hand and kept you; I have given you as a covenant to the people, a light to the nations, to open the eyes that are blind, to bring out the prisoners from the dungeon, from the prison those who sit in darkness. I am the Lord, that is my name; my glory I give to no other, nor my praise to graven images. Behold, the former things have come to pass, and new things I now declare; before they spring forth I tell you of them."

Psalm 36:5-10 [page 632]

A Reading (Lesson) from the Letter to the Hebrews [11:39—12:3]

All these, the patriarchs, prophets, and heroes of the Old Covenant, though well attested by their faith, did not receive what was promised, since God had foreseen something better for us, that apart from us they should not be made perfect. Therefore, since we are surrounded by so great a cloud of witnesses, let us also lay aside every weight, and sin which clings so closely, and let us run with perseverance the race that is set before us, looking to Jesus the pioneer and perfecter of our faith, who for the joy that was set before him endured the cross, despising the shame, and is seated at the right hand of the throne of God. Consider him who endured from sinners such hostility against himself, so that you may not grow weary or fainthearted.

✝ *The Holy Gospel of Our Lord Jesus Christ*
  According to John [12:1-11]

Six days before the Passover, Jesus came to Bethany, where Laz'arus was, whom Jesus had raised from the dead. There they made him a supper; Martha served, and Laz'arus was one of those at table with him. Mary took a pound of costly ointment of pure nard and anointed the feet of Jesus and wiped his feet with her hair; and the house was filled with the fragrance of the ointment. But Judas Iscariot, one of the disciples (he who was to betray him), said, "Why was this ointment not sold for three hundred denarii and given to the poor?" This he said, not that he cared for the poor but because he was a thief, and as he had the money box he used to take what was put into it. Jesus said, "Let her alone, let her keep it for the day of my burial. The poor you always have with you, but you do not always have me." When the great crowd of the Jews learned that he was there, they came, not only on account of Jesus but also to see Laz'arus, whom he had raised from the dead. So the chief priests planned to put Laz'arus also to death, because on account of him many of the Jews were going away and believing in Jesus.

or this

✝ *The Holy Gospel of Our Lord Jesus Christ*
  According to Mark [14:3-9]

While Jesus was at Bethany in the house of Simon the leper, as he sat at table, a woman came with an alabaster

flask of ointment of pure nard, very costly, and she broke
the flask and poured it over his head. But there were some
who said to themselves indignantly, "Why was the
ointment thus wasted? For this ointment might have been
sold for more than three hundred denarii, and given to the
poor." And they reproached her. But Jesus said, "Let her
alone; why do you trouble her? She has done a beautiful
thing to me. For you always have the poor with you, and
whenever you will, you can do good to them; but you will
not always have me. She has done what she could; she has
anointed my body beforehand for burying. And truly,
I say to you, wherever the gospel is preached in the whole
world, what she has done will be told in memory of her."

Tuesday in Holy Week

A Reading (Lesson) from the Book of Isaiah [49:1-6]

Listen to me, O coastlands, and hearken, you peoples from
afar. The Lord called me from the womb, from the body of
my mother he named my name. He made my mouth like a
sharp sword, in the shadow of his hand he hid me; he made
me a polished arrow, in his quiver he hid me away. And he
said to me, "You are my servant, Israel, in whom I will be
glorified." But I said, "I have labored in vain, I have spent
my strength for nothing and vanity; yet surely my right is
with the Lord, and my recompense with my God." And
now the Lord says, who formed me from the womb to be
his servant, to bring Jacob back to him, and that Israel
might be gathered to him, for I am honored in the eyes of
the Lord, and my God has become my strength—he says:
"It is too light a thing that you should be my servant to raise
up the tribes of Jacob and to restore the preserved of Israel;
I will give you as a light to the nations, that my salvation
may reach to the end of the earth."

Psalm 71:1-12 [page 683]

*A Reading (Lesson) from the First Letter of Paul
to the Corinthians* [1:18-31]

The word of the cross is folly to those who are perishing,
but to us who are being saved it is the power of God. For it
is written,"I will destroy the wisdom of the wise, and the
cleverness of the clever I will thwart." Where is the wise
man? Where is the scribe? Where is the debater of this age?
Has not God made foolish the wisdom of the world? For
since, in the wisdom of God, the world did not know God
through wisdom, it pleased God through the folly of what
we preach to save those who believe. For Jews demand
signs and Greeks seek wisdom, but we preach Christ
crucified, a stumbling block to Jews and folly to Gentiles,
but to those who are called, both Jews and Greeks, Christ
the power of God and the wisdom of God. For the
foolishness of God is wiser than men, and the weakness of
God is stronger than men. For consider your call, brethren;
not many of you were wise according to worldly
standards, not many were powerful, not many were of
noble birth; but God chose what is foolish in the world to
shame the wise, God chose what is weak in the world to
shame the strong, God chose what is low and despised in
the world, even things that are not, to bring to nothing
things that are, so that no human being might boast in the
presence of God. He is the source of your life in Christ
Jesus, whom God made our wisdom, our righteousness
and sanctification and redemption; therefore, as it is
written,"Let him who boasts, boast of the Lord."

✝ *The Holy Gospel of Our Lord Jesus Christ
According to John* [12:37-38, 42-50]

Though Jesus had done so many signs before the people,
yet they did not believe in him; it was that the word spoken
by the prophet Isaiah might be fulfilled,"Lord, who has
believed our report, and to whom has the arm of the Lord

been revealed?" Nevertheless many even of the authorities believed in him, but for fear of the Pharisees they did not confess it, lest they should be put out of the synagogue: for they loved the praise of men more than the praise of God. And Jesus cried out and said, "He who believes in me, believes not in me but in him who sent me. And he who sees me sees him who sent me. I have come as light into the world, that whoever believes in me may not remain in darkness. If any one hears my sayings and does not keep them I do not judge him; for I did not come to judge the world but to save the world. He who rejects me and does not receive my sayings has a judge; the word that I have spoken will be his judge on the last day. For I have not spoken on my own authority; the Father who sent me has himself given me commandment what to say and what to speak. And I know that his commandment is eternal life. What I say, therefore, I say as the Father has bidden me."

or this

✝ *The Holy Gospel of Our Lord Jesus Christ According to Mark* [11:15-19]

Jesus and those who followed came to Jerusalem. And Jesus entered the temple and began to drive out those who sold and those who bought in the temple, and he overturned the tables of the money-changers and the seats of those who sold pigeons; and he would not allow any one to carry anything through the temple. And he taught, and said to them, "Is it not written, 'My house shall be called a house of prayer for all nations'? But you have made it a den of robbers." And the chief priests and the scribes heard it and sought a way to destroy him; for they feared him, because all the multitude was astonished at his teaching. And when evening came they went out of the city.

Wednesday in Holy Week

A Reading (Lesson) from the Book of Isaiah [50:4-9a]

The Lord God has given me the tongue of those who are taught, that I may know how to sustain with a word him that is weary. Morning by morning he wakens, he wakens my ear to hear as those who are taught. The Lord God has opened my ear, and I was not rebellious, I turned not backward. I gave my back to the smiters, and my cheeks to those who pulled out the beard; I hid not my face from shame and spitting. For the Lord God helps me; therefore I have not been confounded; therefore I have set my face like a flint, and I know that I shall not be put to shame; he who vindicates me is near. Who will contend with me? Let us stand up together. Who is my adversary? Let him come near to me. Behold, the Lord God helps me; who will declare me guilty?

Psalm 69:7-15, 22-23 [page 679]

A Reading (Lesson) from the Letter to the Hebrews [9:11-15, 24-28]

When Christ appeared as a high priest of the good things that have come, then through the greater and more perfect tent (not made with hands, that is, not of this creation) he entered once for all into the Holy Place, taking not the blood of goats and calves but his own blood, thus securing an eternal redemption. For if the sprinkling of defiled persons with the blood of goats and bulls and with the ashes of a heifer sanctifies for the purification of the flesh, how much more shall the blood of Christ, who through the eternal Spirit offered himself without blemish to God, purify your conscience from dead works to serve the living God. Therefore he is the mediator of a new covenant, so that those who are called may receive the promised eternal inheritance, since a death has occurred which redeems them from the transgressions under the first covenant. For Christ has entered, not into a sanctuary made with hands, a copy of the true one, but into heaven itself, now to appear in the presence of God on our behalf. Nor was it to offer himself repeatedly, as the high priest enters the Holy Place yearly with blood not his own; for then he would have had to suffer repeatedly since the foundation of the world. But as it is, he has appeared once for all at the end of the age to put away sin by the sacrifice of himself. And just as it is appointed for men to die once, and after that comes judgment, so Christ, having been offered once to bear the sins of many, will appear a second time, not to deal with sin but to save those who are eagerly waiting for him.

✝ *The Holy Gospel of Our Lord Jesus Christ According to John* [13:21-35]

At supper with his friends, Jesus was troubled in spirit, and testified, "Truly, truly, I say to you, one of you will betray me." The disciples looked at one another, uncertain of whom he spoke. One of his disciples, whom Jesus loved, was lying close to the breast of Jesus; so Simon Peter beckoned to him and said, "Tell us who it is of whom he speaks." So lying thus, close to the breast of Jesus, he said to him, "Lord, who is it?" Jesus answered, "It is he to whom I shall give this morsel when I have dipped it." So when he had dipped the morsel, he gave it to Judas, the son of Simon Iscariot. Then after the morsel, Satan entered into him. Jesus said to him, "What you are going to do, do quickly." Now no one at the table knew why he said this to him. Some thought that, because Judas had the money box, Jesus was telling him, "Buy what we need for the feast"; or, that he should give something to the poor. So, after receiving the morsel, he immediately went out; and it was night. When he had gone out, Jesus said, "Now is the

Son of man glorified, and in him God is glorified; if God is glorified in him, God will also glorify him in himself, and glorify him at once. Little children, yet a little while I am with you. You will seek me; and as I said to the Jews so now I say to you,'Where I am going you cannot come.' A new commandment I give to you, that you love one another; even as I have loved you, that you also love one another. By this all men will know that you are my disciples, if you have love for one another."

or this

✝ *The Holy Gospel of Our Lord Jesus Christ According to Matthew* [26:1-5, 14-25]

Jesus said to his disciples,"You know that after two days the Passover is coming, and the Son of man will be delivered up to be crucified." Then the chief priests and the elders of the people gathered in the palace of the high priest, who was called Ca'iaphas, and took counsel together in order to arrest Jesus by stealth and kill him. But they said,"Not during the feast, lest there be a tumult among the people." Then one of the twelve, who was called Judas Iscariot, went to the chief priests, and said,"What will you give me if I deliver him to you?" And they paid him thirty pieces of silver. And from that moment he sought an opportunity to betray him. Now on the first day of Unleavened Bread the disciples came to Jesus, saying,"Where will you have us prepare for you to eat the passover?" He said,"Go into the city to a certain one, and say to him,'The Teacher says, My time is at hand; I will keep the passover at your house with my disciples.'" And the disciples did as Jesus had directed them, and they prepared the passover. When it was evening, he sat at table with the twelve disciples; and as they were eating, he said,"Truly, I say to you, one of you will betray me." And they were very sorrowful, and began to say to him one after another,"Is it I, Lord?" He answered,"He who has dipped his hand in the dish with me, will betray me. The Son of man goes as it is written of him, but woe to that man by whom the Son of man is betrayed! It would have been better for that man if he had not been born." Judas, who betrayed him, said,"Is it I, Master?" He said to him,"You have said so."

Maundy Thursday

A Reading (Lesson) from the Book of Exodus [12:1-14a]

The Lord said to Moses and Aaron in the land of Egypt,"This month shall be for you the beginning of months; it shall be the first month of the year for you. Tell all the congregation of Israel that on the tenth day of this month they shall take every man a lamb according to their fathers' houses, a lamb for a household; and if the household is too small for a lamb, then a man and his neighbor next to his house shall take according to the number of persons; according to what each can eat you shall make your count for the lamb. Your lamb shall be without blemish, a male a year old; you shall take it from the sheep or from the goats; and you shall keep it until the fourteenth day of this month, when the whole assembly of the congregation of Israel shall kill their lambs in the evening. Then they shall take some of the blood, and put it on the two doorposts and the lintel of the houses in which they eat them. They shall eat the flesh that night, roasted; with unleavened bread and bitter herbs they shall eat it. Do not eat any of it raw or boiled with water, but roasted, its head with its legs and its inner parts. And you shall let none of it remain until the morning, anything that remains until the morning you shall burn. In this manner you shall eat it: your loins girded, your sandals on your feet, and your staff in your hand; and you shall eat it in haste. It is the Lord's passover. For I will pass through the land of Egypt that night, and I will smite all the first-born in the land of Egypt, both man and beast; and on all the gods of Egypt I will execute judgments: I am the Lord. The blood shall be a sign for you, upon the houses where you are; and when I see the blood, I will pass over you, and no plague shall fall upon you to destroy you, when I smite the land of Egypt. This day shall be for you a memorial day, and you shall keep it as a feast to the Lord."

Psalm 78:14-20, 23-25 [page 696]

A Reading (Lesson) from the First Letter of Paul to the Corinthians [11:23-26 (27-32)]

I received from the Lord what I also delivered to you, that the Lord Jesus on the night when he was betrayed took bread, and when he had given thanks, he broke it, and said,"This is my body which is for you. Do this in remembrance of me." In the same way also the cup, after supper, saying,"This cup is the new covenant in my blood. Do this, as often as you drink it, in remembrance of me." For as often as you eat this bread and drink the cup, you proclaim the Lord's death until he comes.

Whoever, therefore, eats the bread or drinks the cup of the Lord in an unworthy manner will be guilty of profaning the body and blood of the Lord. Let a man examine himself, and so eat of the bread and drink of the cup. For any one who eats and drinks without discerning the body eats and drinks judgment upon himself. That is why many of you are weak and ill, and some have died. But if we judged ourselves truly, we should not be judged. But when we are judged by the Lord, we are chastened so that we may not be condemned along with the world.

✝ *The Holy Gospel of Our Lord Jesus Christ*
According to John [13:1-15]

Now before the feast of the Passover, when Jesus knew
that his hour had come to depart out of this world to the
Father, having loved his own who were in the world, he
loved them to the end. And during supper, when the devil
had already put it into the heart of Judas Iscariot, Simon's
son, to betray him, Jesus, knowing that the Father had
given all things into his hands, and that he had come from
God and was going to God, rose from supper, laid aside his
garments, and girded himself with a towel. Then he poured
water into a basin, and began to wash the disciples' feet,
and to wipe them with the towel with which he was
girded. He came to Simon Peter; and Peter said to him,
"Lord, do you wash my feet?" Jesus answered him,
"What I am doing you do not know now, but afterward you
will understand." Peter said to him, "You shall never wash
my feet." Jesus answered him, "If I do not wash you, you
have no part in me." Simon Peter said to him, "Lord, not
my feet only but also my hands and my head!" Jesus said to
him, "He who has bathed does not need to wash, except for
his feet, but he is clean all over; and you are clean, but not
every one of you." For he knew who was to betray him;
that was why he said, "You are not all clean." When he had
washed their feet, and taken his garments, and resumed his
place, he said to them, "Do you know what I have done to
you? You call me Teacher and Lord; and you are right, for
so I am. If I then, your Lord and Teacher, have washed
your feet, you also ought to wash one another's feet.
For I have given you an example, that you also should
do as I have done to you."

or the following

✝ *The Holy Gospel of Our Lord Jesus Christ*
According to Luke [22:14-30]

And when the hour came, Jesus sat at table, and the
apostles with him. And he said to them, "I have earnestly
desired to eat this passover with you before I suffer; for
I tell you I shall not eat it until it is fulfilled in the kingdom
of God." And he took a cup, and when he had given thanks
he said, "Take this, and divide it among yourselves; for
I tell you that from now on I shall not drink of the fruit of
the vine until the kingdom of God comes." And he took
bread, and when he had given thanks he broke it, and gave
it to them, saying, "This is my body which is given for you.
Do this in remembrance of me." And likewise the cup after
supper, saying, "This cup which is poured out for you is the
new covenant in my blood. But behold the hand of him
who betrays me is with me on the table. For the Son of man
goes as it has been determined; but woe to that man by
whom he is betrayed!" And they began to question one
another, which of them it was that would do this.
A dispute also arose among them, which of them was to be
regarded as the greatest. And he said to them, "The kings of
the Gentiles exercise lordship over them; and those in
authority over them are called benefactors. But not so with
you; rather let the greatest among you become as the
youngest, and the leader as one who serves. For which is
the greater, one who sits at table, or one who serves? Is it
not the one who sits at table? But I am among you as one
who serves. You are those who have continued with me in
my trials; and I assign to you, as my Father assigned to me,
a kingdom, that you may eat and drink at my table in my
kingdom, and sit on thrones judging the twelve tribes of
Israel."

Good Friday

A Reading (Lesson) from the Book of Isaiah [52:13 — 53:12]

Behold, my servant shall prosper, he shall be exalted and lifted up, and shall be very high. As many were astonished at him—his appearance was so marred, beyond human semblance, and his form beyond that of the sons of men— so shall he startle many nations; kings shall shut their mouths because of him; for that which has not been told them they shall see, and that which they have not heard they shall understand. Who has believed what we have heard? And to whom has the arm of the Lord been revealed? For he grew up before him like a young plant, and like a root out of dry ground; he had no form or comeliness that we should look at him, and no beauty that we should desire him. He was despised and rejected by men; a man of sorrows, and acquainted with grief; and as one from whom men hide their faces he was despised, and we esteemed him not. Surely he has borne our griefs and carried our sorrows; yet we esteemed him stricken, smitten by God, and afflicted. But he was wounded for our transgressions, he was bruised for our iniquities; upon him was the chastisement that made us whole, and with his stripes we are healed. All we like sheep have gone astray; we have turned every one to his own way; and the Lord has laid on him the iniquity of us all. He was oppressed, and he was afflicted, yet he opened not his mouth; like a lamb that is led to the slaughter, and like a sheep that before its shearers is dumb, so he opened not his mouth. By oppression and judgment he was taken away; and as for his generation, who considered that he was cut off out of the land of the living, stricken for the transgression of my people? And they made his grave with the wicked and with a rich man in his death, although he had done no violence, and there was no deceit in his mouth. Yet it was the will of the Lord to bruise him; he has put him to grief; when he makes himself an offering for sin, he shall see his offspring, he shall prolong his days; the will of the Lord shall prosper in his hand; he shall see the fruit of the travail of his soul and be satisfied; by his knowledge shall the righteous one, my servant, make many to be accounted righteous; and, he shall bear their iniquities. Therefore I will divide him a portion with the great, and he shall divide the spoil with the strong; because he poured out his soul to death, and was numbered with the transgressors; yet he bore the sin of many, and made intercession for the transgressors.

or this

A Reading (Lesson) from the Book of Genesis [22:1-18]

God tested Abraham, and said to him, "Abraham!" And he said, "Here am I." He said, "Take your son, your only son Isaac, whom you love, and go to the land of Mori'ah, and offer him there as a burnt offering upon one of the mountains of which I shall tell you." So Abraham rose early in the morning, saddled his ass, and took two of his young men with him, and his son Isaac; and he cut the wood for the burnt offering, and arose and went to the place of which God had told him. On the third day Abraham lifted up his eyes and saw the place afar off. Then Abraham said to his young men, "Stay here with the ass; I and the lad will go yonder and worship, and come again to you." And Abraham took the wood of the burnt offering, and laid it on Isaac his son; and he took in his hand the fire and the knife. So they went both of them together. And Isaac said to his father Abraham, "My father!" And he said, "Here am I, my son." He said, "Behold, the fire and the wood; but where is the lamb for a burnt offering?" Abraham said, "God will provide himself the lamb for a burnt offering, my son." So they went both of them together. When they came to the place of which God had told him, Abraham built an altar there, and laid the wood in order, and bound Isaac his son, and laid him on the altar, upon the wood. Then Abraham put forth his hand, and took the knife to slay his son. But the angel of the Lord called to him from heaven and said, "Abraham, Abraham!" And he said, "Here am I." He said, "Do not lay your hand on the lad or do anything to him; for now I know that you fear God, seeing you have not withheld your son, your only son, from me." And Abraham lifted up his eyes and looked, and behold, behind him was a ram, caught in a thicket by his horns; and Abraham went and took the ram, and offered it up as a burnt offering instead of his son. So Abraham called the name of that place The Lord will provide; as it is said to this day, "On the mount of the Lord it shall be provided." And the angel of the Lord called to Abraham a second time from heaven, and said, "By myself I have sworn, says the Lord, because you have done this, and have not withheld your son, your only son, I will indeed bless you, and I will multiply your descendants as the stars of heaven and as the sand which is on the seashore. And your descendants shall possess the gate of their enemies, and by your descendants shall all the nations of the earth bless themselves, because you have obeyed my voice."

or this

A Reading (Lesson) from the Book of Wisdom [2:1,12-24]

The ungodly reasoned unsoundly, saying to themselves, "Short and sorrowful is our life, and there is no remedy when a man comes to his end, and no one has been known to return from Hades. Let us lie in wait for the righteous man, because he is inconvenient to us and opposes our actions; he reproaches us for sins against the law, and accuses us of sins against our training. He professes to have knowledge of God, and calls himself a child of the Lord. He became to us a reproof of our thoughts; the very sight of him is a burden to us, because his manner of life is unlike that of others, and his ways are strange. We are considered by him as something base, and he avoids our ways as unclean; he calls the last end of the righteous happy, and boasts that God is his father. Let us see if his words are true, and let us test what will happen at the end of his life; for if the righteous man is God's son, he will help him, and will deliver him from the hand of his adversaries. Let us test him with insult and torture, that we may find out how gentle he is, and make trial of his forbearance. Let us condemn him to a shameful death, for, according to what he says, he will be protected." Thus they reasoned, but they were led astray, for their wickedness blinded them, and they did not know the secret purposes of God, nor hope for the wages of holiness, nor discern the prize for blameless souls; for God created man for incorruption, and made him in the image of his own eternity, but through the devil's envy death entered the world, and those who belong to his party experience it.

Psalm 22:1-21 [page 610] or *22:1-11* [page 610] or
Psalm 40:1-14 [page 640] or *Psalm 69:1-23* [page 679]

A Reading (Lesson) from the Letter to the Hebrews [10:1-25]

Since the law has but a shadow of the good things to come instead of the true form of these realities, it can never, by the same sacrifices which are continually offered year after year, make perfect those who draw near. Otherwise, would they not have ceased to be offered? If the worshipers had once been cleansed, they would no longer have any consciousness of sin. But in these sacrifices there is a reminder of sin year after year. For it is impossible that the blood of bulls and goats should take away sins. Consequently, when Christ came into the world, he said,

"Sacrifices and offerings thou has not desired, but a body hast thou prepared for me; in burnt offerings and sin offerings thou hast taken no pleasure. Then I said, 'Lo, I have come to do thy will, O God,' as it is written of me in the roll of the book." When he said above, "Thou hast neither desired nor taken pleasure in sacrifices and offerings and burnt offerings and sin offerings" (these are offered according to the law), then he added, "Lo, I have to come to do thy will." He abolishes the first in order to establish the second. And by that will we have been sanctified through the offering of the body of Jesus Christ once for all. And every priest stands daily at his service, offering repeatedly the same sacrifices, which can never take away sins. But when Christ had offered for all time a single sacrifice for sins, he sat down at the right hand of God, then to wait until his enemies should be made a stool for his feet. For by a single offering he has perfected for all time those who are sanctified. And the Holy Spirit also bears witness to us; for after saying, "This is the covenant that I will make with them after those days, says the Lord: I will put my laws on their hearts, and write them on their minds," then he adds, "I will remember their sins and their misdeeds no more." Where there is forgiveness of these, there is no longer any offering for sin. Therefore, brethren, since we have confidence to enter the sanctuary by the blood of Jesus, by the new and living way which he opened for us through the curtain, that is, through his flesh, and since we have a great priest over the house of God, let us draw near with a true heart in full assurance of faith, with our hearts sprinkled clean from an evil conscience and our bodies washed with pure water. Let us hold fast the confession of our hope without wavering, for he who promised is faithful; and let us consider how to stir up one another to love and good works, not neglecting to meet together, as is the habit of some, but encouraging one another, and all the more as you see the Day drawing near.

The Passion of Our Lord Jesus Christ According to John
[18:1 — 19:37]   or   [19:1-37]

> *The customary responses before and after the Gospel are omitted.*
>
> *The shorter form of the Passion begins on page 94.*
>
> *The Passion may be read by one or more persons.*
>
> *The congregation may be seated for the first part of the Passion. At the verse which mentions the arrival at Golgotha [John 19:17], page 96, all stand.*

Narrator   Jesus went forth with his disciples across the Kidron valley, where there was a garden, which he and his disciples entered. Now Judas, who betrayed him, also knew the place; for Jesus often met there with his disciples. So Judas, procuring a band of soldiers and some officers from the chief priests and the Pharisees, went there with lanterns and torches and weapons. Then Jesus, knowing all that was to befall him, came forward and said to them,

Jesus   Whom do you seek?

Narrator   They answered him,

Reader(s)   Jesus of Nazareth.

Narrator   Jesus said to them,

Jesus   I am he.

Narrator   Judas, who betrayed him, was standing with them. When he said to them, "I am he," they drew back and fell to the ground. Again he asked them,

Jesus   Whom do you seek?

Narrator   And they said,

Reader(s) Jesus of Nazareth.

Narrator Jesus answered them,

Jesus I told you that I am he; so, if you seek me, let these men go.

Narrator This was to fulfill the word which he had spoken, "Of those whom thou gavest me I lost not one." Then Simon Peter, having a sword, drew it and struck the high priest's slave and cut off his right ear. The slave's name was Malchus. Jesus said to Peter,

Jesus Put your sword into its sheath; shall I not drink the cup which the Father has given me?

Narrator So the band of soldiers and their captain and the officers of the Jews seized Jesus and bound him. First they led him to Annas; for he was the father-in-law of Ca'iaphas, who was high priest that year. It was Ca'iaphas who had given counsel to the Jews that it was expedient that one man should die for the people. Simon Peter followed Jesus, and so did another disciple. As this disciple was known to the high priest, he entered the court of the high priest along with Jesus, while Peter stood outside at the door. So the other disciple, who was known to the high priest, went out and spoke to the maid who kept the door, and brought Peter in. The maid who kept the door said to Peter,

Reader Are not you also one of this man's disciples?

Narrator And he said,

Reader I am not.

Narrator Now the servants and officers had made a charcoal fire, because it was cold, and they were standing and warming themselves; Peter also was with them, standing and warming himself. The high priest then questioned Jesus about his disciples and his teaching. Jesus answered him,

Jesus I have spoken openly to the world; I have always taught in synagogues and in the temple, where all Jews come together; I have said nothing secretly. Why do you ask me? Ask those who have heard· me, what I said to them; they know what I said.

Narrator When he had said this, one of the officers standing by struck Jesus with his hand, saying,

Reader Is that how you answer the high priest?

Narrator Jesus answered him,

Jesus If I have spoken wrongly, bear witness to the wrong; but if I have spoken rightly, why do you strike me?

Narrator Annas then sent him bound to Ca'iaphas the high priest. Now Simon Peter was standing and warming himself. They said to him,

Reader(s) Are not you also one of his disciples?

Narrator He denied it and said,

Reader I am not.

Narrator One of the servants of the high priest, a kinsman of the man whose ear Peter had cut off, asked,

Reader Did I not see you in the garden with him?

Narrator Peter again denied it; and at once the cock crowed. Then they led Jesus from the house of Ca'iaphas to the praetorium. It was early. They themselves did not enter the praetorium, so that they might not be defiled, but might eat the passover. So Pilate went out to them and said,

Reader	What accusation do you bring against this man?
Narrator	They answered him,
Reader(s)	If this man were not an evildoer, we would not have handed him over.
Narrator	Pilate said to them,
Reader	Take him yourselves and judge him by your own law.
Narrator	The Jews said to him,
Reader(s)	It is not lawful for us to put any man to death.
Narrator	This was to fulfill the word which Jesus had spoken to show by what death he was to die. Pilate entered the praetorium again and called Jesus, and he said to him,
Reader	Are you the King of the Jews?
Narrator	Jesus answered him,
Jesus	Do you say this of your own accord, or did others say it to you about me?
Narrator	Pilate answered,
Reader	Am I a Jew? Your own nation and the chief priests have handed you over to me; what have you done?
Narrator	Jesus answered him,
Jesus	My kingship is not of this world; if my kingship were of this world, my servants would fight, that I might not be handed over to the Jews; but my kingship is not from the world.
Narrator	Pilate said to him,
Reader	So you are a king?
Narrator	Jesus answered,

Jesus	You say that I am a king. For this I was born, and for this I have come into the world, to bear witness to the truth. Every one who is of the truth hears my voice.
Narrator	Pilate said to him,
Reader	What is truth?
Narrator	After he said this, he went out to the Jews again, and told them,
Reader	I find no crime in him. But you have a custom that I should release one man for you at the Passover; will you have me release for you the King of the Jews?
Narrator	They cried out again,
Crowd	Not this man, but Barab′bas!
Narrator	Now Barab′bas was a robber.

The shorter form of the Passion begins here [John 19:1-37]

Narrator	Pilate took Jesus and scourged him. And the soldiers plaited a crown of thorns, and put it on his head, and arrayed him in a purple robe; they came up to him, saying,
Reader(s)	Hail, King of the Jews!
Narrator	And struck him with their hands. Pilate went out again, and said to them,
Reader	See, I am bringing him out to you, that you may know that I find no crime in him.
Narrator	So Jesus came out, wearing the crown of thorns and the purple robe. Pilate said to them,
Reader	Behold the man!

Narrator When the chief priests and the officers saw him, they cried out, saying,

Reader(s) Crucify him, crucify him!

Narrator Pilate said to them,

Reader Take him yourselves and crucify him for I find no crime in him.

Narrator The Jews answered him,

Reader(s) We have a law, and by that law he ought to die, because he has made himself the Son of God.

Narrator When Pilate heard these words, he was the more afraid; he entered the praetorium again and said to Jesus,

Reader Where are you from?

Narrator But Jesus gave no answer. Pilate therefore said to him,

Reader You will not speak to me? Do you not know that I have power to release you, and power to crucify you?

Narrator Jesus answered him,

Jesus You would have no power over me unless it had been given you from above; therefore he who delivered me to you has the greater sin.

Narrator Upon this Pilate sought to release him, but the Jews cried out,

Crowd If you release this man, you are not Caesar's friend; every one who makes himself a king sets himself against Caesar.

Narrator When Pilate heard these words, he brought Jesus out and sat down on the judgment seat at a place called the Pavement, and in Hebrew, Gab'batha.

Now it was the day of Preparation of the Passover; it was about the sixth hour. He said to the Jews,

Reader   Behold your King!

Narrator   They cried out,

Crowd   Away with him, away with him, crucify him!

Narrator   Pilate said to them,

Reader   Shall I crucify your King?

Narrator   The chief priests answered,

Reader(s) We have no king but Caesar.

Narrator   Then he handed him over to them to be crucified.

All stand.

Narrator   So they took Jesus, and he went out, bearing his own cross, to the place of a skull, which is called in Hebrew Gol'gotha. There they crucified him, and with him two others, one on either side, and Jesus between them. Pilate also wrote a title and put it on the cross; it read, "Jesus of Nazareth, the King of the Jews." Many of the Jews read this title, for the place where Jesus was crucified was near the city; and it was written in Hebrew, in Latin, and in Greek. The chief priests of the Jews then said to Pilate,

Reader(s) Do not write, "The King of the Jews," but, "This man said, I am King of the Jews."

Narrator   Pilate answered,

Reader   What I have written I have written.

Narrator   When the soldiers had crucified Jesus they took his garments and made four parts, one for each soldier; also his tunic. But the tunic was without seam, woven from top to bottom; so they said to one another,

Reader(s) Let us not tear it, but cast lots for it to see whose it shall be.

Narrator This was to fulfill the scripture, "They parted my garments among them, and for my clothing they cast lots." So the soldiers did this. But standing by the cross of Jesus were his mother, and his mother's sister, Mary the wife of Clopas, and Mary Mag'dalene. When Jesus saw his mother, and the disciple whom he loved standing near, he said to his mother,

Jesus Woman, behold your son!

Narrator Then he said to the disciple,

Jesus Behold your mother!

Narrator And from that hour the disciple took her to his own home. After this, Jesus, knowing that all was now finished, to fulfill the scripture said,

Jesus I thirst.

Narrator A bowl full of vinegar stood there; so they put a sponge full of the vinegar on hyssop and held it to his mouth. When Jesus had received the vinegar, he said,

Jesus It is finished.

Narrator And he bowed his head and gave up his spirit.

Silence may be kept

Narrator Since it was the day of Preparation, in order to prevent the bodies from remaining on the cross on the sabbath (for that sabbath was a high day), the Jews asked Pilate that their legs might be broken, and that they might be taken away. So the soldiers came and broke the legs of the first, and of the other who had been crucified with him; but when they came to Jesus and saw that he was already dead, they did not break his legs. But one of the soldiers pierced his side with a spear, and at once there came out blood and water. He who saw it has borne witness—his testimony is true, and he knows that he tells the truth—that you also may believe. For these things took place that the scripture might be fulfilled,"Not a bone of him shall be broken." And again another scripture says,"They shall look on him whom they have pierced."

Holy Saturday

A Reading (Lesson) from the Book of Job [14:1-14]

Man that is born of a woman is of few days, and full of trouble. He comes forth like a flower, and withers; he flees like a shadow, and continues not. And dost thou open thy eyes upon such a one and bring him into judgment with thee? Who can bring a clean thing out of an unclean? There is not one. Since his days are determined, and the number of his months is with thee, and thou hast appointed his bounds that he cannot pass, look away from him, and desist, that he may enjoy, like a hireling, his day. For there is hope for a tree, if it be cut down, that it will sprout again, and that its shoots will not cease. Though its root grow old in the earth, and its stump die in the ground, yet at the scent of water it will bud and put forth branches like a young plant. But man dies, and is laid low; man breathes his last, and where is he? As waters fail from a lake, and a river wastes away and dries up, so man lies down and rises not again; till the heavens are no more he will not awake, or be roused out of his sleep. Oh that thou wouldest hide me in Sheol, that thou wouldest conceal me until thy wrath be past, that thou wouldest appoint me a set time, and remember me! If a man die, shall he live again? All the days of my service I would wait, till my release should come.

Psalm 130 [page 784]   or   *Psalm 31:1-5* [page 622]

A Reading (Lesson) from the First Letter of Peter [4:1-8]

Since Christ suffered in the flesh, arm yourselves with the same thought, for whoever has suffered in the flesh has ceased from sin, so as to live for the rest of the time in the flesh no longer by human passions but by the will of God. Let the time that is past suffice for doing what the Gentiles like to do, living in licentiousness, passions, drunkenness, revels, carousing, and lawless idolatry. They are surprised that you do not now join them in the same wild profligacy, and they abuse you; but they will give account to him who is ready to judge the living and the dead. For this is why the gospel was preached even to the dead, that though judged in the flesh like men, they might live in the spirit like God. The end of all things is at hand; therefore keep sane and sober for your prayers. Above all hold unfailing your love for one another, since love covers a multitude of sins.

✝ *The Holy Gospel of Our Lord Jesus Christ According to Matthew* [27:57-66]

When it was evening, there came a rich man from Arimathe'a, named Joseph, who also was a disciple of Jesus. He went to Pilate and asked for the body of Jesus. Then Pilate ordered it to be given to him. And Joseph took the body, and wrapped it in a clean linen shroud, and laid it in his own new tomb, which he had hewn in the rock; and he rolled a great stone to the door of the tomb, and departed. Mary Mag'dalene and the other Mary were there, sitting opposite the sepulchre. Next day, that is, after the day of Preparation, the chief priests and the Pharisees gathered before Pilate and said,"Sir, we remember how that impostor said, while he was still alive,'After three days I will rise again.'Therefore order the sepulchre to be made secure until the third day, lest his disciples go and steal him away, and tell the people,'He has risen from the dead,' and the last fraud will be worse than the first." Pilate said to them,"You have a guard of soldiers; go, make it as secure as you can." So they went and made the sepulchre secure by sealing the stone and setting a guard.

or this

✝ *The Holy Gospel of Our Lord Jesus Christ According to John* [19:38-42]

Joseph of Arimathe'a, who was a disciple of Jesus, but secretly, for fear of the Jews, asked Pilate that he might take away the body of Jesus, and Pilate gave him leave. So he came and took away his body. Nicode'mus also, who had at first come to him by night, came bringing a mixture of myrrh and aloes about a hundred pounds' weight. They took the body of Jesus, and bound it in linen cloths with the spices, as is the burial custom of the Jews. Now in the place where he was crucified there was a garden, and in the garden a new tomb where no one had ever been laid. So because of the Jewish day of Preparation, as the tomb was close at hand, they laid Jesus there.

The Great Vigil of Easter

At the Liturgy of the Word

*At least two of the following Lessons are read, of which one is
always the Lesson from Exodus. After each Lesson, the Psalm or
Canticle listed, or some other suitable psalm, canticle, or hymn
may be sung. A period of silence may be kept; and the Collect
provided (pages 288-291 of the Prayer Book), or some other
suitable Collect, may be said.*

[The Story of Creation]

A Reading (Lesson) from the Book of Genesis [1:1 — 2:2]

In the beginning God created the heavens and the earth.
The earth was without form and void, and darkness was
upon the face of the deep; and the Spirit of God was
moving over the face of the waters. And God said,
"Let there be light"; and there was light. And God saw that
the light was good; and God separated the light from the
darkness. God called the light Day, and the darkness he
called Night. And there was evening and there was
morning, one day. And God said,"Let there be a firmament
in the midst of the waters, and let it separate the waters
from the waters." And God made the firmament and
separated the waters which were under the firmament from
the waters which were above the firmament. And it was so.
And God called the firmament Heaven. And there was
evening and there was morning, a second day. And God
said,"Let the waters under the heavens be gathered
together into one place, and let the dry land appear." And
it was so. God called the dry land Earth, and the waters

that were gathered together he called Seas. And God saw that it was good. And God said,"Let the earth put forth vegetation, plants yielding seed, and fruit trees bearing fruit in which is their seed, each according to its kind, upon the earth." And it was so. The earth brought forth vegetation, plants yielding seed according to their own kinds, and trees bearing fruit in which is their seed, each according to its kind. And God saw that it was good. And there was evening and there was morning, a third day. And God said,"Let there be lights in the firmament of the heavens to separate the day from the night; and let them be for signs and for seasons and for days and years, and let them be lights in the firmament of the heavens to give light upon the earth." And it was so. And God made the two great lights, the greater light to rule the day, and the lesser light to rule the night; he made the stars also. And God set them in the firmament of the heavens to give light upon the earth, to rule over the day, and over the night, and to separate the light from the darkness. And God saw that it was good. And there was evening and there was morning, a fourth day. And God said,"Let the waters bring forth swarms of living creatures, and let birds fly above the earth across the firmament of the heavens." So God created the great sea monsters and every living creature that moves, with which the waters swarm, according to their kinds, and every winged bird according to its kind. And God saw that it was good. And God blessed them, saying,

"Be fruitful and multiply and fill the waters in the seas, and let birds multiply on the earth." And there was evening and there was morning, a fifth day. And God said,"Let the earth bring forth living creatures according to their kinds: cattle and creeping things and beasts of the earth according to their kinds." And it was so. And God made the beasts of the earth according to their kinds and the cattle according to their kinds, and everything that creeps upon the ground according to its kind. And God saw that it was good. Then

God said, "Let us make man in our image, after our likeness; and let them have dominion over the fish of the sea, and over the birds of the air, and over the cattle, and over all the earth, and over every creeping thing that creeps upon the earth." So God created man in his own image, in the image of God he created him; male and female he created them. And God blessed them, and God said to them, "Be fruitful and multiply, and fill the earth and subdue it; and have dominion over the fish of the sea and over the birds of the air and over every living thing that moves upon the earth." And God said, "Behold, I have given you every plant yielding seed which is upon the face of all the earth, and every tree with seed in its fruit; you shall have them for food. And to every beast of the earth, and to every bird of the air, and to everything that creeps on the earth, everything that has the breath of life, I have given every green plant for food." And it was so. And God saw everything that he had made, and behold, it was very good. And there was evening and there was morning, a sixth day. Thus the heavens and the earth were finished, and all the host of them. And on the seventh day God finished his work which he had done, and he rested on the seventh day from all his work which he had done.

Psalm 33:1-11 [page 626]   or   *Psalm 36:5-10* [page 632]

[The Flood]

A Reading (Lesson) from the Book of Genesis
[7:1-5, 11-18; 8:6-18; 9:8-13]

The Lord said to Noah, "Go into the ark, you and all your household, for I have seen that you are righteous before me in this generation. Take with you seven pairs of all clean animals, the male and his mate; and a pair of the animals that are not clean, the male and his mate; and seven pairs of the birds of the air also, male and female, to keep their kind alive upon the face of all the earth. For in seven days I will send rain upon the earth forty days and forty nights; and every living thing that I have made I will blot out from the face of the ground." And Noah did all that the Lord had commanded him. In the six hundredth year of Noah's life, in the second month, on the seventeenth day of the month, on that day all the fountains of the great deep burst forth, and the windows of the heavens were opened. And rain fell upon the earth forty days and forty nights. On the very same day Noah and his sons, Shem and Ham and Japheth, and Noah's wife and the three wives of his sons with them entered the ark, they and every beast according to its kind, and all the cattle according to their kinds, and every creeping thing that creeps on the earth according to its kind, and every bird according to its kind, every bird of every sort. They went into the ark with Noah, two and two of all flesh in which there was the breath of life. And they that entered, male and female of all flesh, went in as God had commanded him; and the Lord shut him in. The flood continued forty days upon the earth; and the waters increased, and bore up the ark, and it rose high above the earth. The waters prevailed and increased greatly upon the earth; and the ark floated on the face of the waters. At the end of forty days Noah opened the window of the ark which he had made, and sent forth a raven; and it went to and fro until the waters were dried up from the earth. Then he sent forth a dove from him, to see if the waters had subsided from the face of the ground; but the dove found no place to set her foot, and she returned to him to the ark, for the waters were still on the face of the whole earth. So he put forth his hand and took her and brought her into the ark with him. He waited another seven days, and again he sent forth the dove out of the ark; and the dove came back to him in the evening, and lo, in her mouth a freshly plucked olive leaf; so Noah knew that the waters had subsided from the earth. Then he waited another seven days, and sent forth the dove; and she did not return to him any more. In the six hundred and first year, in the first month, the first day of the month, the waters were dried from off the earth; and Noah removed the covering of the ark, and looked, and behold the face of the ground was dry. In the second month, on the twenty-seventh day of the month, the earth was dry. Then God said to Noah, "Go forth from the ark, you and your wife, and your sons and your sons' wives with you. Bring forth with you every living thing that is with you of all flesh—birds and animals and every creeping thing that creeps on the earth—that they may breed abundantly on the earth, and be fruitful and multiply upon the earth." So Noah went forth, and his sons and his wife and his sons' wives with him. Then God said to Noah and to his sons with him, "Behold, I establish my covenant with you and your descendants after you, and with every living creature that is with you, the birds, the cattle, and every beast of the earth with you, as many as came out of the ark. I establish my covenant with you, that never again shall all flesh be cut off by the waters of a flood, and never again shall there be a flood to destroy the earth." And God said, "This is the sign of the covenant which I make between me and you and every living creature that is with you, for all future generations: I set my bow in the cloud, and it shall be a sign of the covenant between me and the earth."

Psalm 46 [page 649]

[Abraham's sacrifice of Isaac] •

A Reading (Lesson) from the Book of Genesis [22:1-18]

God tested Abraham, and said to him, "Abraham!" And he said, "Here am I." He said, "Take your son, your only son

Isaac, whom you love, and go to the land of Mori'ah, and offer him there as a burnt offering upon one of the mountains of which I shall tell you." So Abraham rose early in the morning, saddled his ass, and took two of his young men with him, and his son Isaac; and he cut the wood for the burnt offering, and arose and went to the place of which God had told him. On the third day Abraham lifted up his eyes and saw the place afar off. Then Abraham said to his young men, "Stay here with the ass; I and the lad will go yonder and worship, and come again to you." And Abraham took the wood of the burnt offering, and laid it on Isaac his son; and he took in his hand the fire and the knife. So they went both of them together. And Isaac said to his father Abraham, "My father!" And he said, "Here am I, my son." He said, "Behold, the fire and the wood; but where is the lamb for a burnt offering?" Abraham said, "God will provide himself the lamb for a burnt offering, my son." So they went both of them together. When they came to the place of which God had told him, Abraham built an altar there, and laid the wood in order, and bound Isaac his son, and laid him on the altar, upon the wood. Then Abraham put forth his hand, and took the knife to slay his son. But the angel of the Lord called to him from heaven, and said, "Abraham, Abraham!" And he said, "Here am I." He said, "Do not lay your hand on the lad or do anything to him; for now I know that you fear God, seeing you have not withheld your son, your only son, from me." And Abraham lifted up his eyes and looked, and behold, behind him was a ram, caught in a thicket by his horns; and Abraham went and took the ram, and offered it up as a burnt offering instead of his son. So Abraham called the name of that place The Lord will provide; as it is said to this day, "On the mount of the Lord it shall be provided." And the angel of the Lord called to Abraham a second time from heaven, and said, "By myself I have sworn, says the Lord, because you have done this, and have not withheld your son, your only son, I will indeed bless you, and I will multiply your descendants as the stars of heaven and as the sand which is on the seashore. And your descendants shall possess the gate of their enemies, and by your descendants shall all the nations of the earth bless themselves, because you have obeyed my voice."

Psalm 33:12-22 [page 626] or *Psalm 16* [page 599]

[Israel's deliverance at the Red Sea] ✝

A Reading (Lesson) from the Book of Exodus [14:10—15:1]

When Pharaoh drew near, the people of Israel lifted up their eyes, and behold, the Egyptians were marching after them; and they were in great fear. And the people of Israel cried out to the Lord; and they said to Moses, "Is it because there are no graves in Egypt that you have taken us away to die in the wilderness? What have you done to us, in bringing us out of Egypt? Is not this what we have said to you in Egypt, 'Let us alone and let us serve the Egyptians'? For it would have been better for us to serve the Egyptians than die in the wilderness." And Moses said to the people, "Fear not, stand firm, and see the salvation of the Lord, which he will work for you today; for the Egyptians whom you see today, you shall never see again. The Lord will fight for you, and you have only to be still." The Lord said to Moses, "Why do you cry to me? Tell the people of Israel to go forward. Lift up your rod, and stretch out your hand over the sea and divide it, that the people of Israel may go on dry ground through the sea. And I will harden the hearts of the Egyptians so that they shall go in after them, and I will get glory over Pharaoh and all his host, his chariots, and his horsemen. And the Egyptians shall know that I am the Lord, when I have gotten glory over Pharaoh, his chariots, and his horsemen." Then the angel of God who went before the host of Israel moved and went behind them; and the pillar of cloud moved from before them and stood behind them, coming between the host of Egypt and the host of Israel. And there was the cloud and the darkness; and the night passed without one coming near the other all night. Then Moses stretched out his hand over the sea; and the Lord drove the sea back by a strong east wind all night, and made the sea dry land, and the waters were divided. And the people of Israel went into the midst of the sea on dry ground, the waters being a wall to them on their right hand and on their left. The Egyptians pursued, and went in after them into the midst of the sea, all Pharaoh's horses, his chariots, and his horsemen. And in the morning watch, the Lord in the pillar of fire and of cloud looked down upon the host of the Egyptians, and discomfited the host of the Egyptians, clogging their chariot wheels so that they drove heavily; and the Egyptians said, "Let us flee from before Israel; for the Lord fights for them against the Egyptians." Then the Lord said to Moses, "Stretch out your hand over the sea, that the water may come back upon the Egyptians, upon their chariots, and upon their horsemen." So Moses stretched forth his hand over the sea, and the sea returned to its wonted flow when the morning appeared; and the Egyptians fled into it, and the Lord routed the Egyptians in the midst of the sea. The waters returned and covered the chariots and the horsemen and all the host of Pharaoh that had followed them into the sea; not so much as one of them remained. But the people of Israel walked on dry ground through the sea, the waters being a wall to them on their right hand and on their left. Thus the Lord saved Israel that day from the hand of the Egyptians; and Israel saw the Egyptians dead upon the seashore. And Israel saw the great work which the Lord did against the Egyptians, and the people feared the Lord; and they believed in the Lord and in his servant Moses. Then Moses and the people of Israel sang this song to the Lord, saying, "I will sing to the Lord, for he has triumphed gloriously; the horse and his rider he has thrown into the sea."

Canticle 8, The Song of Moses [page 85]

[God's Presence in a renewed Israel]

A Reading (Lesson) from the Book of Isaiah [4:2-6]

In that day the branch of the Lord shall be beautiful and glorious, and the fruit of the land shall be the pride and glory of the survivors of Israel. And he who is left in Zion and remains in Jerusalem will be called holy, every one who has been recorded for life in Jerusalem, when the Lord shall have washed away the filth of the daughters of Zion, and cleansed the bloodstains of Jerusalem from its midst by a spirit of judgment and by a spirit of burning. Then the Lord will create over the whole site of Mount Zion and over her assemblies a cloud by day, and smoke and the shining of a flaming fire by night; for over all the glory there will be a canopy and a pavilion. It will be for a shade by day from the heat, and for a refuge and a shelter from the storm and rain.

Psalm 122 [page 779]

[Salvation offered freely to all] ●

A Reading (Lesson) from the Book of Isaiah [55:1-11]

Thus says the Lord: "Ho, every one who thirsts, come to the waters; and he who has no money, come, buy and eat! Come, buy wine and milk without money and without price. Why do you spend your money for that which is not bread, and your labor for that which does not satisfy?

Hearken diligently to me, and eat what is good, and delight yourselves in fatness. Incline your ear, and come to me; hear, that your soul may live; and I will make with you an everlasting covenant, my steadfast, sure love for David. Behold, I made him a witness to the peoples, a leader and commander for the peoples. Behold, you shall call nations that you know not, and nations that knew you not shall run to you, because of the Lord your God, and of the Holy One of Israel, for he has glorified you. Seek the Lord while he may be found, call upon him while he is near; let the wicked forsake his way, and the unrighteous man his thoughts; let him return to the Lord, that he may have mercy on him, and to our God, for he will abundantly pardon. For my thoughts are not your thoughts, neither are your ways my ways, says the Lord. For as the heavens are higher than the earth, so are my ways higher than your ways and my thoughts than your thoughts. For as the rain and the snow come down from heaven, and return not thither but water the earth, making it bring forth and sprout, giving seed to the sower and bread to the eater, so shall my word be that goes forth from my mouth; it shall not return to me empty, but it shall accomplish that which I purpose, and prosper in the thing for which I sent it."

Canticle 9, The First Song of Isaiah [Page 86]   or

Psalm 42:1-7 [page 643]

[A new heart and a new spirit]

A Reading (Lesson) from the Book of Ezekiel [36:24-28]

Thus says the Lord God: "I will take you from the nations, and gather you from all the countries, and bring you into your own land. I will sprinkle clean water upon you, and you shall be clean from all your uncleannesses, and from all your idols I will cleanse you. A new heart I will give

you, and a new spirit I will put within you; and I will take
out of your flesh the heart of stone and give you a heart of
flesh. And I will put my spirit within you, and cause you to
walk in my statutes, and be careful to observe my
ordinances. You shall dwell in the land which I gave to
your fathers; and you shall be my people, and I will be
your God."

Psalm 42:1-7 [page 643]   or

Canticle 9, The First Song of Isaiah [Page 86]

[The valley of dry bones]   ✹

A Reading (Lesson) from the Book of Ezekiel [37:1-14]

The hand of the Lord was upon me, and he brought me out
by the Spirit of the Lord, and set me down in the midst of
the valley; it was full of bones. And he led me round
among them; and behold, there were very many upon the
valley; and lo, they were very dry. And he said to me, "Son
of man, can these bones live?" And I answered, "O Lord
God, thou knowest." Again he said to me, "Prophesy to
these bones, and say to them, O dry bones, hear the word
of the Lord. Thus says the Lord God to these bones: Behold,
I will cause breath to enter you, and you shall live. And I
will lay sinews upon you, and will cause flesh to come
upon you, and cover you with skin, and put breath in you,
and you shall live; and you shall know that I am the
Lord." So I prophesied as I was commanded; and as I
prophesied, there was a noise, and behold, a rattling; and
the bones came together, bone to its bone. And as I looked,
there were sinews on them, and flesh had come upon them,
and skin had covered them; but there was no breath in
them. Then he said to me, "Prophesy to the breath,
prophesy, son of man, and say to the breath, Thus says the
Lord God: Come from the four winds, O breath, and

breathe upon these slain, that they may live." So I prophesied as he commanded me, and the breath came into them, and they lived, and stood upon their feet, an exceedingly great host. Then he said to me, "Son of man, these bones are the whole house of Israel. Behold, they say, 'Our bones are dried up, and our hope is lost; we are clean cut off.' Therefore prophesy, and say to them, Thus says the Lord God: Behold, I will open your graves, and raise you from your graves, O my people; and I will bring you home into the land of Israel. And you shall know that I am the Lord, when I open your graves, and raise you from your graves, O my people. And I will put my Spirit within you, and you shall live, and I will place you in your own land; then you shall know that I, the Lord, have spoken, and I have done it, says the Lord."

Psalm 30 [page 621] or *Psalm 143* [page 798]

[The gathering of God's people] ✷

A Reading (Lesson) from the Book of Zephaniah [3:12-20]

Thus says the Lord: "I will leave in the midst of you a people humble and lowly. They shall seek refuge in the name of the Lord, those who are left in Israel; they shall do no wrong and utter no lies, nor shall there be found in their mouth a deceitful tongue. For they shall pasture and lie down, and none shall make them afraid." Sing aloud, O daughter of Zion; shout, O Israel! Rejoice and exult with all your heart, O daughter of Jerusalem! The Lord has taken away the judgments against you, he has cast out your enemies. The King of Israel, the Lord, is in your midst; you shall fear evil no more. On that day it shall be said to Jerusalem: "Do not fear, O Zion; let not your hands grow weak. The Lord, your God, is in your midst, a warrior who gives victory; he will rejoice over you with gladness, he will renew you in his love; he will exult over you with loud singing as on a day of festival. I will remove disaster from you, so that you will not bear reproach for it. Behold, at that time I will deal with all your oppressors. And I will save the lame, and gather the outcast, and I will change their shame into praise and renown in all the earth. At that time I will bring you home, at the time when I gather you together; yea, I will make you renowned and praised among all the peoples of the earth, when I restore your fortunes before your eyes," says the Lord.

Psalm 98 [page 727] or *Psalm 126* [page 782]

At the Eucharist

A Reading (Lesson) from the Letter of Paul to the Romans [6:3-11]

Do you not know that all of us who have been baptized into Christ Jesus were baptized into his death? We were buried therefore with him by baptism into death, so that as Christ was raised from the dead by the glory of the Father, we too might walk in newness of life. For if we have been united with him in a death like his, we shall certainly be united with him in a resurrection like his. We know that our old self was crucified with him so that the sinful body might be destroyed, and we might no longer be enslaved to sin. For he who has died is freed from sin. But if we have died with Christ, we believe that we shall also live with him. For we know that Christ being raised from the dead will never die again; death no longer has dominion over him. The death he died, he died to sin, once for all, but the life he lives, he lives to God. So you also must consider yourselves dead to sin and alive to God in Christ Jesus.

"Alleluia" may be sung and repeated.

Psalm 114 [page 756], *or some other suitable psalm or a hymn may be sung.*

✝ *The Holy Gospel of Our Lord Jesus Christ According to Matthew* [28:1-10]

After the sabbath, toward the dawn of the first day of the week, Mary Mag'dalene and the other Mary went to see the sepulchre. And behold, there was a great earthquake; for an angel of the Lord descended from heaven and came and rolled back the stone, and sat upon it. His appearance was like lightning, and his raiment white as snow. And for fear of him the guards trembled and became like dead men. But the angel said to the women, "Do not be afraid; for I know that you seek Jesus who was crucified. He is not here; for he has risen, as he said. Come, see the place where he lay. Then go quickly and tell his disciples that he has risen from the dead, and behold, he is going before you to Galilee; there you will see him. Lo, I have told you." So they departed quickly from the tomb with fear and great joy, and ran to tell his disciples. And behold, Jesus met them and said, "Hail!" And they came up and took hold of his feet and worshiped him. Then Jesus said to them, "Do not be afraid; go and tell my brethren to go to Galilee, and there they will see me."

Easter Day: Early Service

One of the Old Testament Lessons from the Vigil [pages 101-113 above]

Psalm 114 [page 756]

The Epistle: Romans 6:3-11 [page 113 above]

The Holy Gospel: Matthew 28:1-10 [above]

Easter Day: Principal Service

A Reading (Lesson) from the Acts of the Apostles [10:34-43]

Peter opened his mouth and said, "Truly I perceive that God shows no partiality, but in every nation any one who fears him and does what is right is acceptable to him. You know the word which he sent to Israel, preaching good news of peace by Jesus Christ (he is Lord of all), the word which was proclaimed throughout all Judea, beginning from Galilee after the baptism which John preached: how God anointed Jesus of Nazareth with the Holy Spirit and with power; how he went about doing good and healing all that were oppressed by the devil, for God was with him. And we are witnesses to all that he did both in the country of the Jews and in Jerusalem. They put him to death by hanging him on a tree; but God raised him on the third day and made him manifest; not to all the people but to us who were chosen by God as witnesses, who ate and drank with him after he rose from the dead. And he commanded us to preach to the people, and to testify that he is the one ordained by God to be judge of the living and the dead. To him all the prophets bear witness that every one who believes in him receives forgiveness of sins through his name."

or this

A reading (Lesson) from the Book of Isaiah [51:9-11]

Awake, awake, put on strength, O arm of the Lord; awake, as in days of old, the generations of long ago. Was it not thou that didst cut Rahab in pieces, that didst pierce the dragon? Was it not thou that didst dry up the sea, the waters of the great deep; that didst make the depths of the sea, a way for the redeemed to pass over? And the ransomed of the Lord shall return, and come to Zion with singing;

everlasting joy shall be upon their heads; they shall obtain joy and gladness, and sorrow and sighing shall flee away.

Psalm 118:14-29 [page 761] or *118:14-17, 22-24* [page 761]

A Reading (Lesson) from the Letter of Paul to the Colossians [3:1-4]

Since you have been raised with Christ, seek the things that are above, where Christ is, seated at the right hand of God. Set your minds on things that are above, not on things that are on earth. For you have died, and your life is hid with Christ in God. When Christ who is our life appears, then you also will appear with him in glory.

or this

Acts 10:34-43 [page 115 above]

✝ *The Holy Gospel of Our Lord Jesus Christ According to Luke* [24:1-10]

On the first day of the week, at early dawn, the women who had come with Jesus from Galilee went to the tomb, taking the spices which they had prepared. And they found the stone rolled away from the tomb, but when they went in they did not find the body. While they were perplexed about this, behold, two men stood by them in dazzling apparel; and as they were frightened and bowed their faces to the ground, the men said to them, "Why do you seek the living among the dead? Remember how he told you, while he was still in Galilee, that the Son of man must be delivered into the hands of sinful men, and be crucified, and on the third day rise." And they remembered his words, and returning from the tomb they told all this to the eleven and to all the rest. Now it was Mary Mag'dalene and Jo-an'na and Mary the mother of James and the other women with them who told this to the apostles.

Easter Day: Evening Service

A Reading (Lesson) from the Acts of the Apostles
[5:29a,30-32]

Peter and the apostles said to the high priest and the council,"The God of our fathers raised Jesus whom you killed by hanging him on a tree. God exalted him at his right hand as Leader and Savior, to give repentance to Israel and forgiveness of sins, and we are witnesses to these things, and so is the Holy Spirit whom God has given to those who obey him."

or this

A Reading (Lesson) from the Book of Daniel [12:1-3]

The Lord spoke to Daniel in a vision and said,"At that time shall arise Michael, the great prince who has charge of your people. And there shall be a time of trouble, such as never has been since there was a nation till that time; but at that time your people shall be delivered, every one whose name shall be found written in the book. And many of those who sleep in the dust of the earth shall awake, some to everlasting life, and some to shame and everlasting contempt. And those who are wise shall shine like the brightness of the firmament; and those who turn many to righteousness, like the stars for ever and ever."

Psalm 114 [page 756]   or   *Psalm 136* [page 789]   or

Psalm 118:14-17, 22-24 [page 761]

A Reading (Lesson) from the First Letter of Paul to the Corinthians [5:6b-8]

Do you not know that a little leaven leavens the whole lump? Cleanse out the old leaven that you may be a new lump, as you really are unleavened. For Christ, our paschal lamb, has been sacrificed. Let us, therefore, celebrate the festival, not with the old leaven, the leaven of malice and evil, but with the unleavened bread of sincerity and truth.

or this

Acts 5:29a,30-32 [page 117 above]

✝ *The Holy Gospel of Our Lord Jesus Christ According to Luke* [24:13-35]

That very day, the first day of the week, two of the disciples were going to a village named Emma'us, about seven miles from Jerusalem, and talking with each other about all these things that had happened. While they were talking and discussing together, Jesus himself drew near and went with them. But their eyes were kept from recognizing him. And he said to them,"What is this conversation which you are holding with each other as you walk?" And they stood still, looking sad. Then one of them, named Cle'opas, answered him,"Are you the only visitor to Jerusalem who does not know the things that have happened there in these days?" And he said to them,"What things?" And they said to him,"Concerning Jesus of Nazareth, who was a prophet mighty in deed and word before God and all the people, and how our chief priests and rulers delivered him up to be condemned to death, and crucified him. But we had hoped that he was the one to redeem Israel. Yes, and besides all this, it is now the third day since this happened. Moreover, some women of our company amazed us. They were at the tomb early in the morning and did not find his body; and they came back saying that they had even seen a vision of angels, who said that he was alive. Some of those who were with us went to the tomb, and found it just as the women had said; but him they did not see." And he said to them,"O foolish men, and slow of heart to believe all that the prophets have spoken! Was it not necessary that the

Christ should suffer these things and enter into his glory?" And beginning with Moses and all the prophets, he interpreted to them in all the scriptures the things concerning himself. So they drew near to the village to which they were going. He appeared to be going further, but they constrained him, saying, "Stay with us, for it is toward evening and the day is now far spent." So he went in to stay with them. When he was at table with them, he took the bread and blessed, and broke it, and gave it to them. And their eyes were opened and they recognized him; and he vanished out of their sight. They said to each other, "Did not our hearts burn within us while he talked to us on the road, while he opened to us the scriptures?" And they rose that same hour and returned to Jerusalem; and they found the eleven gathered together and those who were with them, who said, "The Lord has risen indeed, and has appeared to Simon!" Then they told what had happened on the road, and how he was known to them in the breaking of the bread.

Monday in Easter Week

A Reading (Lesson) from the Acts of the Apostles [2:14,22b-32]

Peter, standing with the eleven, lifted up his voice and addressed the multitude, "Men of Judea and all who dwell in Jerusalem, let this be known to you, and give ear to my words: Jesus of Nazareth, a man attested to you by God with mighty works and wonders and signs which God did through him in your midst, as you yourselves know—this Jesus, delivered up according to the definite plan and foreknowledge of God, you crucified and killed by the hands of lawless men. But God raised him up, having loosed the pangs of death, because it was not possible for him to be held by it. For David says concerning him, 'I saw the Lord always before me, for he is at my right hand that I may not be shaken; therefore my heart was glad, and my tongue rejoiced; moreover my flesh will dwell in hope. For thou wilt not abandon my soul to Hades, nor let thy Holy One see corruption. Thou hast made known to me the ways of life; thou wilt make me full of gladness with thy presence.' Brethren, I may say to you confidently of the patriarch David that he both died and was buried, and his tomb is with us to this day. Being therefore a prophet, and knowing that God had sworn with an oath to him that he would set one of his descendants upon his throne, he foresaw and spoke of the resurrection of the Christ, that he was not abandoned to Hades, nor did his flesh see corruption. This Jesus God raised up, and of that we all are witnesses."

Psalm 16:8-11 [page 600] or *Psalm 118:19-24* [page 762]

✝ *The Holy Gospel of Our Lord Jesus Christ According to Matthew* [28:9-15]

Behold, Jesus met Mary Mag'dalene and the other Mary and said, "Hail!" And they came up and took hold of his feet and worshiped him. Then Jesus said to them, "Do not be afraid; go and tell my brethren to go to Galilee, and there they will see me." While they were going, behold, some of the guard went into the city and told the chief priests all that had taken place. And when they had assembled with the elders and taken counsel, they gave a sum of money to the soldiers and said, "Tell people, 'His disciples came by night and stole him away while we were asleep.' And if this comes to the governor's ears, we will satisfy him and keep you out of trouble." So they took the money and did as they were directed; and this story has been spread among the Jews to this day.

Tuesday in Easter Week

A Reading (Lesson) from the Acts of the Apostles [2:36-41]

Peter said to the multitude, "Let all the house of Israel therefore know assuredly that God has made him both Lord and Christ, this Jesus whom you crucified." Now when they heard this they were cut to the heart, and said to Peter and the rest of the apostles, "Brethren, what shall we do?" And Peter said to them, "Repent, and be baptized every one of you in the name of Jesus Christ for the forgiveness of your sins; and you shall receive the gift of the Holy Spirit. For the promise is to you and to your children and to all that are far off, every one whom the Lord our God calls to him." And he testified with many other words and exhorted them, saying, "Save yourselves from this crooked generation." So those who received his word were baptized, and there were added that day about three thousand souls.

Psalm 33:18-22 [page 627]   or   *Psalm 118:19-24* [page 762]

✝ *The Holy Gospel of Our Lord Jesus Christ According to John* [20:11-18]

Mary Mag'dalene stood weeping outside the tomb, and as she wept she stooped to look into the tomb; and she saw two angels in white, sitting where the body of Jesus had lain, one at the head and one at the feet. They said to her, "Woman, why are you weeping?" She said to them, "Because they have taken away my Lord, and I do not know where they have laid him." Saying this, she turned round and saw Jesus standing, but she did not know that it was Jesus. Jesus said to her, "Woman, why are you weeping? Whom do you seek?" Supposing him to be the gardener, she said to him, "Sir, if you have carried him away, tell me where you have laid him, and I will take him away." Jesus said to her, "Mary." She turned and said to him in Hebrew, "Rab-bo'ni!" (which means Teacher). Jesus said to her, "Do not hold me, for I have not yet ascended to the Father; but go to my brethren and say to them, I am ascending to my Father and your Father, to my God and your God." Mary Mag'dalene went and said to the disciples, "I have seen the Lord"; and she told them that he had said these things to her.

Wednesday in Easter Week

A Reading (Lesson) from the Acts of the Apostles [3:1-10]

Now Peter and John were going up to the temple at the hour of prayer, the ninth hour. And a man lame from birth was being carried, whom they laid daily at that gate of the temple which is called Beautiful to ask alms of those who entered the temple. Seeing Peter and John about to go into the temple, he asked for alms. And Peter directed his gaze at him, with John, and said, "Look at us." And he fixed his attention upon them, expecting to receive something from them. But Peter said, "I have no silver and gold, but I give you what I have; in the name of Jesus Christ of Nazareth, walk." And he took him by the right hand and raised him up; and immediately his feet and ankles were made strong. And leaping up he stood and walked and entered the temple with them, walking and leaping and praising God. And all the people saw him walking and praising God, and recognized him as the one who sat for alms at the Beautiful Gate of the temple; and they were filled with wonder and amazement at what had happened to him.

Psalm 105:1-8 [page 738]   or   *Psalm 118:19-24* [page 762]

✝ *The Holy Gospel of Our Lord Jesus Christ According to Luke* [24:13-35] [page 118 above]

Thursday in Easter Week

A Reading (Lesson) from the Acts of the Apostles [3:11-26]

While the lame man whom Peter and John had healed clung to them, all the people ran together to them in the portico called Solomon's, astounded. And when Peter saw it he addressed the people, "Men of Israel, why do you wonder at this, or why do you stare at us, as though by our own power or piety we had made him walk? The God of Abraham and of Isaac and of Jacob, the God of our fathers, glorified his servant Jesus, whom you delivered up and denied in the presence of Pilate, when he had decided to release him. But you denied the Holy and Righteous One, and asked for a murderer to be granted to you, and killed the Author of life, whom God raised from the dead. To this we are witnesses. And his name, by faith in his name, has made this man strong whom you see and know; and the faith which is through Jesus has given the man this perfect health in the presence of you all. And now, brethren, I know that you acted in ignorance, as did also your rulers. But what God foretold by the mouth of all the prophets, that his Christ should suffer, he thus fulfilled. Repent therefore, and turn again, that your sins may be blotted out, that times of refreshing may come from the presence of the Lord, and that he may send the Christ appointed for you, Jesus, whom heaven must receive until the time for establishing all that God spoke by the mouth of his holy prophets from of old. Moses said, 'The Lord God will raise up for you a prophet from your brethren as he raised me up. You shall listen to him in whatever he tells you. And it shall be that every soul that does not listen to that prophet shall be destroyed from the people.' And all the prophets who have spoken, from Samuel and those who came afterwards, also proclaimed these days. You are the sons of the prophets and of the covenant which God gave to your fathers, saying to Abraham, 'And in your posterity shall all the families of the earth be blessed.' God, having raised up his servant, sent him to you first, to bless you in turning every one of you from your wickedness."

Psalm 8 [page 592] or *Psalm 114* [page 756] or *Psalm 118:19-24* [page 762]

✝ *The Holy Gospel of Our Lord Jesus Christ According to Luke* [24:36b-48]

While the disciples were telling how they had seen Jesus risen from the dead, Jesus himself stood among them. But they were startled and frightened, and supposed that they saw a ghost. And he said to them, "Why are you troubled, and why do questionings rise in your hearts? See my hands and my feet, that it is I myself; handle me, and see; for a spirit has not flesh and bones as you see that I have." And while they still disbelieved for joy, and wondered, he said to them, "Have you anything here to eat?" They gave him a piece of broiled fish, and he took it and ate before them. Then he said to them, "These are my words which I spoke to you, while I was still with you, that everything written about me in the law of Moses and the prophets and the psalms must be fulfilled." Then he opened their minds to understand the scriptures, and said to them, "Thus it is written, that the Christ should suffer and on the third day rise from the dead, and that repentance and forgiveness of sins should be preached in his name to all nations, beginning from Jerusalem. You are witnesses of these things."

Friday in Easter Week

A Reading (Lesson) from the Acts of the Apostles [4:1-12]

As Peter and John were speaking to the people, the priests and the captain of the temple and the Sad'ducees came upon them, annoyed because they were teaching the people and proclaiming in Jesus the resurrection from the dead. And they arrested them and put them in custody until the morrow, for it was already evening. But many of those who heard the word believed; and the number of the men came to about five thousand. On the morrow their rulers and elders and scribes were gathered together in Jerusalem, with Annas the high priest and Ca'iaphas and John and Alexander, and all who were of the high-priestly family. And when they had set them in the midst, they inquired, "By what power or by what name did you do this?" Then Peter, filled with the Holy Spirit, said to them, "Rulers of the people and elders, if we are being examined today concerning a good deed done to a cripple, by what means this man has been healed, be it known to you all, and to all the people of Israel, that by the name of Jesus Christ of Nazareth, whom you crucified, whom God raised from the dead, by him this man is standing before you well. This is the stone which was rejected by you builders, but which has become the head of the corner. And there is salvation in no one else, for there is no other name under heaven given among men by which we must be saved."

Psalm 116:1-8 [page 759] or *Psalm 118:19-24* [page 762]

✝ *The Holy Gospel of Our Lord Jesus Christ According to John* [21:1-14]

After this Jesus revealed himself again to the disciples by the Sea of Tibe'ri-as; and he revealed himself in this way. Simon Peter, Thomas called the Twin, Nathan'a-el of Cana in Galilee, the sons of Zeb'edee, and two others of his disciples were together. Simon Peter said to them, "I am going fishing." They said to him, "We will go with you." They went out and got into the boat; but that night they caught nothing. Just as day was breaking, Jesus stood on the beach; yet the disciples did not know that it was Jesus. Jesus said to them, "Children, have you any fish?" They answered him, "No." He said to them, "Cast the net on the right side of the boat, and you will find some." So they cast it, and now they were not able to haul it in, for the quantity of fish. That disciple whom Jesus loved said to Peter, "It is the Lord!" When Simon Peter heard that it was the Lord, he put on his clothes, for he was stripped for work, and sprang into the sea. But the other disciples came in the boat, dragging the net full of fish, for they were not far from the land, but about a hundred yards off. When they got out on land, they saw a charcoal fire there, with fish lying on it, and bread. Jesus said to them, "Bring some of the fish that you have just caught." So Simon Peter went aboard and hauled the net ashore, full of large fish, a hundred and fifty-three of them; and although there were so many, the net was not torn. Jesus said to them, "Come and have breakfast." Now none of the disciples dared ask him, "Who are you?" They knew it was the Lord. Jesus came and took the bread and gave it to them, and so with the fish. This was now the third time that Jesus was revealed to the disciples after he was raised from the dead.

Saturday in Easter Week

A Reading (Lesson) from the Acts of the Apostles [4:13-21]

Now when the rulers and elders and scribes saw the boldness of Peter and John, and perceived that they were uneducated, common men, they wondered; and they recognized that they had been with Jesus. But seeing the man that had been healed standing beside them, they had nothing to say in opposition. But when they had commanded them to go aside out of the council, they conferred with one another, saying, "What shall we do with these men? For that a notable sign has been performed through them is manifest to all the inhabitants of Jerusalem, and we cannot deny it. But in order that it may spread no further among the people, let us warn them to speak no more to any one in this name." So they called them and charged them not to speak or teach at all in the name of Jesus. But Peter and John answered them, "Whether it is right in the sight of God to listen to you rather than to God, you must judge; for we cannot but speak of what we have seen and heard." And when they had further threatened them, they let them go, finding no way to punish them, because of the people; for all men praised God for what had happened.

Psalm 118:14-18 [page 871] or *118:19-24* [page 872]

✝ *The Holy Gospel of Our Lord Jesus Christ According to Mark* [16:9-15, 20]

Now when Jesus rose early on the first day of the week, he appeared first to Mary Mag'dalene, from whom he had cast out seven demons. She went out and told those who had been with him, as they mourned and wept. But when they heard that he was alive and had been seen by her, they would not believe it. After this he appeared in another form to two of them as they were walking into the country. And they went back and told the rest, but they did not believe them. Afterward he appeared to the eleven themselves as they sat at table; and he upbraided them for their unbelief and hardness of heart, because they had not believed those who saw him after he had risen. And he said to them, "Go into all the world and preach the gospel to the whole creation." And they went forth and preached everywhere, while the Lord worked with them and confirmed the message by the signs that attended it.

Second Sunday of Easter

A Reading (Lesson) from the Acts of the Apostles
[5:12a, 17-22, 25-29]

Now many signs and wonders were done among the
people by the hands of the apostles. But the high priest rose
up and all who were with him, that is, the party of the
Sad'ducees, and filled with jealousy they arrested the
apostles and put them in the common prison. But at night
an angel of the Lord opened the prison doors and brought
them out and said, "Go and stand in the temple and speak
to the people all the words of this Life." And when they
heard this, they entered the temple at daybreak and taught.
Now the high priest came and those who were with him
and called together the council and all the senate of Israel,
and sent to the prison to have them brought. But when the
officers came, they did not find them in the prison, and
they returned and reported. And some one came and told
them, "The men whom you put in prison are standing in
the temple and teaching the people." Then the captain with
the officers went and brought them, but without violence,
for they were afraid of being stoned by the people. And
when they had brought them, they set them before the
council. And the high priest questioned them, saying, "We
strictly charged you not to teach in this name, yet here you
have filled Jerusalem with your teaching and you intend to
bring this man's blood upon us." But Peter and the apostles
answered, "We must obey God rather than men."

or this

A Reading (Lesson) from the Book of Job [42:1-6]

Then Job answered the Lord: "I know that thou canst do all
things, and that no purpose of thine can be thwarted. 'Who
is this that hides counsel without knowledge?' Therefore

I have uttered what I did not understand, things too
wonderful for me, which I did not know.'Hear, and I will
speak; I will question you, and you declare to me.' I had
heard of thee by the hearing of the ear, but now my eye
sees thee; therefore I despise myself, and repent in dust and
ashes."

Psalm 111 [page 754]   or   *Psalm 118:19-24* [page 762]

A Reading (Lesson) from the Revelation to John [1:(1-8)9-19]

The revelation of Jesus Christ, which God gave him to
show to his servants what must soon take place; and he
made it known by sending his angel to his servant John,
who bore witness to the word of God and to the
testimony of Jesus Christ, even to all that he saw.
Blessed is he who reads aloud the words of the
prophecy, and blessed are those who hear, and who
keep what is written therein; for the time is near. John to
the seven churches that are in Asia: Grace to you and
peace from him who is and who was and who is to
come, and from the seven spirits who are before his
throne, and from Jesus Christ the faithful witness, the
first-born of the dead, and the ruler of kings on earth. To
him who loves us and has freed us from our sins by his
blood and made us a kingdom, priests to his God and
Father, to him be glory and dominion for ever and ever.
Amen. Behold, he is coming with the clouds, and every
eye will see him, every one who pierced him; and all
tribes of the earth will wail on account of him. Even so.
Amen. "I am the Alpha and the Omega," says the Lord
God, who is and who was and who is to come, the
Almighty.

I John, your brother, who share with you in Jesus the
tribulation and the kingdom and the patient endurance,
was on the island called Patmos on account of the word of

God and the testimony of Jesus. I was in the Spirit on the Lord's day, and I heard behind me a loud voice like a trumpet saying, "Write what you see in a book and send it to the seven churches, to Ephesus and to Smyrna and to Per'gamum and to Thyati'ra and to Sardis and to Philadelphia and to La-odice'a." Then I turned to see the voice that was speaking to me, and on turning I saw seven golden lampstands, and in the midst of the lampstands one like a son of man, clothed with a long robe and with a golden girdle round his breast; his head and his hair were white as white wool, white as snow; his eyes were like a flame of fire, his feet were like burnished bronze, refined as in a furnace, and his voice was like the sound of many waters; in his right hand he held seven stars, from his mouth issued a sharp two-edged sword, and his face was like the sun shining in full strength. When I saw him, I fell at his feet as though dead. But he laid his right hand upon me, saying, "Fear not, I am the first and the last, and the living one; I died, and behold I am alive for evermore, and I have the keys of Death and Hades. Now write what you see, what is and what is to take place hereafter.

or this

Acts 5:12a, 17-22, 25-29 [page 128 above]

✝ *The Holy Gospel of Our Lord Jesus Christ According to John* [20:19-31]

On the evening of that day, the first day of the week, the doors being shut where the disciples were, for fear of the Jews, Jesus came and stood among them and said to them, "Peace be with you." When he had said this, he showed them his hands and his side. Then the disciples were glad when they saw the Lord. Jesus said to them again, "Peace be with you. As the Father has sent me, even so I send you." And when he had said this, he breathed on them and said to them, "Receive the Holy Spirit. If you forgive the sins of any, they are forgiven; if you retain the sins of any, they are retained." Now Thomas, one of the twelve, called the Twin, was not with them when Jesus came. So the other disciples told him, "We have seen the Lord." But he said to them, "Unless I see in his hands the print of the nails, and place my finger in the mark of the nails, and place my hand in his side, I will not believe." Eight days later, his disciples were again in the house, and Thomas was with them. The doors were shut, but Jesus came and stood among them, and said, "Peace be with you." Then he said to Thomas, "Put your finger here, and see my hands; and put out your hand, and place it in my side; do not be faithless, but believing." Thomas answered him, "My Lord and my God!" Jesus said to him, "Have you believed because you have seen me? Blessed are those who have not seen and yet believe." Now Jesus did many other signs in the presence of the disciples, which are not written in this book; but these are written that you may believe that Jesus is the Christ, the Son of God, and that believing you may have life in his name.

Third Sunday of Easter

A Reading (Lesson) from the Acts of the Apostles [9:1-19a]

But Saul, still breathing threats and murder against the disciples of the Lord, went to the high priest and asked him for letters to the synagogues at Damascus, so that if he found any belonging to the Way, men or women, he might bring them bound to Jerusalem. Now as he journeyed he approached Damascus, and suddenly a light from heaven flashed about him. And he fell to the ground and heard a voice saying to him, "Saul, Saul, why do you persecute me?" And he said, "Who are you, Lord?" And he said, "I am Jesus, whom you are persecuting; but rise and enter the city, and you will be told what you are to do." The men who were traveling with him stood speechless, hearing the voice but seeing no one. Saul arose from the ground; and when his eyes were opened, he could see nothing; so they led him by the hand and brought him into Damascus. And for three days he was without sight, and neither ate nor drank. Now there was a disciple at Damascus named Anani'as. The Lord said to him in a vision,"Anani'as." And he said,"Here I am, Lord." And the Lord said to him,"Rise and go to the street called Straight, and inquire in the house of Judas for a man of Tarsus named Saul; for behold, he is praying, and he has seen a man named Anani'as come in and lay his hands on him so that he might regain his sight." But Anani'as answered,"Lord, I have heard from many about this man, how much evil he has done to thy saints at Jerusalem; and here he has authority from the chief priests to bind all who call upon thy name." But the Lord said to him,"Go, for he is a chosen instrument of mine to carry my name before the Gentiles and kings and the sons of Israel; for I will show him how much he must suffer for the sake of my name." So Anani'as departed and entered the house. And laying his hands on him he said, "Brother Saul, the Lord Jesus who appeared to you on the road by which you came, has sent me that you may regain your sight and be filled with the Holy Spirit." And immediately something like scales fell from his eyes and he regained his sight. Then he rose and was baptized, and took food and was strengthened.

or this

A Reading (Lesson) from the Book of Jeremiah [32:36-41]

"Thus says the Lord, the God of Israel, concerning this city of which you say,'It is given into the hand of the king of Babylon by sword, by famine, and by pestilence': Behold, I will gather them from all the countries to which I drove them in my anger and my wrath and in great indignation;

I will bring them back to this place, and I will make them dwell in safety. And they shall be my people, and I will be their God. I will give them one heart and one way, that they may fear me for ever, for their own good and the good of their children after them. I will make with them an everlasting covenant, that I will not turn away from doing good to them; and I will put the fear of me in their hearts, that they may not turn from me. I will rejoice in doing them good, and I will plant them in this land in faithfulness, with all my heart and all my soul."

Psalm 33 [page 626] or *33:1-11* [page 626]

A Reading (Lesson) from the Revelation to John [5:6-14]

Between the throne and the four living creatures and among the elders, I saw a Lamb standing, as though it had been slain, with seven horns and with seven eyes, which are the seven spirits of God sent out into all the earth; and he went and took the scroll from the right hand of him who was seated on the throne. And when he had taken the scroll, the four living creatures and the twenty-four elders fell down before the Lamb, each holding a harp, and with golden bowls full of incense, which are the prayers of the saints; and they sang a new song, saying, "Worthy art thou to take the scroll and to open its seals, for thou wast slain and by thy blood didst ransom men for God from every tribe and tongue and people and nation, and hast made them a kingdom and priests to our God, and they shall reign on earth." Then I looked, and I heard around the throne and the living creatures and the elders the voice of many angels, numbering myriads of myriads and thousands of thousands, saying with a loud voice, "Worthy is the Lamb who was slain, to receive power and wealth and wisdom and might and honor and glory and blessing!" And I heard every creature in heaven and on earth and under the earth and in the sea, and all therein, saying, "To him who sits upon the throne and to the Lamb be blessing and honor and glory and might for ever and ever!" And the four living creatures said, "Amen!" and the elders fell down and worshiped.

or this

Acts 9:1-19a [page 131 above]

✝ *The Holy Gospel of Our Lord Jesus Christ*
　 According to John [21:1-14]

Jesus revealed himself again to the disciples by the Sea of Tibe′ri-as; and he revealed himself in this way. Simon Peter, Thomas called the Twin, Nathan′a-el of Cana in Galilee, the sons of Zeb′edee, and two others of his disciples were together. Simon Peter said to them, "I am going fishing." They said to him, "We will go with you." They went out and got into the boat; but that night they caught nothing. Just as day was breaking, Jesus stood on the beach; yet the disciples did not know that it was Jesus. Jesus said to them, "Children, have you any fish?" They answered him, "No." He said to them, "Cast the net on the right side of the boat, and you will find some." So they cast it, and now they were not able to haul it in, for the quantity of fish. That disciple whom Jesus loved said to Peter, "It is the Lord!" When Simon Peter heard that it was the Lord, he put on his clothes, for he was stripped for work, and sprang into the sea. But the other disciples came in the boat, dragging the net full of fish, for they were not far from the land, but about a hundred yards off. When they got out on land, they saw a charcoal fire there, with fish lying on it, and bread. Jesus said to them, "Bring some of the fish that you have just caught." So Simon Peter went aboard and hauled the net ashore, full of large fish, a hundred and fifty-three of them; and although there were so many, the net was not torn. Jesus said to them,"Come and have breakfast." Now none of the disciples dared ask him,"Who are you?" They knew it was the Lord. Jesus came and took the bread and gave it to them, and so with the fish. This was now the third time that Jesus was revealed to the disciples after he was raised from the dead.

Fourth Sunday of Easter

A Reading (Lesson) from the Acts of the Apostles
[13:15-16, 26-33 (34-39)]

When Paul and Barnabas came to Antioch of Pisid'ia, they went on the sabbath day into the synagogue, and after the reading of the law and the prophets, the rulers of the synagogue sent to them, saying,"Brethren, if you have any word of exhortation for the people, say it." So Paul stood up, and motioning with his hands said: "Men of Israel, and you that fear God, listen: Brethren, sons of the family of Abraham, and those among you that fear God, to us has been sent the message of this salvation. For those who live in Jerusalem and their rulers, because they did not recognize Jesus nor understand the utterances of the prophets which are read every sabbath, fulfilled these by condemning him. Though they could charge him with nothing deserving death, yet they asked Pilate to have him killed. And when they had fulfilled all that was written of him, they took him down from the tree, and laid him in a tomb. But God raised him from the dead; and for many days he appeared to those who came up with him from Galilee to Jerusalem, who are now his witnesses to the people. And we bring you the good news that what God promised to the fathers, this he has fulfilled to us their children by raising Jesus; as also it is written in the second psalm,'Thou art my Son, today I have begotten thee.'"

"And as for the fact that he raised him from the dead, no more to return to corruption, he spoke in this way,'I will give you the holy and sure blessings of David.' Therefore he says also in another psalm,'Thou wilt not let thy Holy One see corruption.' For David, after he had served the counsel of God in his own generation, fell asleep, and was laid with his fathers, and saw corruption; but he whom God raised up saw no corruption. Let it be known to you therefore, brethren, that through this man forgiveness of sins is proclaimed to you, and by him every one that believes is freed from everything from which you could not be freed by the law of Moses."

or this

A Reading (Lesson) from the Book of Numbers [27:12-23]

The Lord said to Moses,"Go up into this mountain of Ab'arim, and see the land which I have given to the people of Israel. And when you have seen it, you also shall be gathered to your people, as your people, as your brother Aaron was gathered, because you rebelled against my word in the wilderness of Zin during the strife of the congregation, to sanctify me at the waters before their eyes." (These are the waters of Mer'ibah of Kadesh in the wilderness of Zin.) Moses said to the Lord,"Let the Lord, the God of the spirits of all flesh, appoint a man over the congregation, who shall go out before them and come in before them, who shall lead them out and bring them in; that the congregation of the Lord may not be as sheep which have no shepherd." And the Lord said to Moses "Take Joshua the son of Nun, a man in whom is the spirit, and lay your hand upon him; cause him to stand before Elea'zar the priest and all the congregation, and you shall commission him in their sight. You shall invest him with some of your authority, that all the congregation of the people of Israel may obey. And he shall stand before

Elea'zar the priest, who shall inquire for him by the judgment of the Urim before the Lord; at his word they shall go out, and at his word they shall come in, both he and all the people of Israel with him, the whole congregation." And Moses did as the Lord commanded him; he took Joshua and caused him to stand before Elea'zar the priest and the whole congregation, and he laid his hands upon him, and commissioned him as the Lord directed through Moses.

Psalm 100 [page 729]

A Reading (Lesson) from the Revelation to John [7:9-17]

After this I looked, and behold, a great multitude which no man could number, from every nation, from all tribes and peoples and tongues, standing before the throne and before the Lamb, clothed in white robes, with palm branches in their hands, and crying out with a loud voice, "Salvation belongs to our God who sits upon the throne, and to the Lamb!" And all the angels stood round the throne and round the elders and the four living creatures, and they fell on their faces before the throne and worshiped God, saying, "Amen! Blessing and glory and wisdom and thanksgiving and honor and power and might be to our God for ever and ever! Amen." Then one of the elders addressed me, saying, "Who are these, clothed in white robes, and whence have they come?" I said to him, "Sir, you know." And he said to me, "These are they who have come out of the great tribulation; they have washed their robes and made them white in the blood of the Lamb. Therefore are they before the throne of God, and serve him day and night within his temple; and he who sits upon the throne will shelter them with his presence. They shall hunger no more, neither thirst any more; the sun shall not strike them, not any scorching heat. For the Lamb in the midst of the throne will be their shepherd, and he will guide them to springs of living water; and God will wipe away every tear from their eyes."

or this

Acts 13:15-16, 26-33 (34-39) [page 135 above]

✠ *The Holy Gospel of Our Lord Jesus Christ According to John* [10:22-30]

It was the feast of the Dedication at Jerusalem; it was winter, and Jesus was walking in the temple, in the portico of Solomon. So the Jews gathered round him and said to him,"How long will you keep us in suspense? If you are the Christ, tell us plainly." Jesus answered them,"I told you, and you do not believe. The works that I do in my Father's name, they bear witness to me; but you do not believe, because you do not belong to my sheep. My sheep hear my voice, and I know them, and they follow me; and I give them eternal life, and they shall never perish, and no one shall snatch them out of my hand. My Father, who has given them to me, is greater than all, and no one is able to snatch them out of the Father's hand. I and the Father are one."

Fifth Sunday of Easter

A Reading (Lesson) from the Acts of the Apostles [13:44-52]

The next sabbath after Paul first spoke in the synagogue at Antioch of Pisid'ia, almost the whole city gathered together to hear the word of God. But when the Jews saw the multitudes, they were filled with jealousy, and contradicted what was spoken by Paul, and reviled him. And Paul and Barnabas spoke out boldly, saying,"It was necessary that the word of God should be spoken first to you. Since you thrust it from you, and judge yourselves unworthy of eternal life, behold, we turn to the Gentiles. For so the Lord has commanded us, saying,'I have set you to be a light for the Gentiles, that you may bring salvation to the uttermost parts of the earth.' " And when the Gentiles heard this, they were glad and glorified the word of God; and as many as were ordained to eternal life believed. And the word of the Lord spread throughout all the region. But the Jews incited the devout women of high standing and the leading men of the city, and stirred up persecution against Paul and Barnabas, and drove them out of their district. But they shook off the dust from their feet against them, and went to Ico'nium. And the disciples were filled with joy and with the Holy Spirit.

or this

A Reading (Lesson) from the Book of Leviticus [19:1-2,9-18]

The Lord said to Moses,"Say to all the congregation of the people of Israel, You shall be holy; for I the Lord your God am holy. When you reap the harvest of your land, you shall not reap your field to its very border, neither shall you gather the gleanings after your harvest. And you shall not strip your vineyard bare, neither shall you gather the fallen grapes of your vineyard; you shall leave them for the poor and for the sojourner: I am the Lord your God. You shall not steal, nor deal falsely, nor lie to one another. And you shall not swear by my name falsely, and so profane the name of your God: I am the Lord. You shall not oppress your neighbor or rob him. The wages of a hired servant shall not remain with you all night until the morning. You shall not curse the deaf or put a stumbling block before the blind, but you shall fear your God: I am the Lord. You shall do no injustice in judgment; you shall not be partial to the poor or defer to the great, but in righteousness shall you judge your neighbor. You shall not go up and down as a slanderer among your people, and you shall not stand forth against the life of your neighbor: I am the Lord. You shall not hate your brother in your heart, but you shall reason with your neighbor, lest you bear sin because of him. You shall not take vengeance or bear any grudge against the sons of your own people, but you shall love your neighbor as yourself: I am the Lord."

Psalm 145 [page 801]   or   *145:1-9* [page 801]

A Reading (Lesson) from the Revelation to John [19:1, 4-9]

After this I heard what seemed to be the loud voice of a great multitude in heaven, crying, "Hallelujah! Salvation and glory and power belong to our God." And the twenty-four elders and the four living creatures fell down and worshiped God who is seated on the throne, saying, "Amen. Hallelujah!" And from the throne came a voice crying, "Praise our God, all you his servants, you who fear him, small and great." Then I heard what seemed to be the voice of a great multitude, like the sound of many waters and like the sound of mighty thunderpeals, crying, "Hallelujah! For the Lord our God the Almighty reigns. Let us rejoice and exult and give him the glory, for the marriage of the Lamb has come, and his Bride has made herself ready; it was granted her to be clothed with fine linen, bright and pure" — for the fine linen is the righteous deeds of the saints. And the angel said to me, "Write this: Blessed are those who are invited to the marriage supper of the Lamb." And he said to me, "These are true words of God."

or this

Acts 13:44-52 [page 138 above]

✝ *The Holy Gospel of Our Lord Jesus Christ*
According to John [13:31-35]

At the last supper, when Judas had gone out, Jesus said, "Now is the Son of man glorified, and in him God is glorified; if God is glorified in him, God will also glorify him in himself, and glorify him at once. Little children, yet a little while I am with you. You will seek me; and as I said to the Jews so now I say to you,'Where I am going you cannot come.' A new commandment I give to you, that you love one another; even as I have loved you, that you also love one another. By this all men will know that you are my disciples, if you have love for one another."

Sixth Sunday of Easter

A Reading (Lesson) from the Acts of the Apostles [14:8-18]

Now at Lystra there was a man sitting, who could not use his feet; he was a cripple from birth, who had never walked. He listened to Paul speaking; and Paul, looking intently at him and seeing that he had faith to be made well, said in a loud voice,"Stand upright on your feet." And he sprang up and walked. And when the crowds saw what Paul had done, they lifted up their voices, saying in Lycao'nian,"The gods have come down to us in the likeness of men!" Barnabas they called Zeus, and Paul, because he was the chief speaker, they called Hermes. And the priest of Zeus, whose temple was in front of the city, brought oxen and garlands to the gates and wanted to offer sacrifice with the people. But when the apostles Barnabas and Paul heard of it, they tore their garments and rushed out among the multitude, crying "Men, why are you doing this? We also are men, of like nature with you, and bring you good news, that you should turn from these vain things to a living God who made the heaven and the earth and the sea and all that is in them. In past generations he allowed all the nations to walk in their own ways; yet he did not leave himself without witness, for he did good and gave you from heaven rains and fruitful seasons, satisfying your hearts with food and gladness." With these words they scarcely restrained the people from offering sacrifice to them.

or this

A Reading (Lesson) from the Book of Joel [2:21-27]

The Lord said to his people: "Fear not, O land; be glad and rejoice, for the Lord has done great things! Fear not, you beasts of the field, for the pastures of the wilderness are green; the tree bears its fruit, the fig tree and the vine give their full yield. Be glad, O sons of Zion, and rejoice in the Lord, your God; for he has given the early rain for your vindication, he has poured down for you abundant rain, the early and the latter rain, as before. The threshing floors shall be full of grain, the vats shall overflow with wine and oil. I will restore to you the years which the swarming locust has eaten, the hopper, the destroyer, and the cutter, my great army, which I sent among you. You shall eat in plenty and be satisfied, and praise the name of the Lord your God, who has dealt wondrously with you. And my people shall never again be put to shame. You shall know that I am in the midst of Israel, and that I, the Lord, am your God and there is none else. And my people shall never again be put to shame."

Psalm 67 [page 675]

A Reading (Lesson) from the Revelation to John
[21:22—22:5]

And I saw no temple in the holy city, for its temple is the Lord God the Almighty and the Lamb. And the city has no need of sun or moon to shine upon it, for the glory of God is its light, and its lamp is the Lamb. By its light shall the nations walk; and the kings of the earth shall bring their glory into it, and its gates shall never be shut by day—and there shall be no night there; they shall bring into it the glory and the honor of the nations. But nothing unclean shall enter it, nor any one who practices abomination or falsehood, but only those who are written in the Lamb's book of life. Then he showed me the river of the water of life, bright as crystal, flowing from the throne of God and of the Lamb through the middle of the street of the city; also, on either side of the river, the tree of life with its twelve kinds of fruit, yielding its fruit each month; and the leaves of the tree were for the healing of the nations. There shall no more be anything accursed, but the throne of God and of the Lamb shall be in it, and his servants shall worship him; they shall see his face, and his name shall be on their foreheads. And night shall be no more; they need no light of lamp or sun, for the Lord God will be their light, and they shall reign for ever and ever.

or this

Acts 14:8-18 [page 141 above]

✝ *The Holy Gospel of Our Lord Jesus Christ*
  According to John [14:23-29]

Jesus said to Judas (not Iscariot),"If a man loves me, he will keep my word, and my Father will love him, and we will come to him and make our home with him. He who does not love me does not keep my words; and the word which you hear is not mine but the Father's who sent me. These things I have spoken to you, while I am still with you. But the Counselor, the Holy Spirit, whom the Father will send in my name, he will teach you all things, and bring to your remembrance all that I have said to you. Peace I leave with you; my peace I give to you; not as the world gives do I give to you. Let not your hearts be troubled, neither let them be afraid. You heard me say to you,'I go away, and I will come to you.' If you loved me, you would have rejoiced, because I go to the Father; for the Father is greater than I. And now I have told you before it takes place, so that when it does take place, you may believe."

Ascension Day

A Reading (Lesson) from the Acts of the Apostles [1:1-11]

In the first book, O The-oph'ilus, I have dealt with all that Jesus began to do and teach, until the day when he was taken up, after he had given commandment through the Holy Spirit to the apostles whom he had chosen. To them he presented himself alive after his passion by many proofs, appearing to them during forty days, and speaking of the kingdom of God. And while staying with them he charged them not to depart from Jerusalem, but to wait for the promise of the Father, which, he said,"you heard from me, for John baptized with water, but before many days you shall be baptized with the Holy Spirit." So when they had come together, they asked him,"Lord, will you at this time restore the kingdom to Israel?" He said to them,"It is not for you to know times or seasons which the Father has fixed by his own authority. But you shall receive power when the Holy Spirit has come upon you; and you shall be my witnesses in Jerusalem and in all Judea and Samar'ia and to the end of the earth." And when he has said this, as they were looking on, he was lifted up, and a cloud took him out of their sight. And while they were gazing into heaven as he went, behold, two men stood by them in white robes, and said,"Men of Galilee, why do you stand looking into heaven? This Jesus, who was taken up from you into heaven, will come in the same way as you saw him go into heaven."

or this

A Reading (Lesson) from the Second Book of the Kings [2:1-15]

Now when the Lord was about to take Eli'jah up to heaven by a whirlwind, Eli'jah and Eli'sha were on their way from Gilgal. And Eli'jah said to Eli'sha,"Tarry here, I pray you; for the Lord has sent me as far as Bethel." But Eli'sha said,"As the Lord lives, and as you yourself live, I will not leave you." So they went down to Bethel. And the sons of the prophets who were in Bethel came out to Eli'sha, and said to him,"Do you know that today the Lord will take away your master from over you?" And he said,"Yes, I know it; hold your peace." Eli'jah said to him,"Eli'sha, tarry here, I pray you; for the Lord has sent me to Jericho." But he said,"As the Lord lives, and as you yourself live, I will not leave you." So they came to Jericho. The sons of the prophets who were at Jericho drew near to Eli'sha, and said to him,"Do you know that today the Lord will take away your master from over you?" And he answered,"Yes, I know it; hold your peace." Then Eli'jah said to him,"Tarry here, I pray you; for the Lord has sent me to the Jordan." But he said,"As the Lord lives, and as you yourself live, I will not leave you." So the two of them went on. Fifty men of the sons of the prophets also went, and stood at some distance from them, as they both were standing by the Jordan. Then Eli'jah took his mantle, and rolled it up, and struck the water, and the water was parted to the one side and to the other, till the two of them could go over on dry ground. When they had crossed, Eli′jah said to Eli′sha, "Ask what I shall do for you, before I am taken from you." And Eli′sha said, "I pray you, let me inherit a double share of your spirit." And he said, "You have asked a hard thing; yet, if you see me as I am being taken from you, it shall be so for you; but if you do not see me, it shall not be so." And as they still went on and talked, behold, a chariot of fire and horses of fire separated the two of them. And Eli′jah went up by a whirlwind into heaven. And Eli′sha saw it and he cried, "My father, my father! the chariots of Israel and its horsemen!" And he saw him no more. Then he took hold of his own clothes and rent them in two pieces. And he took up the mantle of Eli′jah that had fallen from him, and went back and stood on the bank of the Jordan. Then he took the mantle of Eli′jah that had fallen from him, and struck the water, saying, "Where is the Lord, the God of Eli′jah?" And when he had struck the water, the water was parted to the one side and to the other; and Eli′sha went over. Now when the sons of the prophets who were at Jericho saw him over against them, they said, "The spirit of Eli′jah rests on Eli′sha." And they came to meet him, and bowed to the ground before him.

Psalm 47 [page 650] or *Psalm 110:1-5* [page 753]

A Reading (Lesson) from the Letter of Paul to the Ephesians [1:15-23]

Because I have heard of your faith in the Lord Jesus and your love toward all the saints, I do not cease to give thanks for you, remembering you in my prayers, that the God of our Lord Jesus Christ, the Father of glory, may give you a spirit of wisdom and of revelation in the knowledge of him, having the eyes of your hearts enlightened, that you may know what is the hope to which he has called you, what are the riches of his glorious inheritance in the saints, and what is the immeasurable greatness of his power in us who believe, according to the working of his great might which he accomplished in Christ when he raised him from the dead and made him sit at his right hand in the heavenly places, far above all rule and authority and power and dominion, and above every name that is named, not only in this age but also in that which is to come; and he has put all things under his feet and has made him the head over all things for the church, which is his body, the fullness of him who fills all in all.

or this

Acts 1:1-11 [page 144 above]

✝ The Holy Gospel of Our Lord Jesus Christ According to Luke [24:49-53]

Jesus said to his disciples, "Behold, I send the promise of my Father upon you; but stay in the city, until you are clothed with power from on high." Then he led them out as far as Bethany, and lifting up his hands he blessed them. While he blessed them, he parted from them, and was carried up into heaven. And they returned to Jerusalem with great joy, and were continually in the temple blessing God.

or this

✝ The Holy Gospel of Our Lord Jesus Christ According to Mark [16:9-15, 19-20]

Now when Jesus rose early on the first day of the week, he appeared first to Mary Mag'dalene, from whom he had cast out seven demons. She went out and told those who had been with him, as they mourned and wept. But when they heard that he was alive and had been seen by her, they would not believe it. After this he appeared in another form to two of them, as they were walking into the country. And they went back and told the rest, but they did not believe them. Afterward he appeared to the eleven themselves as they sat at table; and he upbraided them for their unbelief and hardness of heart, because they had not believed those who saw him after he had risen. And he said to them, "Go into all the world and preach the gospel to the whole creation." So then the Lord Jesus, after he had spoken to them, was taken up into heaven, and sat down at the right hand of God. And they went forth and preached everywhere, while the Lord worked with them and confirmed the message by the signs that attended it.

Seventh Sunday of Easter

A Reading (Lesson) from the Acts of the Apostles [16:16-34]

With Paul and Silas, we came to Philippi of Macedo'nia, a Roman colony, and as we were going to the place of prayer, we were met by a slave girl who had a spirit of divination and brought her owners much gain by soothsaying. She followed Paul and us, crying, "These men are servants of the Most High God, who proclaim to you the way of salvation." And this she did for many days. But Paul was annoyed, and turned and said to the spirit, "I charge you in the name of Jesus Christ to come out of her." And it came out that very hour. But when her owners saw that their hope of gain was gone, they seized Paul and Silas and dragged them into the market place before the rulers; and when they had brought them to the magistrates they said, "These men are Jews and they are disturbing our city. They advocate customs which it is not lawful for us Romans to accept or practice." The crowd joined in attacking them; and the magistrates tore the garments off them and gave orders to beat them with rods. And when they had inflicted many blows upon them, they threw them into prison, charging the jailer to keep them safely. Having received this charge, he put them into the inner prison and fastened their feet in the stocks. But about midnight Paul and Silas were praying and singing hymns to God, and the prisoners were listening to them, and suddenly there was a great earthquake, so that the foundations of the prison were shaken; and immediately all the doors were opened and every one's fetters were unfastened. When the jailer woke and saw that the prison doors were open, he drew his sword and was about to kill himself, supposing that the prisoners had escaped. But Paul cried with a loud voice, "Do not harm yourself, for we are all here." And he called for lights and rushed in, and trembling with fear he fell down before Paul and Silas, and brought them out and said, "Men, what must I do to be saved?" And they said, "Believe in the Lord Jesus, and you will be saved, you and your household." And they spoke the word of the Lord to him and to all that were in his house. And he took them the same hour of the night, and washed their wounds, and he was baptized at once, with all his family. Then he brought them up into his house, and set food before them; and he rejoiced with all his household that he had believed in God.

or this

Reading (Lesson) from the First Book of Samuel [12:19-24]

After Saul was made King, the people greatly feared the Lord, and all the people said to Samuel, "Pray for your servants to the Lord your God, that we may not die; for we have added to all our sins this evil, to ask for ourselves a king." And Samuel said to the people, "Fear not; you have done all this evil, yet do not turn aside from following the Lord, but serve the Lord with all your heart; and do not turn aside after vain things which cannot profit or save, for they are vain. For the Lord will not cast away his people, for his great name's sake, because it has pleased the Lord to make you a people for himself. Moreover as for me, far be it from me that I should sin against the Lord by ceasing to pray for you; and I will instruct you in the good and the right way. Only fear the Lord, and serve him faithfully with all your heart; for consider what great things he has done for you.

Psalm 68:1-20 [page 676]   or   *Psalm 47* [page 650]

A Reading (Lesson) from the Revelation to John
[22:12-14, 16-17, 20]

At the end of the visions I heard these words, "Behold, I am coming soon, bringing my recompense, to repay every one for what he has done. I am the Alpha and the Omega, the first and the last, the beginning and the end." Blessed are those who wash their robes, that they may have the right to the tree of life and that they may enter the city by the gates. "I Jesus have sent my angel to you with this testimony for the churches. I am the root and the offspring of David, the bright morning star." The Spirit and the Bride say, "Come." And let him who hears say, "Come." And let him who is thirsty come, let him who desires take the water of life without price. He who testifies to these things says, "Surely I am coming soon." Amen. Come, Lord Jesus!

or this

Acts 16:16-34 [page 148 above]

✝ *The Holy Gospel of Our Lord Jesus Christ According to John* [17:20-26]

Jesus prayed for his disciples, and then he said, "I do not pray for these only, but also for those who believe in me through their word, that they may all be one; even as thou, Father, art in me, and I in thee, that they also may be in us, so that the world may believe that thou hast sent me. The glory which thou hast given me I have given to them that they may be one even as we are one, I in them and thou in me, that they may become perfectly one, so that the world may know that thou hast sent me and hast loved them even as thou hast loved me. Father, I desire that they also whom thou hast given me, may be with me where I am, to behold my glory which thou hast given me in thy love for me before the foundation of the world. O righteous Father, the world has not known thee, but I have known thee; and these know that thou hast sent me. I made known to them thy name, and I will make it known, that the love with which thou hast loved me may be in them, and I in them."

Day of Pentecost: Early or Vigil Service

A Reading (Lesson) from the Book of Genesis [11:1-9]

Now the whole earth had one language and few words. And as men migrated from the east, they found a plain in the land of Shinar and settled there. And they said to one another,"Come, let us make bricks, and burn them thoroughly." And they had brick for stone, and bitumen for mortar. Then they said,"Come, let us build ourselves a city, and a tower with its top in the heavens, and let us make a name for ourselves, lest we be scattered abroad upon the face of the whole earth." And the Lord came down to see the city and the tower, which the sons of men had built. And the Lord said,"Behold, they are one people, and they have all one language; and this is only the beginning of what they will do; and nothing that they propose to do will now be impossible for them. Come, let us go down, and there confuse their language, that they may not understand one another's speech." So the Lord scattered them abroad from there over the face of all the earth, and they left off building the city. Therefore its name was called Babel, because there the Lord confused the language of all the earth; and from there the Lord scattered them abroad over the face of all the earth.

Psalm 33:12-22 [page 626]

or this

A Reading (Lesson) from the Book of Exodus
[19:1-9a, 16-20a; 20:18-20]

On the third new moon after the people of Israel had gone forth out of the land of Egypt, on that day they came into the wilderness of Sinai. And when they set out from Reph'idim and came into the wilderness of Sinai, they encamped in the wilderness; and there Israel encamped before the mountain. And Moses went up to God, and the Lord called to him out of the mountain, saying,"Thus you shall say to the house of Jacob, and tell the people of Israel: You have seen what I did to the Egyptians, and how I bore you on eagles' wings and brought you to myself. Now therefore, if you will obey my voice and keep my covenant, you shall be my own possession among all peoples; for all the earth is mine, and you shall be to me a kingdom of priests and a holy nation. These are the words which you shall speak to the children of Israel." So Moses came and called the elders of the people, and set before them all these words which the Lord had commanded him. And all the people answered together and said,"All that the Lord has spoken we will do." And Moses reported the words of the people to the Lord. And the Lord said to Moses,"Lo, I am coming to you in a thick cloud, that the people may hear when I speak with you, and may also believe you for ever." On the morning of the third day there were thunders and lightnings, and a thick cloud upon the mountain, and a very loud trumpet blast, so that all the people who were in the camp trembled. Then Moses brought the people out of the camp to meet God; and they took their stand at the foot of the mountain. And Mount Sinai was wrapped in smoke, because the Lord descended upon it in fire; and the smoke of it went up like the smoke of a kiln, and the whole mountain quaked greatly. And as the sound of the trumpet grew louder and louder, Moses spoke, and God answered him in thunder. And the Lord came down upon Mount Sinai, to the top of the mountain. Now when all the people perceived the thunderings and the lightnings and the sound of the trumpet and the mountain smoking, the people were afraid and trembled; and they stood afar off, and said to Moses,"You speak to us, and we will hear; but let not God speak to us, lest we die." And Moses said to the people, "Do not fear; for God has come to prove you, and that the fear of him may be before your eyes, that you may not sin."

Canticle 2 or 13, A Song of Praise [page 49 or 90]

or this

A Reading (Lesson) from the Book of Ezekiel [37:1-14]

The hand of the Lord was upon me, and he brought me out by·the Spirit of the Lord, and set me down in the midst of the valley; it was full of bones. And he led me round among them; and behold, there were very many upon the valley; and lo, they were very dry. And he said to me,"Son of man, can these bones live?" And I answered,"O Lord God, thou knowest." Again he said to me,"Prophesy to these bones, and say to them, O dry bones, hear the word of the Lord. Thus says the Lord God to these bones: Behold, I will cause breath to enter you, and you shall live. And I will lay sinews upon you, and will cause flesh to come upon you, and cover you with skin, and put breath in you, and you shall live; and you shall know that I am the Lord." So I prophesied as I was commanded; and as I prophesied, there was a noise and behold, a rattling; and the bones came together, bone to its bone. And as I looked, there were sinews on them, and flesh had come upon them, and skin had covered them; but there was no breath in them. Then he said to me, "Prophesy to the breath, prophesy, son of man, and say to the breath, Thus says the Lord God: Come from the four winds, O breath, and breathe upon these slain, that they may live." So I prophesied as he commanded me, and the breath came into them, and they lived, and stood upon their feet, an exceedingly great host. Then he said to me, "Son of man, these bones are the whole house of Israel. Behold, they say, 'Our bones are dried up, and our hope is lost; we are clean cut off.' Therefore prophesy, and say to them, Thus says the Lord God: Behold, I will open your graves and raise you from your graves, O my people; and I will bring you home into the land of Israel. And you shall know that I am the Lord, when I open your graves, and raise you from your graves, O my people. And I will put my Spirit within you, and you shall live, and I will place you in your own land; then you shall know that I, the Lord, have spoken, and I have done it, says the Lord."

Psalm 130 [page 784]

or this

A Reading (Lesson) from the Book of Joel [2:28-32]

The Lord said to his people, "It shall come to pass afterward, that I will pour out my spirit on all flesh; your sons and daughters shall prophesy, your old men shall dream dreams, and your young men shall see visions. Even upon the menservants and maidservants in those days, I will pour out my spirit. And I will give portents in the heavens and on the earth, blood and fire and columns of smoke. The sun shall be turned to darkness, and the moon to blood, before the great and terrible day of the Lord comes. And it shall come to pass that all who call upon the name of the Lord shall be delivered; for in Mount Zion and in Jerusalem there shall be those who escape, as the Lord has said, and among the survivors shall be those whom the Lord calls."

Canticle 9, The First Song of Isaiah [page 86]

or this

Acts 2:1-11 [page 156 below]

Psalm 104:25-32 [page 736]

or this

A Reading (Lesson) from the Letter of Paul to the Romans [8:14-17,22-27]

All who are led by the Spirit of God are sons of God. For you did not receive the spirit of slavery to fall back into fear, but you have received the spirit of sonship. When we cry,"Abba! Father!" it is the Spirit himself bearing witness with our spirit that we are children of God, and if children, then heirs, heirs of God and fellow heirs with Christ, provided we suffer with him in order that we may also be glorified with him. We know that the whole creation has been groaning in travail together until now; and not only the creation, but we ourselves, who have the first fruits of the Spirit, groan inwardly as we wait for adoption as sons, the redemption of our bodies. For in this hope we were saved. Now hope that is seen is not hope. For who hopes for what he sees? But if we hope for what we do not see, we wait for it with patience. Likewise the Spirit helps us in our weakness; for we do not know how to pray as we ought, but the Spirit himself intercedes for us with sighs too deep for words. And he who searches the hearts of men knows what is in the mind of the Spirit, because the Spirit intercedes for the saints according to the will of God.

✝ *The Holy Gospel of Our Lord Jesus Christ According to John* [7:37-39a]

On the last day of the feast, the great day, Jesus stood up and proclaimed, "If any one thirst, let him come to me and drink. He who believes in me, as the scripture has said, 'Out of his heart shall flow rivers of living water.'" Now this he said about the Spirit, which those who believed in him were to receive.

Day of Pentecost: Principal Service

A Reading (Lesson) from the Acts of the Apostles [2:1-11]

When the day of Pentecost had come, the disciples were all together in one place. And suddenly a sound came from heaven like the rush of a mighty wind, and it filled all the house where they were sitting. And there appeared to them tongues as of fire, distributed and resting on each one of them. And they were all filled with the Holy Spirit and began to speak in other tongues, as the Spirit gave them utterance. Now there were dwelling in Jerusalem Jews, devout men from every nation under heaven. And at this sound the multitude came together, and they were bewildered, because each one heard them speaking in his own language. And they were amazed and wondered, saying, "Are not all these who are speaking Galileans? And how is it that we hear, each of us in his own native language? Par'thians and Medes and Elamites and residents of Mesopota'mia, Judea and Cappado'cia, Pontus and Asia, Phryg'ia and Pamphyl'ia, Egypt and the parts of Libya belonging to Cyre'ne, and visitors from Rome, both Jews and proselytes, Cretans and Arabians, we hear them telling in our own tongues the mighty works of God."

or the following

A Reading (Lesson) from the Book of Joel [2:28-32]
[page 154 above]

Psalm 104:25-37 [page 736] or *104:25-32* [page 736] or
Psalm 33:12-15, 18-22 [page 626]

*A Reading (Lesson) From the First Letter of Paul
to the Corinthians* [12:4-13]

Now there are varieties of gifts, but the same Spirit; and
there are varieties of service, but the same Lord; and there
are varieties of working, but it is the same God who
inspires them all in every one. To each is given the
manifestation of the Spirit for the common good. To one is
given through the Spirit the utterance of wisdom, and to
another the utterance of knowledge according to the same
Spirit, to another faith by the same Spirit, to another gifts
of healing by the one Spirit, to another the working of
miracles, to another prophecy, to another the ability to
distinguish between spirits, to another various kinds of
tongues, to another the interpretation of tongues. All these
are inspired by one and the same Spirit, who apportions to
each one individually as he wills. For just as the body is one
and has many members, and all the members of the body,
though many, are one body, so it is with Christ. For by one
Spirit we were all baptized into one body—Jews or Greeks,
slaves or free—and all were made to drink of one Spirit.

or this

Acts 2:1-11 [page 156 above]

✝ *The Holy Gospel of Our Lord Jesus Christ
According to John* [20:19-23]

On the evening of that day, the first day of the week, the
doors being shut where the disciples were, for fear of the

Jews, Jesus came and stood among them and said to them, "Peace be with you." When he had said this, he showed them his hands and his side. Then the disciples were glad when they saw the Lord. Jesus said to them again, "Peace be with you. As the Father has sent me, even so I send you." And when he had said this, he breathed on them, and said to them, "Receive the Holy Spirit. If you forgive the sins of any, they are forgiven; if you retain the sins of any, they are retained."

or this

✝ *The Holy Gospel of Our Lord Jesus Christ*
According to John [14:8-17]

Philip said to Jesus, "Lord, show us the Father, and we shall be satisfied." Jesus said to him, "Have I been with you so long, and yet you do not know me, Philip? He who has seen me has seen the Father; how can you say, 'Show us the Father'? Do you not believe that I am in the Father and the Father in me? The words that I say to you I do not speak on my own authority; but the Father who dwells in me does his works. Believe me that I am in the Father and the Father in me; or else believe me for the sake of the works themselves. Truly, truly, I say to you, he who believes in me will also do the works that I do; and greater works than these will he do, because I go to the Father. Whatever you ask in my name, I will do it, that the Father may be glorified in the Son; if you ask anything in my name, I will do it. If you love me, you will keep my commandments. And I will pray the Father, and he will give you another Counselor, to be with you for ever, even the Spirit of truth, whom the world cannot receive, because it neither sees him nor knows him; you know him, for he dwells with you, and will be in you."

Trinity Sunday

A Reading (Lesson) from the Book of Isaiah   [6:1-8]

In the year that King Uzzi'ah died, I saw the Lord sitting upon a throne, high and lifted up; and his train filled the temple. Above him stood the seraphim; each had six wings: with two he covered his face, and with two he covered his feet, and with two he flew. And one called to another and said:"Holy, holy, holy is the Lord of hosts; the whole earth is full of his glory." And the foundations of the thresholds shook at the voice of him who called, and the house was filled with smoke. And I said: "Woe is me! For I am lost; for I am a man of unclean lips, and I dwell in the midst of a people of unclean lips; for my eyes have seen the King, the Lord of hosts!" Then flew one of the seraphim to me, having in his hand a burning coal which he had taken with tongs from the altar. And he touched my mouth, and said: "Behold, this has touched your lips; your guilt is taken away, and your sin forgiven." And I heard the voice of the Lord saying,"Whom shall I send, and who will go for us?" Then I said,"Here am I! Send me."

Psalm 29   [page 620]   or
Benedictus es, Canticle 2 or 13   [page 49 or 90]

A Reading (Lesson) from the Revelation to John   [4:1-11]

After this I looked, and lo, in heaven an open door! And the first voice, which I had heard speaking to me like a trumpet, said,"Come up hither, and I will show you what must take place after this." At once I was in the Spirit, and lo, a throne stood in heaven, with one seated on the throne! And he who sat there appeared like jasper and carnelian, and round the throne was a rainbow that looked like an emerald. Round the throne were twenty-four thrones, and seated on the thrones were twenty-four elders, clad in white garments, with golden crowns upon their heads. From the throne issue flashes of lightning, and voices and peals of thunder, and before the throne burn seven torches of fire, which are the seven spirits of God; and before the throne there is as it were a sea of glass, like crystal. And round the throne, on each side of the throne, are four living creatures, full of eyes in front and behind: the first living creature like a lion, the second living creature like an ox, the third living creature with the face of a man, and the fourth living creature like a flying eagle. And the four living creatures, each of them with six wings, are full of eyes all round and within, and day and night they never cease to sing,"Holy, holy, holy, is the Lord God Almighty, who was and is and is to come!" And whenever the living creatures give glory and honor and thanks to him who is seated on the throne, who lives for ever and ever, the twenty-four elders fall down before him who is seated on the throne and worship him who lives for ever and ever; they cast their crowns before the throne, singing,"Worthy art thou, our Lord and God, to receive glory and honor and power, for thou didst create all things, and by thy will they existed and were created."

✝ *The Holy Gospel of Our Lord Jesus Christ According to John* [16: (5-11)12-15]

Jesus said,"Now I am going to him who sent me; yet none of you asks me,'Where are you going?' But because I have said these things to you, sorrow has filled your hearts. Nevertheless I tell you the truth: it is to your advantage that I go away, for if I do not go away, the Counselor will not come to you; but if I go, I will send him to you. And when he comes, he will convince the world concerning sin and righteousness and judgment: concerning sin, because they do not believe in me; concerning righteousness, because I go to the Father, and you will see me no more; concerning judgment, because the ruler of this world is judged."

[*Jesus said,*] "I have yet many things to say to you, but you cannot bear them now. When the Spirit of truth comes, he will guide you into all the truth; for he will not speak on his own authority, but whatever he hears he will speak, and he will declare to you the things that are to come. He will glorify me, for he will take what is mine and declare it to you. All that the Father has is mine; therefore I said that he will take what is mine and declare it to you."

Proper 1 *The Sunday Closest to May 11*
[*Same as on the Sixth Sunday after the Epiphany, pages 37-39*]

Proper 2 *The Sunday Closest to May 18*
[*Same as on the Seventh Sunday after the Epiphany, pages 39-42*]

Proper 3 *The Sunday Closest to May 25*
[*Same as on the Eighth Sunday after the Epiphany, pages 42-44*]

Proper 4 *The Sunday Closest to June 1*

A Reading (Lesson) from the First Book of the Kings
[8:22-23, 27-30, 41-43]

Then Solomon stood before the altar of the Lord in the presence of all the assembly of Israel, and spread forth his hands toward heaven; and said, "O Lord, God of Israel, there is no God like thee, in heaven above or on earth beneath, keeping covenant and showing steadfast love to thy servants who walk before thee with all their heart. But will God indeed dwell on the earth? Behold, heaven and the highest heaven cannot contain thee; how much less this house which I have built! Yet have regard to the prayer of thy servant and to his supplication, O Lord my God, hearkening to the cry and to the prayer which thy servant prays before thee this day; that thy eyes may be open night and day toward this house, the place of which thou hast said, 'My name shall be there,' that thou mayest hearken to the prayer which thy servant offers toward this place. And hearken thou to the supplication of thy servant and of thy people Israel, when they pray toward this place; and when thou hearest, forgive. Likewise when a foreigner, who is not of thy people Israel, comes from a far country for thy name's sake (for they shall hear of thy great name, and thy mighty hand, and of thy outstretched arm), when he comes and prays toward this house, hear thou in heaven thy dwelling place, and do according to all for which the foreigner calls to thee; in order that all the peoples of the earth may know thy name and fear thee, as do thy people Israel, and that they may know that this house which I have built is called by thy name."

Psalm 96 [page 725] or *96:1-9* [page 725]

A Reading (Lesson) from the Letter of Paul to the Galatians [1:1-10]

Paul an apostle—not from men nor through man, but through Jesus Christ and God the Father, who raised him from the dead—and all the brethren who are with me, to the churches of Galatia: Grace to you and peace from God the Father and our Lord Jesus Christ, who gave himself for our sins to deliver us from the present evil age, according to the will of our God and Father; to whom be the glory for ever and ever. Amen. I am astonished that you are so quickly deserting him who called you in the grace of Christ and turning to a different gospel—not that there is another gospel, but there are some who trouble you and want to pervert the gospel of Christ. But even if we, or an angel from heaven, should preach to you a gospel contrary to that which we preached to you, let him be accursed. As we have said before, so now I say again, if any one is preaching to you a gospel contrary to that which you received, let him be accursed. Am I now seeking the favor of men, or of God? Or am I trying to please men? If I were still pleasing men, I should not be a servant of Christ.

✝ *The Holy Gospel of Our Lord Jesus Christ According to Luke* [7:1-10]

After Jesus had ended all his sayings in the hearing of the people he entered Caper'na-um. Now a centurion had a slave who was dear to him, who was sick and at the point of death. When he heard of Jesus, he sent to him elders of the Jews, asking him to come and heal his slave. And when they came to Jesus, they besought him earnestly, saying, "He is worthy to have you do this for him, for he loves our nation, and he built us our synagogue." And Jesus went with them. When he was not far from the house, the centurion sent friends to him, saying to him, "Lord, do not trouble yourself, for I am not worthy to have you come under my roof; therefore I did not presume to come to you. But say the word, and let my servant be healed. For I am a man set under authority with soldiers under me: and I say to one, 'Go,' and he goes; and to another, 'Come,' and he comes; and to my slave, 'Do this,' and he does it." When Jesus heard this he marveled at him, and turned and said to the multitude that followed him, "I tell you, not even in Israel have I found such faith." And when those who had been sent returned to the house, they found the slave well.

Proper 5 *The Sunday Closest to June 8*

A Reading (Lesson) from the First Book of the Kings [17:17-24]

The son of the mistress of the house at Zar'ephath became ill; and his illness was so severe that there was no breath left in him. And she said to Eli'jah, "What have you against me, O man of God? You have come to me to bring my sin to remembrance, and to cause the death of my son!" And he said to her, "Give me your son." And he took him from her bosom, and carried him up into the upper chamber, where he lodged, and laid him upon his own bed. And he cried to the Lord, "O Lord my God, hast thou brought calamity even upon the widow with whom I sojourn, by slaying her son?" Then he stretched himself upon the child three times, and cried to the Lord, "O Lord my God, let this child's soul come into him again." And the Lord hearkened to the voice of Eli'jah; and the soul of the child came into him again, and he revived. And Eli'jah took the child, and brought him down from the upper chamber into the house, and delivered him to his mother; and Eli'jah said, "See, your son lives." And the woman said to Eli'jah, "Now I know that you are a man of God, and that the word of the Lord in your mouth is truth."

Psalm 30 [page 621] or *30:1-6, 12-13* [page 621]

A Reading (Lesson) from the Letter of Paul to the Galatians [1:11-24]

I would have you know, brethren, that the gospel which was preached by me is not man's gospel. For I did not receive it from man, nor was I taught it, but it came through a revelation of Jesus Christ. For you have heard of my former life in Judaism, how I persecuted the church of God violently and tried to destroy it; and I advanced in Judaism beyond many of my own age among my people, so extremely zealous was I for the traditions of my fathers. But when he who had set me apart before I was born, and had called me through his grace, was pleased to reveal his Son to me, in order that I might preach him among the Gentiles, I did not confer with flesh and blood, nor did I go up to Jerusalem to those who were apostles before me, but I went away into Arabia; and again I returned to

Damascus. Then after three years I went up to Jerusalem to visit Cephas, and remained with him fifteen days. But I saw none of the other apostles except James the Lord's brother. (In what I am writing to you, before God, I do not lie!) Then I went into the regions of Syria and Cili'cia. And I was still not known by sight to the churches of Christ in Judea; they only heard it said, "He who once persecuted us is now preaching the faith he once tried to destroy." And they glorified God because of me.

✝ *The Holy Gospel of Our Lord Jesus Christ According to Luke* [7:11-17]

Soon after healing the centurion's slave, Jesus went to a city called Na'in, and his disciples and a great crowd went with him. As he drew near to the gate of the city, behold, a man who had died was being carried out, the only son of his mother, and she was a widow; and a large crowd from the city was with her. And when the Lord saw her, he had compassion on her and said to her, "Do not weep." And he came and touched the bier, and the bearers stood still. And he said, "Young man, I say to you, arise." And the dead man sat up, and began to speak. And he gave him to his mother. Fear seized them all; and they glorified God, saying, "A great prophet has arisen among us!" and "God has visited his people!" And this report concerning him spread through the whole of Judea and all the surrounding country.

Proper 6   *The Sunday Closest to June 15*

A Reading (Lesson) from the Second Book of Samuel [11:26 — 12:10, 13-15]

When the wife of Uri'ah heard that Uri'ah her husband was dead, she made lamentation for her husband. And when the mourning was over, David sent and brought her to his house, and she became his wife, and bore him a son. But the thing that David had done displeased the Lord. And the Lord sent Nathan to David. He came to him, and said to him, "There were two men in a certain city, the one rich and the other poor. The rich man had very many flocks and herds; but the poor man had nothing but one little ewe lamb, which he had bought. And he brought it up, and it grew up with him and with his children; it used to eat of his morsel, and drink from his cup, and lie in his bosom, and it was like a daughter to him. Now there came a traveler to the rich man, and he was unwilling to take one of his own flock or herd to prepare for the wayfarer who had come to him, but he took the poor man's lamb, and prepared it for the man who had come to him." Then David's anger was greatly kindled against the man; and he said to Nathan, "As the Lord lives, the man who has done this deserves to die; and he shall restore the lamb fourfold; because he did this thing, and because he had no pity." Nathan said to David, "You are the man. Thus says the Lord, the God of Israel, 'I anointed you king over Israel, and I delivered you out of the hand of Saul; and I gave you your master's house, and your master's wives into your bosom, and gave you the house of Israel and of Judah; and if this were too little, I would add to you as much more. Why have you despised the word of the Lord, to do what is evil in his sight? You have smitten Uri′ah the Hittite with the sword, and have taken his wife to be your wife, and have slain him with the sword of the Ammonites. Now therefore the sword shall never depart from your house, because you have despised me, and have taken the wife of Uri′ah the Hittite to be your wife.'" David said to Nathan, "I have sinned against the Lord." And Nathan said to David, "The Lord also has put away your sin; you shall not die. Nevertheless, because by this deed you have utterly scorned the Lord, the child that is born to you shall die."

Then Nathan went to his house. And the Lord struck the child that Uri'ah's wife bore to David, and it became sick.

Psalm 32 [page 624]   or   *32:1-8* [page 624]

*A Reading (Lesson) from the Letter of Paul
to the Galatians* [2:11-21]

When Cephas came to Antioch I opposed him to his face, because he stood condemned. For before certain men came from James, he ate with the Gentiles; but when they came he drew back and separated himself, fearing the circumcision party. And with him the rest of the Jews acted insincerely, so that even Barnabas was carried away by their insincerity. But when I saw that they were not straightforward about the truth of the gospel, I said to Cephas before them all, "If you, though a Jew, live like a Gentile and not like a Jew, how can you compel the Gentiles to live like Jews?" We ourselves, who are Jews by birth and not Gentile sinners, yet who know that a man is not justified by works of the law but through faith in Jesus Christ, even we have believed in Christ Jesus, in order to be justified by faith in Christ, and not by works of the law, because by works of the law shall no one be justified. But if, in our endeavor to be justified in Christ, we ourselves were found to be sinners, is Christ then an agent of sin? Certainly not! But if I build up again those things which I tore down, then I prove myself a transgressor. For I through the law died to the law, that I might live to God. I have been crucified with Christ; it is no longer I who live, but Christ who lives in me; and the life I now live in the flesh I live by faith in the Son of God, who loved me and gave himself for me. I do not nullify the grace of God; for if justification were through the law, then Christ died to no purpose.

✝ *The Holy Gospel of Our Lord Jesus Christ*
According to Luke [7:36-50]

One of the Pharisees asked Jesus to eat with him, and he went into the Pharisee's house, and took his place at table. And behold, a woman of the city, who was a sinner, when she learned that he was at table in the Pharisee's house, brought an alabaster flask of ointment, and standing behind him at his feet, weeping, she began to wet his feet with her tears, and wiped them with the hair of her head, and kissed his feet, and anointed them with the ointment. Now when the Pharisee who had invited him saw it, he said to himself,"If this man were a prophet, he would have known who and what sort of woman this is who is touching him, for she is a sinner." And Jesus answering said to him,"Simon, I have something to say to you." And he answered,"What is it, Teacher?" Jesus said,"A certain creditor had two debtors; one owed five hundred denarii, and the other fifty. When they could not pay, he forgave them both. Now which of them will love him more?" Simon answered,"The one, I suppose, to whom he forgave more." And he said to him,"You have judged rightly." Then turning toward the woman he said to Simon,"Do you see this woman? I entered your house, you gave me no water for my feet, but she has wet my feet with her tears and wiped them with her hair. You gave me no kiss, but from the time I came in she has not ceased to kiss my feet. You did not anoint my head with oil, but she has anointed my feet with ointment. Therefore I tell you, her sins, which are many, are forgiven, for she loved much; but he who is forgiven little, loves little." And he said to her,"Your sins are forgiven." Then those who were at table with him began to say among themselves,"Who is this, who even forgives sins?" And he said to the woman,"Your faith has saved you; go in peace."

Proper 7   *The Sunday Closest to June 22*

A Reading (Lesson) from the Book of Zechariah
[12:8-10; 13:1]

"On the day of the siege against Jerusalem," says the Lord,
"I will put a shield about the inhabitants of Jerusalem
so that the feeblest among them on that day shall be like
David, and the house of David shall be like God, like the
angel of the Lord, at their head. And on that day I will seek
to destroy all the nations that come against Jerusalem. And
I will pour out on the house of David and the inhabitants
of Jerusalem a spirit of compassion and supplication, so
that, when they look on him whom they have pierced, they
shall mourn for him, as one mourns for an only child, and
weep bitterly over him, as one weeps over a first-born. On
that day there shall be a fountain opened for the house of
David and the inhabitants of Jerusalem to cleanse them
from sin and uncleanness."

Psalm 63:1-8   [page 670]

*A Reading (Lesson) from the Letter of Paul
to the Galatians* [3:23-29]

Now before faith came, we were confined under the law,
kept under restraint until faith should be revealed. So that
the law was our custodian until Christ came, that we might
be justified by faith. But now that faith has come, we are
no longer under a custodian; for in Christ Jesus you are all
sons of God, through faith. For as many of you, as were
baptized into Christ have put on Christ. There is neither
Jew nor Greek, there is neither slave nor free, there is
neither male nor female; for you are all one in Christ Jesus.
And if you are Christ's, then you are Abraham's offspring,
heirs according to promise.

✝ *The Holy Gospel of Our Lord Jesus Christ*
According to Luke [9:18-24]

Now it happened that as Jesus was praying alone the disciples were with him; and he asked them, "Who do the people say that I am?" And they answered, "John the Baptist; but others say, Eli'jah; and others, that one of the old prophets has risen." And he said to them, "But who do you say that I am?" And Peter answered, "The Christ of God." But he charged and commanded them to tell this to no one, saying, "The Son of man must suffer many things, and be rejected by the elders and chief priests and scribes, and be killed, and on the third day be raised." And he said to all, "If any man would come after me, let him deny himself and take up his cross daily and follow me. For whoever would save his life will lose it; and whoever loses his life for my sake, he will save it."

Proper 8   *The Sunday Closest to June 29*

A Reading (Lesson) from the First Book of the Kings
[19:15-16, 19-21]

The Lord said to Eli'jah, "Go, return on your way to the wilderness of Damascus; and when you arrive, you shall anoint Haz'ael to be king over Syria; and Jehu the son of Nimshi you shall anoint to be king over Israel; and Eli'sha the son of Shaphat of A'bel-meho'lah you shall anoint to be prophet in your place." So he departed from there, and found Eli'sha the son of Shaphat, who was plowing, with twelve yoke of oxen before him, and he was with the twelfth. Eli'jah passed by him and cast his mantle upon him. And he left the oxen, and ran after Eli'jah, and said, "Let me kiss my father and my mother, and then I will follow you." And he said to him, "Go back again; for what have I done to you?" And he returned from following him, and took the yoke of oxen, and slew them, and boiled their flesh with the yokes of the oxen, and gave it to the people, and they ate. Then he arose and went after Eli'jah, and ministered to him.

Psalm 16 [page 599]   or   *16:5-11* [page 600]

A Reading (Lesson) from the Letter of Paul to the Galatians [5:1, 13-25]

For freedom Christ has set us free; stand fast therefore, and do not submit again to a yoke of slavery. For you were called to freedom, brethren; only do not use your freedom as an opportunity for the flesh, but through love be servants of one another. For the whole law is fulfilled in one word, "You shall love your neighbor as yourself." But if you bite and devour one another take heed that you are not consumed by one another. But I say, walk by the Spirit, and do not gratify the desires of the flesh. For the desires of the flesh are against the Spirit, and the desires of the Spirit are against the flesh; for these are opposed to each other, to prevent you from doing what you would. But if you were led by the Spirit you are not under the law. Now the works of the flesh are plain: fornication, impurity, licentiousness, idolatry, sorcery, enmity, strife, jealousy, anger, selfishness, dissension, party spirit, envy, drunkenness, carousing, and the like. I warn you, as I warned you before, that those who do such things shall not inherit the kingdom of God. But the fruit of the Spirit is love, joy, peace, patience, kindness, goodness, faithfulness, gentleness, self-control; against such there is no law. And those who belong to Christ Jesus have crucified the flesh with its passions and desires. If we live by the Spirit, let us also walk by the Spirit.

✝ *The Holy Gospel of Our Lord Jesus Christ*
According to Luke [9:51-62]

When the days drew near for Jesus to be received up, he set his face to go to Jerusalem. And he sent messengers ahead of him, who went and entered a village of the Samaritans, to make ready for him; but the people would not receive him, because his face was set toward Jcrusalem. And when his disciples James and John saw it, they said, "Lord, do you want us to bid fire come down from heaven and consume them?" But he turned and rebuked them. And they went on to another village. As they were going along the road, a man said to him, "I will follow you wherever you go." And Jesus said to him, "Foxes have holes, and birds of the air have nests; but the Son of man has nowhere to lay his head." To another he said, "Follow me." But he said, "Lord, let me first go and bury my father." But he said to him, "Leave the dead to bury their own dead; but as for you, go and proclaim the kingdom of God." Another said, "I will follow you, Lord; but let me first say farewell to those at my home." Jesus said to him, "No one who puts his hand to the plow and looks back is fit for the kingdom of God."

Proper 9 *The Sunday Closest to July 6*

A Reading (Lesson) from the Book of Isaiah [66:10-16]

Thus says the Lord, "Rejoice with Jerusalem, and be glad for her, all you who love her; rejoice with her in joy, all you who mourn over her; that you may suck and be satisfied with her consoling breasts; that you may drink deeply with delight from the abundance of her glory." For thus says the Lord: "Behold, I will extend prosperity to her like a river, and the wealth of the nations like an overflowing stream; and you shall suck, you shall be carried upon her hip, and dandled upon her knees. As one whom his mother comforts, so I will comfort you; you shall be comforted in Jerusalem. You shall see, and your heart shall rejoice; your bones shall flourish like the grass; and it shall be known that the hand of the Lord is with his servants, and his indignation is against his enemies. For behold, the Lord will come in fire, and his chariots like the storm-wind, to render his anger in fury, and his rebuke with flames of fire. For by fire will the Lord execute judgment, and by his sword, upon all flesh; and those slain by the Lord shall be many."

Psalm 66 [page 673]   or   *66:1-8* [page 673]

A Reading (Lesson) from the Letter of Paul
to the Galatians [6:(1-10)14-18]

Brethren, if a man is overtaken in any trespass, you who are spiritual should restore him in a spirit of gentleness. Look to yourself, lest you too be tempted. Bear one another's burdens, and so fulfill the law of Christ. For if any one thinks he is something, when he is nothing, he deceives himself. But let each one test his own work, and then his reason to boast will be in himself alone and not in his neighbor. For each man will have to bear his own load. Let him who is taught the word share all good things with him who teaches. Do not be deceived; God is not mocked, for whatever a man sows, that he will also reap. For he who sows to his own flesh will from the flesh reap corruption; but he who sows to the Spirit will from the Spirit reap eternal life. And let us not grow weary in well-doing, for in due season we shall reap, if we do not lose heart. So then, as we have opportunity, let us do good to all men, and especially to those who are of the household of faith.

Far be it from me to glory except in the cross of our Lord Jesus Christ, by which the world has been crucified to me, and I to the world. For neither circumcision counts for anything, nor uncircumcision, but a new creation. Peace and mercy be upon all who walk by this rule, upon the Israel of God. Henceforth let no man trouble me; for I bear on my body the marks of Jesus. The grace of our Lord Jesus Christ be with your spirit, brethren. Amen.

✝ *The Holy Gospel of Our Lord Jesus Christ According to Luke* [10:1-12, 16-20]

After this the Lord appointed seventy others, and sent them on ahead of him, two by two, into every town and place where he himself was about to come. And he said to them, "The harvest is plentiful, but the laborers are few; pray therefore the Lord of the harvest to send out laborers into his harvest. Go your way; behold, I send you out as lambs in the midst of wolves. Carry no purse, no bag, no sandals; and salute no one on the road. Whatever house you enter, first say, 'Peace be to this house!' And if a son of peace is there, your peace shall rest upon him; but if not, it shall return to you. And remain in the same house, eating and drinking what they provide, for the laborer deserves his wages; do not go from house to house. Whenever you enter a town and they receive you, eat what is set before you; heal the sick in it and say to them, 'The kingdom of God has come near to you.' But whenever you enter a town and they do not receive you, go into its streets and say, 'Even the dust of your town that clings to our feet, we wipe off against you; nevertheless know this, that the kingdom of God has come near.' I tell you, it shall be more tolerable on that day for Sodom than for that town. He who hears you hears me, and he who rejects you rejects me, and he who rejects me rejects him who sent me." The seventy returned with joy, saying, "Lord, even the demons are subject to us in your name!" And he said to them,
"I saw Satan fall like lightning from heaven. Behold, I have given you authority to tread upon serpents and scorpions,

and over all the power of the enemy; and nothing shall hurt you. Nevertheless do not rejoice in this, that the spirits are subject to you; but rejoice that your names are written in heaven."

Proper 10 *The Sunday Closest to July 13*

A Reading (Lesson) from the Book of Deuteronomy [30:9-14]

Moses said to the people of Israel, "The Lord your God will make you abundantly prosperous in all the work of your hand, in the fruit of your body, and in the fruit of your cattle, and in the fruit of your ground; for the Lord will again take delight in prospering you, as he took delight in your fathers, if you obey the voice of the Lord your God, to keep his commandments and his statutes which are written in this book of the law, if you turn to the Lord your God, with all your heart and with all your soul. For this commandment which I command you this day is not too hard for you, neither is it far off. It is not in heaven, that you should say, 'Who will go up for us to heaven, and bring it to us, that we may hear it and do it?' Neither is it beyond the sea, that you should say, 'Who will go over the sea for us, and bring it to us, that we may hear it and do it?' But the word is very near you; it is in your mouth and in your heart, so that you can do it."

Psalm 25 [page 614] or *25:3-9* [page 614]

A Reading (Lesson) from the Letter of Paul to the Colossians [1:1-14]

Paul, an apostle of Christ Jesus by the will of God, and Timothy our brother, to the saints and faithful brethren in Christ at Colos'sae: Grace to you and peace from God our Father. We always thank God, the Father of our Lord Jesus Christ, when we pray for you, because we have heard of your faith in Christ Jesus and of the love which you have for all the saints, because of the hope laid up for you in heaven. Of this you have heard before in the word of the truth, the gospel which has come to you, as indeed in the whole world it is bearing fruit and growing—so among yourselves, from the day you heard and understood the grace of God in truth, as you learned it from Ep'aphras our beloved fellow servant. He is a faithful minister of Christ on our behalf and has made known to us your love in the Spirit. And so, from the day we heard of it, we have not ceased to pray for you, asking that you may be filled with the knowledge of his will in all spiritual wisdom and understanding, to lead a life worthy of the Lord, fully pleasing to him, bearing fruit in every good work and increasing in the knowledge of God. May you be strengthened with all power, according to his glorious might, for all endurance and patience with joy, giving thanks to the Father, who has qualified us to share in the inheritance of the saints in light. He has delivered us from the dominion of darkness and transferred us to the kingdom of his beloved Son, in whom we have redemption, the forgiveness of sins.

✝ *The Holy Gospel of Our Lord Jesus Christ According to Luke* [10:25-37]

And behold, a lawyer stood up to put Jesus to the test, saying, "Teacher, what shall I do to inherit eternal life?" He said to him, "What is written in the law? How do you read?" And he answered, "You shall love the Lord your God with all your heart, and with all your soul, and with all your strength, and with all your mind; and your neighbor as yourself." And he said to him, "You have answered right; do this, and you will live." But he, desiring to justify himself, said to Jesus, "And who is my neighbor?" Jesus replied, "A man was going down from Jerusalem to Jericho, and he fell among robbers, who stripped him and beat him, and departed, leaving him half dead. Now by chance a priest was going down that road; and when he saw him he passed by on the other side. So likewise a Levite, when he came to the place and saw him, passed by on the other side. But a Samaritan, as he journeyed, came to where he was; and when he saw him, he had compassion, and went to him and bound up his wounds, pouring on oil and wine; then he set him on his own beast and brought him to an inn, and took care of him. And the next day he took out two denarii and gave them to the innkeeper, saying, 'Take care of him; and whatever more you spend, I will repay you when I come back.' Which of these three, do you think, proved neighbor to the man who fell among the robbers?" He said, "The one who showed mercy on him." And Jesus said to him, "Go and do likewise."

Proper 11 *The Sunday Closest to July 20*

A Reading (Lesson) from the Book of Genesis
[18:1-10a (10b-14)]

The Lord appeared to Abraham by the oaks of Mamre, as he sat at the door of his tent in the heat of the day. He lifted up his eyes and looked, and behold, three men stood in front of him. When he saw them, he ran from the tent door to meet them, and bowed himself to the earth, and said, "My lord, if I have found favor in your sight; do not pass by your servant. Let a little water be brought, and wash your feet, and rest yourselves under the tree, while I fetch a morsel of bread, that you may refresh yourselves, and after that you may pass on—since you have come to your servant." So they said, "Do as you have said." And Abraham hastened into the tent to Sarah, and said, "Make ready quickly three measures of fine meal, knead it, and make cakes." And Abraham ran to the herd, and took a

calf, tender and good, and gave it to the servant, who
hastened to prepare it. Then he took curds, and milk, and
the calf which he had prepared, and set it before them; and
he stood by them under the tree while they ate. They said
to him, "Where is Sarah your wife?" And he said, "She is in
the tent." The Lord said, "I will surely return to you in the
spring, and Sarah your wife shall have a son."

> And Sarah was listening at the tent door behind him.
> Now Abraham and Sarah were old, advanced in age; it
> had ceased to be with Sarah after the manner of women.
> So Sarah laughed to herself, saying, "After I have grown
> old, and my husband is old, shall I have pleasure?" The
> Lord said to Abraham, "Why did Sarah laugh, and say,
> 'Shall I indeed bear a child, now that I am old?' Is anything
> too hard for the Lord? At the appointed time I will
> return to you, in the spring, and Sarah shall have a son."

Psalm 15 [page 599]

*A Reading (Lesson) from the Letter of Paul
to the Colossians* [1:21-29]

You, who once were estranged and hostile in mind, doing
evil deeds, he has now reconciled in his body of flesh by his
death, in order to present you holy and blameless and
irreproachable before him, provided that you continue in
the faith, stable and steadfast, not shifting from the hope of
the gospel which you heard, which has been preached to
every creature under heaven, and of which I, Paul, became
a minister. Now I rejoice in my sufferings for your sake,
and in my flesh I complete what is lacking in Christ's
afflictions for the sake of his body, that is, the church, of
which I became a minister according to the divine office
which was given to me for you, to make the word of God
fully known, the mystery hidden for ages and generations,
but now made manifest to his saints. To them God chose to
make known how great among the Gentiles are the riches

of the glory of this mystery, which is Christ in you, the hope of glory. Him we proclaim, warning every man and teaching every man in all wisdom, that we may present every man mature in Christ. For this I toil, striving with all the energy which he mightily inspires within me.

✝ *The Holy Gospel of Our Lord Jesus Christ According to Luke* [10:38-42]

As Jesus and his disciples went on their way, Jesus entered a village; and a woman named Martha received him into her house. And she had a sister called Mary, who sat at the Lord's feet and listened to his teaching. But Martha was distracted with much serving; and she went to him and said,"Lord, do you not care that my sister has left me to serve alone? Tell her then to help me." But the Lord answered her,"Martha, Martha, you are anxious and troubled about many things; one thing is needful. Mary has chosen the good portion, which shall not be taken away from her."

Proper 12 *The Sunday Closest to July 27*

A Reading (Lesson) from the Book of Genesis [18:20-33]

The Lord said to Abraham,"Because the outcry against Sodom and Gomor′rah is great and their sin is very grave, I will go down to see whether they have done altogether according to the outcry which has come to me; and if not, I will know." So the men turned from there, and went toward Sodom; but Abraham still stood before the Lord. Then Abraham drew near, and said,"Wilt thou indeed destroy the righteous with the wicked? Suppose there are fifty righteous within the city; wilt thou then destroy the place and not spare it for the fifty righteous who are in it? Far be it from thee to do such a thing, to slay the righteous with the wicked, so that the righteous fare as the wicked!

Far be that from thee! Shall not the Judge of all the earth do right?" And the Lord said, "If I find at Sodom fifty righteous in the city, I will spare the whole place for their sake." Abraham answered, "Behold, I have taken upon myself to speak to the Lord, I who am but dust and ashes. Suppose five of the fifty righteous are lacking? Wilt thou destroy the whole city for lack of five?" And he said, "I will not destroy it if I find forty-five there." Again he spoke to him, and said, "Suppose forty are found there." He answered, "For the sake of forty I will not do it." Then he said, "Oh let not the Lord be angry, and I will speak. Suppose thirty are found there." He answered, "I will not do it, if I find thirty there." He said, "Behold, I have taken upon myself to speak to the Lord. Suppose twenty are found there." He answered, "For the sake of twenty I will not destroy it." Then he said. "Oh let not the Lord be angry, and I will speak again but this once. Suppose ten are found there." He answered, "For the sake of ten I will not destroy it." And the Lord went his way, when he had finished speaking to Abraham; and Abraham returned to his place.

Psalm 138 [page 793]

A Reading (Lesson) from the Letter of Paul to the Colossians [2:6-15]

As you received Christ Jesus the Lord, so live in him, rooted and built up in him and established in the faith, just as you were taught, abounding in thanksgiving. See to it that no one makes a prey of you by philosophy and empty deceit, according to human tradition, according to the elemental spirits of the universe, and not according to Christ. For in him the whole fullness of deity dwells bodily, and you have come to fullness of life in him, who is the head of all rule and authority. In him also you were circumcised with a circumcision made without hands, by putting off the body of flesh in the circumcision of Christ; and you were buried with him in baptism, in which you were also raised with him through faith in the working of God, who raised him from the dead. And you, who were dead in trespasses and the uncircumcision of your flesh, God made alive together with him, having forgiven us all our trespasses, having canceled the bond which stood against us with its legal demands; this he set aside, nailing it to the cross. He disarmed the principalities and powers and made a public example of them, triumphing over them in him.

✝ *The Holy Gospel of Our Lord Jesus Christ
According to Luke* [11:1-13]

Jesus was praying in a certain place, and when he ceased, one of his disciples said to him,"Lord, teach us to pray, as John taught his disciples." And he said to them,"When you pray, say: Father, hallowed be thy name. Thy kingdom come. Give us each day our daily bread; and forgive us our sins, for we ourselves forgive every one who is indebted to us; and lead us not into temptation." And he said to them,"Which of you who has a friend will go to him at midnight and say to him,'Friend, lend me three loaves; for a friend of mine has arrived on a journey, and I have nothing to set before him'; and he will answer from within,'Do not bother me; the door is now shut, and my children are with me in bed; I cannot get up and give you anything'? I tell you, though he will not get up and give him anything because he is his friend, yet because of his importunity he will rise and give him whatever he needs. And I tell you, Ask, and it will be given you; seek, and you will find; knock, and it will be opened to you. For every one who asks receives, and he who seeks finds, and to him who knocks it will be opened. What father among you, if his son asks for a fish, will instead of a fish give him a serpent; or if he asks for an egg, will give him a scorpion?

If you then, who are evil, know how to give good gifts to your children, how much more will the heavenly Father give the Holy Spirit to those who ask him!"

Proper 13 *The Sunday closest to August 3*

A Reading (Lesson) from Ecclesiastes
[1:12-14; 2:(1-7, 11) 18-23]

I the Preacher have been king over Israel in Jerusalem. And I applied my mind to seek and to search out by wisdom all that is done under heaven; it is an unhappy business that God has given to the sons of men to be busy with. I have seen everything that is done under the sun; and behold, all is vanity and a striving after wind.

> I said to myself, "Come now, I will make a test of pleasure; enjoy yourself." But behold, this also was vanity. I said of laughter, "It is mad," and of pleasure, "What use is it?" I searched with my mind how to cheer my body with wine—my mind still guiding me with wisdom—and how to lay hold on folly, till I might see what was good for the sons of men to do under heaven during the few days of their life. I made great works; I built houses and planted vineyards for myself; I made myself gardens and parks, and planted in them all kinds of fruit trees. I made myself pools from which to water the forest of growing trees. I bought male and female slaves, and had slaves who were born in my house; I had also great possessions of herds and flocks, more than any who had been before me in Jerusalem. Then I considered all that my hands had done and the toil I had spent in doing it, and behold, all was vanity and a striving after wind, and there was nothing to be gained under the sun.

I hated all my toil in which I had toiled under the sun,

seeing that I must leave it to the man who will come after me; and who knows whether he will be a wise man or a fool? Yet he will be master of all for which I toiled and used my wisdom under the sun. This also is vanity. So I turned about and gave my heart up to despair over all the toil of my labors under the sun, because sometimes a man who has toiled with wisdom and knowledge and skill must leave all to be enjoyed by a man who did not toil for it. This also is vanity and a great evil. What has a man from all the toil and strain with which he toils beneath the sun? For all his days are full of pain, and his work is a vexation; even in the night his mind does not rest. This also is vanity.

Psalm 49 [page 652]   or   *49:1-11* [page 652]

*A Reading (Lesson) from the Letter of Paul
to the Colossians* [3:(5-11) 12-17]

> Put to death what is earthly in you: fornication, impurity, passion, evil desire, and covetousness, which is idolatry. On account of these the wrath of God is coming. In these you once walked, when you lived in them. But now put them all away: anger, wrath, malice, slander, and foul talk from your mouth. Do not lie to one another, seeing that you have put off the old nature with its practices and have put on the new nature, which is being renewed in knowledge after the image of its creator. Here there cannot be Greek and Jew, circumcised and uncircumcised, barbarian, Scyth'ian, slave, free man, but Christ is all, and in all.

Put on then, as God's chosen ones, holy and beloved, compassion, kindness, lowliness, meekness, and patience, forbearing one another and, if one has a complaint against another, forgiving each other; as the Lord has forgiven you, so you also must forgive. And above all these put on love, which binds everything together in perfect harmony. And let the peace of Christ rule in your hearts, to which

indeed you were called in the one body. And be thankful.
Let the word of Christ dwell in you richly, teach and
admonish one another in all wisdom, and sing psalms and
hymns and spiritual songs with thankfulness in your hearts
to God. And whatever you do, in word or deed, do
everything in the name of the Lord Jesus, giving thanks to
God the Father through him.

✝ *The Holy Gospel of Our Lord Jesus Christ*
According to Luke [12:13-21]

One of the multitude said to Jesus,"Teacher, bid my brother
divide the inheritance with me." But he said to him,"Man,
who made me a judge or divider over you?" And he said to
them,"Take heed, and beware of all covetousness; for a
man's life does not consist in the abundance of his
possessions." And he told them a parable, saying,"The
land of a rich man brought forth plentifully; and he
thought to himself,'What shall I do, for I have nowhere to
store my crops?' And he said,'I will do this: I will pull down
my barns, and build larger ones; and there I will store all
my grain and my goods. And I will say to my soul, Soul,
you have ample goods laid up for many years; take your
ease, eat, drink, be merry.' But God said to him,'Fool! This
night your soul is required of you; and the things you have
prepared, whose will they be?' So is he who lays up treasure
for himself, and is not rich toward God."

Proper 14 *The Sunday closest to August 10*

A Reading (Lesson) from the Book of Genesis [15:1-6]

The word of the Lord came to Abram in a vision,"Fear not,
Abram, I am your shield; your reward shall be very
great." But Abram said,"O Lord God, what wilt thou give
me, for I continue childless, and the heir of my house is
Elie'zer of Damascus?" And Abram said,"Behold, thou hast

given me no offspring; and a slave born in my house will be my heir." And behold, the word of the Lord came to him, "This man shall not be your heir; your own son shall be your heir." And he brought him outside and said, "Look toward heaven, and number the stars, if you are able to number them." Then he said to him, "So shall your descendants be." And he believed the Lord; and he reckoned it to him as righteousness.

Psalm 33 [page 626]   or   *33:12-15, 18-22* [page 626]

A Reading (Lesson) from the Letter to the Hebrews
[11:1-3(4-7)8-16]

Now faith is the assurance of things hoped for, the conviction of things not seen. For by it the men of old received divine approval. By faith we understand that the world was created by the word of God, so that what is seen was made out of things which do not appear.

> By faith Abel offered to God a more acceptable sacrifice than Cain, through which he received approval as righteous, God bearing witness by accepting his gifts; he died, but through his faith he is still speaking. By faith Enoch was taken up so that he should not see death; and he was not found, because God had taken him. Now before he was taken he was attested as having pleased God. And without faith it is impossible to please him. For whoever would draw near to God must believe that he exists and that he rewards those who seek him. By faith Noah, being warned by God concerning events as yet unseen, took heed and constructed an ark for the saving of his household; by this he condemned the world and became an heir of the righteousness which comes by faith.

By faith Abraham obeyed when he was called to go out to a place which he was to receive as an inheritance; and he went out, not knowing where he was to go. By faith he sojourned in the land of promise, as in a foreign land, living in tents with Isaac and Jacob, heirs with him of the same promise. For he looked forward to the city which has foundations, whose builder and maker is God. By faith Sarah herself received power to conceive, even when she was past the age, since she considered him faithful who had promised. Therefore from one man, and him as good as dead, were born decendants as many as the stars of heaven and as the innumerable grains of sand by the seashore. These all died in faith, not having received what was promised, but having seen it and greeted it from afar, and having acknowledged that they were strangers and exiles on the earth. For people who speak thus make it clear that they are seeking a homeland. If they had been thinking of that land from which they had gone out, they would have had opportunity to return. But as it is, they desire a better country, that is, a heavenly one. Therefore God is not ashamed to be called their God, for he has prepared for them a city.

✝ *The Holy Gospel of Our Lord Jesus Christ
According to Luke* [12:32-40]

Jesus said to his disciples, "Fear not, little flock, for it is your Father's good pleasure to give you the kingdom. Sell your possessions, and give alms; provide yourselves with purses that do not grow old, with a treasure in the heavens that does not fail, where no thief approaches and no moth destroys. For where your treasure is, there will your heart be also. Let your loins be girded and your lamps burning, and be like men who are waiting for their master to come home from the marriage feast, so that they may open to him at once when he comes and knocks. Blessed are those servants whom the master finds awake when he comes; truly, I say to you, he will gird himself and have them sit at table, and he will come and serve them. If he comes in the second watch, or in the third, and finds them so, blessed are those servants! But know this, that if the householder had known at what hour the thief was coming, he would not have left his house to be broken into. You also must be ready; for the Son of man is coming at an unexpected hour."

Proper 15   *The Sunday Closest to August 17*

A Reading (Lesson) from the Book of Jeremiah [23:23-29]

Thus says the Lord of hosts: "Am I a God at hand and not a God afar off? Can a man hide himself in secret places so that I cannot see him? says the Lord. Do I not fill heaven and earth? says the Lord. I have heard what the prophets have said who prophesy lies in my name, saying, 'I have dreamed, I have dreamed!' How long shall there be lies in the heart of the prophets who prophesy lies, and who prophesy the deceit of their own heart, who think to make my people forget my name by their dreams which they tell one another, even as their fathers forgot my name for Ba'al? Let the prophet who has a dream tell the dream, but let him who has my word speak my word faithfully. What has straw in common with wheat? says the Lord. Is not my word like fire, says the Lord, and like a hammer which breaks the rock in pieces?"

Psalm 82 [page 705]

A Reading (Lesson) from the Letter to the Hebrews [12:1-7 (8-10) 11-14]

Therefore, since we are surrounded by so great a cloud of witnesses, let us also lay aside every weight, and sin which clings so closely, and let us run with perseverance the race that is set before us, looking to Jesus the pioneer and perfecter of our faith, who for the joy that was set before him endured the cross, despising the shame, and is seated at the right hand of the throne of God. Consider him who endured from sinners such hostility against himself, so that you may not grow weary or faint-hearted. In your struggle against sin you have not yet resisted to the point of shedding your blood. And have you forgotten the exhortation which addresses you as sons?—"My son, do not regard lightly the discipline of the Lord, nor lose courage when you are punished by him. For the Lord disciplines him whom he loves, and chastises every son whom he receives." It is for discipline that you have to endure. God is treating you as sons; for what son is there whom his father does not discipline?

> If you are left without discipline, in which all have participated, then you are illegitimate children and not sons. Besides this, we have had earthly fathers to discipline us and we respected them. Shall we not much more be subject to the Father of spirits and live? For they disciplined us for a short time at their pleasure, but he disciplines us for our good, that we may share his holiness.

For the moment all discipline seems painful rather than pleasant; later it yields the peaceful fruit of righteousness to those who have been trained by it. Therefore lift your drooping hands and strengthen your weak knees, and make straight paths for your feet, so that what is lame may not be put out of joint but rather be healed. Strive for peace with all men, and for the holiness without which no one will see the Lord.

✝ *The Holy Gospel of Our Lord Jesus Christ According to Luke* [12:49-56]

Jesus said,"I came to cast fire upon the earth; and would that it were already kindled! I have a baptism to be baptized with; and how I am constrained until it is accomplished! Do you think that I have come to give peace on earth? No, I tell you, but rather division; for henceforth in one house there will be five divided, three against two and two against three; they will be divided, father against son and son against father, mother against daughter and daughter against her mother, mother-in-law against her daughter-in-law and daughter-in-law against her mother-in-law." He also said to the multitudes, "When you see a cloud rising in the west, you say at once, 'A shower is coming'; and so it happens. And when you see the south wind blowing, you say, 'There will be scorching heat'; and it happens. You hypocrites! You know how to interpret the appearance of earth and sky; but why do you not know how to interpret the present time?"

Proper 16 *The Sunday Closest to August 24*

A Reading (Lesson) from the Book of Isaiah [28:14-22]

Hear the word of the Lord, you scoffers, who rule this people in Jerusalem! Because you have said, "We have made a covenant with death, and with Sheol we have an agreement; when the overwhelming scourge passes through, it will not come to us; for we have made lies our refuge, and in falsehood we have taken shelter"; therefore thus says the Lord God, "Behold, I am laying in Zion for a foundation a stone, a tested stone, a precious cornerstone, of a sure foundation: 'He who believes will not be in haste.' And I will make justice the line, and righteousness the plummet; and hail will sweep away the refuge of lies, and waters will overwhelm the shelter." Then your covenant with death will be annulled, and your agreement with Sheol will not stand; when the overwhelming scourge passes through, you will be beaten down by it. As often as it passes through it will take you; for morning by morning it will pass through, by day and by night; and it will be sheer terror to understand the message. For the bed is too short to stretch oneself on it, and the covering too narrow to wrap oneself in it. For the Lord will rise up as on Mount Pera'zim, he will be wroth as in the valley of Gibeon; to do his deed—strange is his deed! and to work his work—alien is his work! Now therefore do not scoff, lest your bonds be made strong; for I have heard a decree of destruction from the Lord God of hosts upon the whole land.

Psalm 46 [page 649]

A Reading (Lesson) from the Letter to the Hebrews
[12:18-19, 22-29]

You have not come to what may be touched, a blazing fire, and darkness, and gloom, and a tempest, and the sound of a trumpet, and a voice whose words made the hearers entreat that no further messages be spoken to them. But you have come to Mount Zion and to the city of the living God, the heavenly Jerusalem, and to innumerable angels in festal gathering, and to the assembly of the first-born who are enrolled in heaven, and to a judge who is God of all, and to the spirits of just men made perfect, and to Jesus, the mediator of a new covenant, and to the sprinkled blood that speaks more graciously than the blood of Abel. See that you do not refuse him who is speaking. For if they did not escape when they refused him who warned them on earth, much less shall we escape if we reject him who warns from heaven. His voice then shook the earth; but now he has promised, "Yet once more I will shake not only the earth but also the heaven." This phrase, "Yet once more," indicates the removal of what is shaken, as of what has been made, in order that what cannot be shaken may remain. Therefore let us be grateful for receiving a kingdom that cannot be shaken, and thus let us offer to God acceptable worship, with reverence and awe; for our God is a consuming fire.

✝ *The Holy Gospel of Our Lord Jesus Christ*
According to Luke [13:22-30]

Jesus went on his way through towns and villages, teaching, and journeying toward Jerusalem. And some one said to him, "Lord, will those who are saved be few?" And he said to them, "Strive to enter by the narrow door; for many, I tell you, will seek to enter and will not be able. When once the householder has risen up and shut the door, you will begin to stand outside and to knock at the door, saying, 'Lord, open to us.' He will answer you, 'I do not know where you come from.' Then you will begin to say, 'We ate and drank in your presence, and you taught in our streets.' But he will say 'I tell you, I do not know where you come from; depart from me, all you workers of iniquity!' There you will weep and gnash your teeth, when you see Abraham and Isaac and Jacob and all the prophets in the kingdom of God and you yourselves thrust out. And men will come from east and west, and from north and south, and sit at table in the kingdom of God. And behold, some are last who will be first, and some are first who will be last."

Proper 17   *The Sunday Closest to August 31*

A Reading (Lesson) from the Book of Ecclesiasticus
[10(7-11)12-18]

Arrogance is hateful before the Lord and before men, and injustice is outrageous to both. Sovereignty passes from nation to nation on account of injustice and insolence and wealth. How can he who is dust and ashes be proud? For even in life his bowels decay. A long illness baffles the physician; the king of today will die tomorrow. For when a man is dead, he will inherit creeping things, and wild beasts and worms.

The beginning of man's pride is to depart from the Lord; his heart has forsaken his Maker. For the beginning of pride is sin, and the man who clings to it pours out abominations. Therefore the Lord brought upon them extraordinary afflictions, and destroyed them utterly. The Lord has cast down the thrones of rulers, and has seated the lowly in their place. The Lord has plucked up the roots of the nations, and has planted the humble in their place. The Lord has overthrown the lands of the nations, and has destroyed them to the foundations of the earth. He has removed some of them and destroyed them, and has extinguished the memory of them from the earth. Pride was not created for men, nor fierce anger for those born of women.

Psalm 112 [page 755]

A Reading (Lesson) from the Letter to the Hebrews [13:1-8]

Let brotherly love continue. Do not neglect to show hospitality to strangers, for thereby some have entertained angels unawares. Remember those who are in prison, as though in prison with them; and those who are ill-treated, since you also are in the body. Let marriage be held in honor among all, and let the marriage bed be undefiled; for God will judge the immoral and adulterous. Keep your life free from love of money, and be content with what you have; for he has said, "I will never fail you nor forsake you." Hence we can confidently say, "The Lord is my helper, I will not be afraid; what can man do to me?" Remember your leaders, those who spoke to you the word of God; consider the outcome of their life, and imitate their faith. Jesus Christ is the same yesterday and today and for ever.

✝ *The Holy Gospel of Our Lord Jesus Christ According to Luke* [14:1, 7-14]

One sabbath when Jesus went to dine at the house of a ruler who belonged to the Pharisees, they were watching him. Now he told a parable to those who were invited, when he marked how they chose the places of honor, saying to them, "When you are invited by any one to a marriage feast, do not sit down in a place of honor, lest a more eminent man than you be invited by him; and he who invited you both will come and say to you, 'Give place to this man,' and then you will begin with shame to take the lowest place. But when you are invited, go and sit in the lowest place, so that when your host comes he may say to you, 'Friend, go up higher'; then you will be honored in the presence of all who sit at table with you. For every one who exalts himself will be humbled, and he who humbles himself will be exalted." He said also to the man who had invited him, "When you give a dinner or a banquet, do not invite your friends or your brothers or your kinsmen or rich neighbors, lest they also invite you in return, and you be repaid. But when you give a feast, invite the poor, the maimed, the lame, the blind, and you will be blessed, because they cannot repay you. You will be repaid at the resurrection of the just."

Proper 18   *The Sunday Closest to September 7*

A Reading (Lesson) from the Book of Deuteronomy [30:15-20]

Moses said to all Israel the words which the Lord commanded him: "See, I have set before you this day life and good, death and evil. If you obey the commandments of the Lord your God which I command you this day, by loving the Lord your God, by walking in his ways, and by keeping his commandments and his statutes and his ordinances, then you shall live and multiply, and the Lord your God will bless you in the land which you are entering to take possession of it. But if your heart turns away, and you will not hear, but are drawn away to worship other gods and serve them, I declare to you this day, that you shall perish; you shall not live long in the land which you are going over the Jordan to enter and possess. I call heaven and earth to witness against you this day, that I have set before you life and death, blessing and curse; therefore choose life, that you and your descendants may live, loving the Lord your God, obeying his voice, and cleaving to him; for that means life to you and length of days, that you may dwell in the land which the Lord swore to your fathers, to Abraham, to Isaac, and to Jacob, to give them."

Psalm 1 [page 585]

A Reading (Lesson) from the Letter of Paul to Philemon
[1-20]

Paul, a prisoner for Christ Jesus, and Timothy our brother, to Phile'mon our beloved fellow worker, and Ap'phia our sister and Archip'pus our fellow soldier, and the church in your house: Grace to you and peace from God our Father and the Lord Jesus Christ. I thank my God always when I remember you in my prayers, because I hear of your love and of the faith which you have toward the Lord Jesus and all the saints, and I pray that the sharing of your faith may promote the knowledge of all the good that is ours in Christ. For I have derived much joy and comfort from your love, my brother, because the hearts of the saints have been refreshed through you. Accordingly, though I am bold enough in Christ to command you to do what is required, yet for love's sake I prefer to appeal to you—I, Paul, an ambassador and now a prisoner also for Christ Jesus—I appeal to you for my child, Ones'imus, whose father I have become in my imprisonment. (Formerly he was useless to you, but now he is indeed useful to you and to me.) I am sending him back to you, sending my very heart. I would have been glad to keep him with me, in order that he might serve me on your behalf during my imprisonment for the gospel; but I preferred to do nothing without your consent in order that your goodness might not be by compulsion but of your own free will. Perhaps this is why he was parted from you for a while, that you might have him back for ever, no longer as a slave but more than a slave, as a beloved brother, especially to me but how much more to you, both in the flesh and in the Lord. So if you consider me your partner, receive him as you would receive me. If he has wronged you at all, or owes you anything, charge that to my account. I, Paul, write this with my own hand, I will repay it—to say nothing of your owing me even your own self. Yes, brother, I want some benefit from you in the Lord. Refresh my heart in Christ.

✝ *The Holy Gospel of Our Lord Jesus Christ According to Luke* [14:25-33]

Great multitudes accompanied Jesus; and he turned and said to them, "If any one comes to me and does not hate his own father and mother and wife and children and brothers and sisters, yes, and even his own life, he cannot be my disciple. Whoever does not bear his own cross and come after me, cannot be my disciple. For which of you, desiring to build a tower, does not first sit down and count the cost, whether he has enough to complete it? Otherwise, when he has laid a foundation, and is not able to finish, all who see it begin to mock him, saying, 'This man began to build, and was not able to finish.' Or what king, going to encounter another king in war, will not sit down first and take counsel whether he is able with ten thousand to meet him who comes against him with twenty thousand? And if not,

while the other is yet a great way off, he sends an embassy
and asks terms of peace. So therefore, whoever of you does
not renounce all that he has cannot be my disciple."

Proper 19 *The Sunday Closest to September 14*

A Reading (Lesson) from the Book of Exodus [32:1, 7-14]

When the people saw that Moses delayed to come down
from the mountain, the people gathered themselves
together to Aaron, and said to him,"Up, make us gods,
who shall go before us; as for this Moses, the man who
brought us up out of the land of Egypt, we do not know
what has become of him." And the Lord said to Moses,
"Go down; for your people, whom you brought up out of
the land of Egypt, have corrupted themselves; they have
turned aside quickly out of the way which I commanded
them; they have made for themselves a molten calf, and
have worshiped it and sacrificed to it, and said,'These are
your gods, O Israel, who brought you up out of the land of
Egypt!'"And the Lord said to Moses,"I have seen this
people, and behold, it is a stiff-necked people; now
therefore let me alone, that my wrath may burn hot against
them and I may consume them; but of you I will make a
great nation."But Moses besought the Lord his God, and
said,"O Lord, why does thy wrath burn hot against thy
people, whom thou hast brought forth out of the land of
Egypt with great power and with a mighty hand? Why
should the Egyptians say,'With evil intent did he bring
them forth, to slay them in the mountains, and to consume
them from the face of the earth'? Turn from thy fierce
wrath, and repent of this evil against thy people.
Remember Abraham, Isaac, and Israel, thy servants, to
whom thou didst swear by thine own self, and didst say to
them,'I will multiply your descendants as the stars of
heaven, and all this land that I have promised I will give to

your descendants, and they shall inherit it for ever.'" And the Lord repented of the evil which he thought to do to his people.

Psalm 51:1-18 [page 656]   or   *51:1-11* [page 656]

A Reading (Lesson) from the First Letter of Paul to Timothy [1:12-17]

I thank him who has given me strength for this, Christ Jesus our Lord, because he judged me faithful by appointing me to his service, though I formerly blasphemed and persecuted and insulted him; but I received mercy because I had acted ignorantly in unbelief, and the grace of our Lord overflowed for me with the faith and love that are in Christ Jesus. The saying is sure and worthy of full acceptance, that Christ Jesus came into the world to save sinners. And I am the foremost of sinners; but I received mercy for this reason, that in me, as the foremost, Jesus Christ might display his perfect patience for an example to those who were to believe in him for eternal life. To the King of ages, immortal, invisible, the only God, be honor and glory for ever and ever. Amen.

✝ *The Holy Gospel of Our Lord Jesus Christ According to Luke* [15:1-10]

Now the tax collectors and sinners were all drawing near to hear Jesus. And the Pharisees and the scribes murmured, saying, "This man receives sinners and eats with them." So he told them this parable: "What man of you, having a hundred sheep, if he has lost one of them, does not leave the ninety-nine in the wilderness, and go after the one which is lost, until he finds it? And when he has found it, he lays it on his shoulders, rejoicing. And when he comes home, he calls together his friends and his neighbors, saying to them, 'Rejoice with me, for I have found my sheep which was lost.' Just so, I tell you, there will be more joy in heaven over one sinner who repents than over ninety-nine righteous persons who need no repentance. Or what woman, having ten silver coins, if she loses one coin, does not light a lamp and sweep the house and seek diligently until she finds it? And when she has found it, she calls together her friends and neighbors, saying, 'Rejoice with me, for I have found the coin which I had lost.' Just so, I tell you, there is joy before the angels of God over one sinner who repents."

Proper 20 *The Sunday Closest to September 21*

A Reading (Lesson) from the Book of Amos [8:4-7 (8-12)]

Hear this, you who trample upon the needy, and bring the poor of the land to an end, saying, "When will the new moon be over, that we may sell grain? And the sabbath, that we may offer wheat for sale, that we may make the ephah small and the shekel great, and deal deceitfully with false balances, that we may buy the poor for silver and the needy for a pair of sandals, and sell the refuse of the wheat?" The Lord has sworn by the pride of Jacob: "Surely I will never forget any of their deeds."

"Shall not the land tremble on this account, and every one mourn who dwells in it, and all of it rise like the Nile, and be tossed about and sink again, like the Nile of Egypt? And on that day," says the Lord God, "I will make the sun go down at noon, and darken the earth in broad daylight. I will turn your feasts into mourning, and all your songs into lamentation; I will bring sackcloth upon all loins, and baldness on every head; I will make it like the mourning for an only son, and the end of it like a bitter day. Behold, the days are coming," says the Lord God, "When I will send a famine on the land; not a famine of bread, nor a thirst for water, but of hearing the words of the Lord. They shall wander from sea to sea, and from north to east; they shall run to and fro, to seek the word of the Lord, but they shall not find it."

Psalm 138 [page 793]

A Reading (Lesson) from the First Letter of Paul to Timothy [2:1-8]

First of all, then, I urge that supplications, prayers, intercessions, and thanksgivings be made for all men, for kings and all who are in high positions, that we may lead a quiet and peaceable life, godly and respectful in every way. This is good, and it is acceptable in the sight of God our Savior, who desires all men to be saved and to come to the knowledge of the truth. For there is one God, and there is one mediator between God and men, the man Christ Jesus, who gave himself as a ransom for all, the testimony to which was borne at the proper time. For this I was appointed a preacher and apostle (I am telling the truth, I am not lying), a teacher of the Gentiles in faith and truth. I desire, then, that in every place the men should pray, lifting holy hands without anger or quarreling.

✝ *The Holy Gospel of Our Lord Jesus Christ According to Luke* [16:1-13]

Jesus said to the disciples,"There was a rich man who had a steward, and charges were brought to him that this man was wasting his goods. And he called him and said to him,'What is this that I hear about you? Turn in the account of your stewardship, for you can no longer be steward.' And the steward said to himself,'What shall I do, since my master is taking the stewardship away from me? I am not strong enough to dig, and I am ashamed to beg. I have decided what to do, so that people may receive me into their houses when I am put out of the stewardship.' So, summoning his master's debtors one by one, he said to the first, 'How much do you owe my master?' He said, 'A hundred measures of oil.' And he said to him, 'Take your bill, and sit down quickly and write fifty.' Then he said to another, 'And how much do you owe?' He said, 'A hundred measures of wheat.' He said to him, 'Take your bill, and write eighty.' The master commended the dishonest steward for his shrewdness; for the sons of this world are more shrewd in dealing with their own generation than the sons of light. And I tell you, make friends for yourselves by means of unrighteous mammon, so that when it fails they may receive you into the eternal habitations. He who is faithful in a very little is faithful also in much; and he who is dishonest in a very little is dishonest also in much. If then you have not been faithful in the unrighteous mammon, who will entrust to you the true riches? And if you have not been faithful in that which is another's, who will give you that which is your own? No servant can serve two masters; for either he will hate the one and love the other, or he will be devoted to the one and despise the other. You cannot serve God and mammon."

Proper 21 *The Sunday Closest to September 28*

A Reading (Lesson) from the Book of Amos [6:1-7]

Woe to those who are at ease in Zion, and to those who feel secure on the mountain of Samar'ia, the notable men of the first of the nations, to whom the house of Israel come! Pass over to Calneh, and see; and thence go to Hamath the great; then go down to Gath of the Philistines. Are they better than these kingdoms? Or is their territory greater than your territory, O you who put far away the evil day, and bring near the seat of violence? Woe to those who lie upon beds of ivory, and stretch themselves upon their couches, and eat lambs from the flock, and calves from the midst of the stall; who sing idle songs to the sound of the harp, and like David invent for themselves instruments of music; who drink wine in bowls, and anoint themselves with the finest oils, but are not grieved over the ruin of Joseph! Therefore they shall now be the first of those to go into exile, and the revelry of those who stretch themselves shall pass away.

Psalm 146 [page 803]   or   *146:4-9* [page 803]

A Reading (Lesson) from the First Letter of Paul to Timothy [6:11-19]

As for you, man of God, aim at righteousness, godliness, faith, love, steadfastness, gentleness. Fight the good fight of the faith; take hold of the eternal life to which you were called when you made the good confession in the presence of many witnesses. In the presence of God who gives life to all things, and of Christ Jesus who in his testimony before Pontius Pilate made the good confession, I charge you to keep the commandment unstained and free from reproach until the appearing of our Lord Jesus Christ; and this will be made manifest at the proper time by the blessed and only Sovereign, the King of kings and Lord of lords, who alone has immortality and dwells in unapproachable light, whom no man has ever seen or can see. To him be honor and eternal dominion. Amen. As for the rich in this world, charge them not to be haughty, nor to set their hopes on uncertain riches but on God, who richly furnishes us with everything to enjoy. They are to do good, to be rich in good deeds, liberal and generous, thus laying up for themselves a good foundation for the future, so that they may take hold of the life which is life indeed.

✝ *The Holy Gospel of Our Lord Jesus Christ*
According to Luke [16:19-31]

Jesus said, "There was a rich man, who was clothed in purple and fine linen and who feasted sumptuously every day. And at his gate lay a poor man named Laz'arus, full of sores, who desired to be fed with what fell from the rich man's table; moreover the dogs came and licked his sores. The poor man died and was carried by the angels to Abraham's bosom. The rich man also died and was buried; and in Hades, being in torment, he lifted up his eyes, and saw Abraham far off and Laz'arus in his bosom. And he called out, 'Father Abraham, have mercy upon me, and send Laz'arus to dip the end of his finger in water and cool my tongue; for I am in anguish in this flame.' But Abraham said, 'Son, remember that you in your lifetime received your good things, and Laz'arus in like manner evil things; but now he is comforted here, and you are in anguish. And besides all this, between us and you a great chasm has been fixed, in order that those who would pass from here to you may not be able, and none may cross from there to us.' And he said, 'Then I beg you, father, to send him to my father's house, for I have five brothers, so that he may warn them, lest they also come into this place of torment.' But Abraham said, 'They have Moses and the prophets; let them hear them.' And he said, 'No, father Abraham; but if some one goes to them from the dead, they will repent.' He said to him, 'If they do not hear Moses and the prophets, neither will they be convinced if some one should rise from the dead.'"

Proper 22 *The Sunday Closest to October 5*

A Reading (Lesson) from the Book of Habak'kuk
[1:1-6(7-11)12-13; 2:1-4]

The oracle of God which Habak'kuk the prophet saw: O Lord, how long shall I cry for help, and thou wilt not hear?

Or cry to thee "Violence!" and thou wilt not save? Why dost thou make me see wrongs and look upon trouble? Destruction and violence are before me; strife and contention arise. So the law is slacked and justice never goes forth. For the wicked surround the righteous, so justice goes forth perverted.—Look among the nations, and see; wonder and be astounded. For I am doing a work in your days that you would not believe if told. For lo, I am rousing the Chalde'ans, that bitter and hasty nation, who march through the breadth of the earth, to seize habitations not their own.

> Dread and terrible are they; their justice and dignity proceed from themselves. Their horses are swifter than leopards, more fierce than the evening wolves; their horsemen press proudly on. Yea, their horsemen come from afar; they fly like an eagle swift to devour. They all come for violence; terror of them goes before them. They gather captives like sand. At kings they scoff, and of rulers they make sport. They laugh at every fortress, for they heap up earth and take it. Then they sweep by like the wind and go on, guilty men, whose own might is their god!

Art thou not from everlasting, O Lord my God, my Holy One? We shall not die. O Lord, thou hast ordained them as a judgment; and thou, O Rock, hast established them for chastisement. Thou who art of purer eyes than to behold evil and canst not look on wrong, why dost thou look on faithless men, and art silent when the wicked swallows up the man more righteous than he?— I will take my stand to watch, and station myself on the tower, and look forth to see what he will say to me, and what I will answer concerning my complaint. And the Lord answered me, "Write the vision; make it plain upon tablets, so he may run who reads it. For still the vision awaits its time; it hastens to the end—it will not lie. If it seem slow, wait for it; it will surely come, it will not delay. Behold, he whose soul is not upright in him shall fail, but the righteous shall live by his faith."

Psalm 37:1-18 [page 633]   or   *37:3-10* [page 633]

A Reading (Lesson) from the Second Letter of Paul to Timothy [1:(1-5)6-14]

> Paul, an apostle of Christ Jesus by the will of God according to the promise of the life which is in Christ Jesus, to Timothy, my beloved child: Grace, mercy, and peace from God the Father and Christ Jesus our Lord. I thank God whom I serve with a clear conscience, as did my fathers, when I remember you constantly in my prayers. As I remember your tears, I long night and day to see you, that I may be filled with joy. I am reminded of your sincere faith, a faith that dwelt first in your grandmother Lo'is and your mother Eunice and now, I am sure, dwells in you. Hence,

I remind you to rekindle the gift of God that is within you through the laying on of my hands; for God did not give us a spirit of timidity, but a spirit of power and love and self-control. Do not be ashamed then of testifying to our Lord, nor of me his prisoner, but share in suffering for the gospel in the power of God, who saved us and called us with a holy calling, not in virtue of our works but in virtue of his own purpose and the grace which he gave us in Christ Jesus ages ago, and now has manifested through the appearing of our Savior Christ Jesus, who abolished death and brought life and immortality to light through the gospel. For this gospel I was appointed a preacher and apostle and teacher, and therefore I suffer as I do. But I am not ashamed, for I know whom I have believed, and I am sure that he is able to guard until that Day what has been entrusted to me. Follow the pattern of the sound words which you have heard from me, in the faith and love which are in Christ Jesus; guard the truth that has been entrusted to you by the Holy Spirit who dwells within us.

✠ *The Holy Gospel of Our Lord Jesus Christ According to Luke* [17:5-10]

The apostles said to the Lord, "Increase our faith!" And the Lord said, "If you had faith as a grain of mustard seed, you could say to this sycamine tree, 'Be rooted up, and be planted in the sea,' and it would obey you. Will any one of you, who has a servant plowing or keeping sheep, say to him when he has come in from the field, 'Come at once and sit down at table'? Will he not rather say to him, 'Prepare supper for me, and gird yourself and serve me, till I eat and drink; and afterward you shall eat and drink'? Does he thank the servant because he did what was commanded? So you also, when you have done all that is commanded you, say, 'We are unworthy servants; we have only done what was our duty.'"

Proper 23   *The Sunday Closest to October 12*

A Reading (Lesson) from the Book of Ruth [1:(1-7)8-19a]

In the days when the judges ruled there was a famine in the land, and a certain man of Bethlehem in Judah went to sojourn in the country of Moab, he and his wife and his two sons. The name of the man was Elim'elech and the name of his wife Na'omi, and the names of his two sons were Mahlon and Chil'ion; they were Eph'rathites from Bethlehem in Judah. They went into the country of Moab and remained there. But Elim'elech, the husband of Na'omi, died, and she was left with her two sons. These took Moabite wives; the name of one was Orpah and the name of the other Ruth. They lived there about ten years; and both Mahlon and Chil'ion died, so that the woman was bereft of her two sons and her husband. Then she started with her daughters-in-law to return from the country of Moab, for she had heard in the country of Moab that the Lord had visited his people and given them food. So she set out from the place where she was, with her two daughters-in-law, and they went on the way to return to the land of Judah.

[*When Na'omi's sons died, and she decided to return to her native Bethlehem,*] Na'omi said to her two daughters-in-law, "Go, return each of you to her mother's house. May the Lord deal kindly with you, as you have dealt with the dead and with me. The Lord grant that you may find a home, each of you in the house of her husband!" Then she kissed them, and they lifted up their voices and wept. And they said to her, "No, we will return with you to your people." But Na'omi said, "Turn back, my daughters, why will you go with me? Have I yet sons in my womb that they may become your husbands? Turn back, my daughters, go your way, for I am too old to have a husband. If I should say I have hope, even if I should have a husband this night and should bear sons, would you therefore wait till they were grown? Would you therefore refrain from marrying? No, my daughters, for it is exceedingly bitter to me for your sake that the hand of the Lord has gone forth against me." Then they lifted up their voices and wept again; and Orpah kissed her mother-in-law, but Ruth clung to her. And she said, "See, your sister-in-law has gone back to her people and to her gods; return after your sister-in-law." But Ruth said, "Entreat me not to leave you or to return from following you; for where you go I will go, and where you lodge I will lodge, your people shall be my people, and your God my God; where you die I will die, and there will I be buried. May the Lord do so to me and more also if even death parts me from you." And when Na'omi saw that she was determined to go with her, she said no more. So the two of them went on until they came to Bethlehem.

Psalm 113   [page 756]

A Reading (Lesson) from the Second Letter of Paul to Timothy [2:(3-7)8-15]

Share in suffering as a good soldier of Christ Jesus. No soldier on service gets entangled in civilian pursuits, since his aim is to satisfy the one who enlisted him. An athlete is not crowned unless he competes according to the rules. It is the hard-working farmer who ought to have the first share of the crops. Think over what I say, for the Lord will grant you understanding in everything.

Remember Jesus Christ, risen from the dead, descended from David, as preached in my gospel, the gospel for which I am suffering and wearing fetters like a criminal. But the word of God is not fettered. Therefore I endure everything for the sake of the elect, that they also may obtain salvation in Christ Jesus with its eternal glory. The saying is sure: If we have died with him, we shall also live with him; if we endure, we shall also reign with him; if we deny him, he also will deny us; if we are faithless, he remains faithful—for he cannot deny himself. Remind them of this, and charge them before the Lord to avoid disputing about words, which does no good, but only ruins the hearers. Do your best to present yourself to God as one approved, a workman who has no need to be ashamed, rightly handling the word of truth.

✝ *The Holy Gospel of Our Lord Jesus Christ According to Luke* [17:11-19]

On the way to Jerusalem Jesus was passing along between Samar'ia and Galilee. And as he entered a village, he was met by ten lepers, who stood at a distance and lifted up

their voices and said, "Jesus, Master, have mercy on us."
When he saw them he said to them, "Go and show
yourselves to the priests." And as they went they were
cleansed. Then one of them, when he saw that he was
healed, turned back, praising God with a loud voice; and
he fell on his face at Jesus' feet, giving him thanks. Now he
was a Samaritan. Then said Jesus, "Were not ten cleansed?
Where are the nine? Was no one found to return and give
praise to God except this foreigner?" And he said to him,
"Rise and go your way; your faith has made you well."

Proper 24   *The Sunday Closest to October 19*

A Reading (Lesson) from the Book of Genesis   [32:3-8, 22-30]

Jacob sent messengers before him to Esau his brother in the
land of Se'ir, the country of Edom, instructing them, "Thus
you shall say to my lord Esau: Thus says your servant
Jacob, 'I have sojourned with Laban, and stayed until now;
and I have oxen, asses, flocks, menservants and
maidservants; and I have sent to tell my lord, in order that
I may find favor in your sight.' " And the messengers
returned to Jacob, saying, "We came to your brother Esau,
and he is coming to meet you, and four hundred men with
him." Then Jacob was greatly afraid and distressed; and he
divided the people that were with him, and the flocks and
herds and camels, into two companies, thinking, "If Esau
comes to the one company and destroys it, then the
company which is left will escape." The same night he
arose and took his two wives, his two maids, and his eleven
children, and crossed the ford of the Jabbok. He took them
and sent them across the stream, and likewise everything
that he had. And Jacob was left alone; and a man wrestled
with him until the breaking of the day. When the man saw
that he did not prevail against Jacob, he touched the
hollow of his thigh; and Jacob's thigh was put out of joint

as he wrestled with him. Then he said, "Let me go, for the day is breaking." But Jacob said, "I will not let you go, unless you bless me." And he said to him, "What is your name?" And he said, "Jacob." Then he said, "Your name shall no more be called Jacob, but Israel, for you have striven with God and with men, and have prevailed." Then Jacob asked him, "Tell me, I pray, your name." But he said, "Why is it that you ask my name?" And there he blessed him. So Jacob called the name of the place Peni'el, saying, "For I have seen God face to face, and yet my life is preserved."

Psalm 121 [page 779]

A Reading (Lesson) from the Second Letter of Paul to Timothy [3:14—4:5]

As for you, continue in what you have learned and have firmly believed, knowing from whom you learned it and how from childhood you have been acquainted with the sacred writings which are able to instruct you for salvation through faith in Christ Jesus. All scripture is inspired by God and profitable for teaching, for reproof, for correction, and for training in righteousness, that the man of God may be complete, equipped for every good work. I charge you in the presence of God and of Christ Jesus who is to judge the living and the dead, and by his appearing and his kingdom: preach the word, be urgent in season and out of season, convince, rebuke, and exhort, be unfailing in patience and in teaching. For the time is coming when people will not endure sound teaching, but having itching ears they will accumulate for themselves teachers to suit their own likings, and will turn away from listening to the truth and wander into myths. As for you, always be steady, endure suffering, do the work of an evangelist, fulfill your ministry.

✝ *The Holy Gospel of Our Lord Jesus Christ*
According to Luke [18:1-8a]

Jesus told this parable to his disciples, to the effect that they ought always to pray and not lose heart. He said, "In a certain city there was a judge who neither feared God nor regarded man; and there was a widow in that city who kept coming to him and saying, 'Vindicate me against my adversary.' For a while he refused; but afterward he said to himself, 'Though I neither fear God nor regard man, yet because this widow bothers me, I will vindicate her, or she will wear me out by her continual coming.'" And the Lord said, "Hear what the unrighteous judge says. And will not God vindicate his elect, who cry to him day and night? Will he delay long over them? I tell you, he will vindicate them speedily."

Proper 25 *The Sunday Closest to October 26*

A Reading (Lesson) from the Book of Jeremiah
[14:(1-6) 7-10, 19-22]

The word of the Lord which came to Jeremiah concerning the drought: "Judah mourns and her gates languish; her people lament on the ground, and the cry of Jerusalem goes up. Her nobles send their servants for water; they come to the cisterns, they find no water, they return with their vessels empty; they are ashamed and confounded and cover their heads. Because of the ground which is dismayed, since there is no rain on the land, the farmers are ashamed, they cover their heads. Even the hind in the field forsakes her newborn calf because there is no grass. The wild asses stand on the bare heights, they pant for air like jackals; their eyes fail because there is no herbage."

Though our iniquities testify against us, act, O Lord, for thy name's sake; for our backslidings are many, we have sinned against thee. O thou hope of Israel, its savior in time of trouble, why shouldst thou be like a stranger in the land, like a wayfarer who turns aside to tarry for a night? Why shouldst thou be like a man confused, like a mighty man who cannot save? Yet thou, O Lord, art in the midst of us, and we are called by thy name; leave us not. Hast thou utterly rejected Judah? Does thy soul loathe Zion? Why hast thou smitten us so that there is no healing for us? We looked for peace, but no good came; for a time of healing, but behold, terror. We acknowledge our wickedness, O Lord, and the iniquity of our fathers, for we have sinned against thee. Do not spurn us, for thy name's sake; do not dishonor thy glorious throne; remember and do not break thy covenant with us. Are there any among the false gods of the nations that can bring rain? Or can the heavens give showers? Art thou not he, O Lord our God? We set our hope on thee, for thou doest all these things.

Psalm 84 [page 707] or *84:1-6* [page 707]

A Reading (Lesson) from the Second Letter of Paul to Timothy [4:6-8, 16-18]

I am already on the point of being sacrificed; the time of my departure has come. I have fought the good fight, I have finished the race, I have kept the faith. Henceforth there is laid up for me the crown of righteousness, which the Lord, the righteous judge, will award to me on that Day, and not only to me but also to all who have loved his appearing. At my first defense no one took my part; all deserted me. May it not be charged against them! But the Lord stood by me and gave me strength to proclaim the message fully, that all the Gentiles might hear it. So I was rescued from the lion's mouth. The Lord will rescue me from every evil and save me for his heavenly kingdom. To him be the glory for ever and ever. Amen.

✝ *The Holy Gospel of Our Lord Jesus Christ*
According to Luke [18:9-14]

Jesus told this parable to some who trusted in themselves that they were righteous and despised others: "Two men went up into the temple to pray, one a Pharisee and the other a tax collector. The Pharisee stood and prayed thus with himself, 'God, I thank thee that I am not like other men, extortioners, unjust, adulterers, or even like this tax collector. I fast twice a week, I give tithes of all that I get.' But the tax collector, standing far off, would not even lift up his eyes to heaven, but beat his breast, saying, 'God, be merciful to me a sinner!' I tell you, this man went down to his house justified rather than the other; for every one who exalts himself will be humbled, but he who humbles himself will be exalted."

Proper 26   *The Sunday Closest to November 2*

A Reading (Lesson) from the Book of Isaiah   [1:10-20]

Hear the word of the Lord, you rulers of Sodom! Give ear to the teaching of our God, you people of Gomor'rah! "What to me is the multitude of your sacrifices? says the Lord; I have had enough of burnt offerings of rams and the fat of fed beasts; I do not delight in the blood of bulls, or of lambs, or of he-goats. When you come to appear before me, who requires of you this trampling of my courts? Bring no more vain offerings; incense is an abomination to me. New moon and sabbath and the calling of assemblies— I cannot endure iniquity and solemn assembly. Your new moons and your appointed feasts my soul hates; they have become a burden to me, I am weary of bearing them. When you spread forth your hands, I will hide my eyes from you; even though you make many prayers, I will not listen; your hands are full of blood. Wash yourselves; make yourselves clean; remove the evil of your doings from before my eyes; cease to do evil, learn to do good; seek justice, correct oppression; defend the fatherless, plead for the widow. Come now, let us reason together, says the Lord: though your sins are like scarlet, they shall be as white as snow; though they are red like crimson, they shall become like wool. If you are willing and obedient, you shall eat the good of the land; but if you refuse and rebel, you shall be devoured by the sword; for the mouth of the Lord has spoken."

Psalm 32 [page 624]   or   *32:1-8* [page 624]

A Reading (Lesson) from the Second Letter of Paul to the Thessalonians [1:1-5(6-10)11-12]

Paul, Silva'nus, and Timothy, to the church of the Thessalo'nians in God our Father and the Lord Jesus Christ: Grace to you and peace from God the Father and the Lord Jesus Christ. We are bound to give thanks to God always for you, brethren, as is fitting, because your faith is growing abundantly, and the love of every one of you for one another is increasing. Therefore we ourselves boast of you in the churches of God for your steadfastness and faith in all your persecutions and in the afflictions which you are enduring. This is evidence of the righteous judgment of God, that you may be made worthy of the kingdom of God, for which you are suffering,

since indeed God deems it just to repay with affliction those who afflict you, and to grant rest with us to you who are afflicted, when the Lord Jesus is revealed from heaven with his mighty angels in flaming fire, inflicting vengence upon those who do not know God and upon those who do not obey the gospel of our Lord Jesus. They shall suffer the punishment of eternal destruction and exclusion from the presence of the Lord and from the glory of his might, when he comes on that day to be glorified in his saints, and to be marveled at in all who have believed, because our testimony to you was believed.

To this end we always pray for you, that our God may make you worthy of his call, and may fulfill every good resolve and work of faith by his power, so that the name of our Lord Jesus may be glorified in you, and you in him, according to the grace of our God and the Lord Jesus Christ.

✝ *The Holy Gospel of Our Lord Jesus Christ According to Luke* [19:1-10]

Jesus entered Jericho and was passing through. And there was a man named Zacchae'us; he was a chief tax collector, and rich. And he sought to see who Jesus was, but could not, on account of the crowd, because he was small of stature. So he ran on ahead and climbed up into a sycamore tree to see him, for he was to pass that way. And when Jesus came to the place, he looked up and said to him, "Zacchae'us, make haste and come down; for I must stay at your house today." So he made haste and came down, and received him joyfully. And when they saw it they all murmured, "He has gone in to be the guest of a man who is a sinner." And Zacchae'us stood and said to the Lord, "Behold, Lord, the half of my goods I give to the poor; and if I have defrauded any one of anything, I restore it fourfold." And Jesus said to him, "Today salvation has come to this house, since he also is a son of Abraham. For the Son of man came to seek and to save the lost."

Proper 27   *The Sunday Closest to November 9*

A Reading (Lesson) from the Book of Job [19:23-27a]

Job said, "Oh that my words were written! Oh that they were inscribed in a book! Oh that with an iron pen and lead they were graven in the rock for ever! For I know that my Redeemer lives, and at last he will stand upon the earth; and after my skin has been thus destroyed, then from my flesh I shall see God, whom I shall see on my side, and my eyes shall behold, and not another."

Psalm 17 [page 600]   or   *17:1-8* [page 600]

A Reading (Lesson) from the Second Letter of Paul to the Thessalonians [2:13—3:5]

We are bound to give thanks to God always for you, brethren beloved by the Lord, because God chose you from the beginning to be saved, through sanctification by the Spirit and belief in the truth. To this he called you through our gospel, so that you may obtain the glory of our Lord Jesus Christ. So then, brethren, stand firm and hold to the traditions which you were taught by us, either by word of mouth or by letter. Now may our Lord Jesus Christ himself, and God our Father, who loved us and gave us eternal comfort and good hope through grace, comfort your hearts and establish them in every good work and word. Finally, brethren, pray for us, that the word of the Lord may speed on and triumph, as it did among you, and that we may be delivered from wicked and evil men; for not all have faith. But the Lord is faithful; he will strengthen you and guard you from evil. And we have confidence in the Lord about you, that you are doing and will do the things which we command. May the Lord direct your hearts to the love of God and to the steadfastness of Christ.

✝ *The Holy Gospel of Our Lord Jesus Christ*
According to Luke [20:27(28-33)34-38]

There came to Jesus some Sad'ducees, those who say that
there is no resurrection,

> and they asked him a question, saying,"Teacher, Moses
> wrote for us that if a man's brother dies, having a wife
> but no children, the man must take the wife and raise up
> children for his brother. Now there were seven brothers;
> the first took a wife, and died without children; and the
> second and the third took her, and likewise all seven left
> no children and died. Afterward the woman also died.
> In the resurrection, therefore, whose wife will the
> woman be? For the seven had her as wife."

And Jesus said to them,"The sons of this age marry and are
given in marriage; but those who are accounted worthy to
attain to that age and to the resurrection from the dead
neither marry nor are given in marriage, for they cannot
die any more, because they are equal to angels and are sons
of God, being sons of the resurrection. But that the dead
are raised, even Moses showed, in the passage about the
bush, where he calls the Lord the God of Abraham and the
God of Isaac and the God of Jacob. Now he is not God of
the dead, but of the living; for all live to him."

Proper 28   *The Sunday Closest to November 16*

A Reading (Lesson) from the Book of Malachi
[3:13—4:2a,5-6]

"Your words have been stout against me," says the Lord.
"Yet you say 'How have we spoken against thee?' You have
said,'It is vain to serve God. What is the good of our
keeping his charge or of walking as in mourning before the
Lord of hosts? Henceforth we deem the arrogant blessed;
evildoers not only prosper but when they put God to the

test they escape.'" Then those who feared the Lord spoke with one another; the Lord heeded and heard them, and a book of remembrance was written before him of those who feared the Lord and thought on his name. "They shall be mine, says the Lord of hosts, my special possession on the day when I act, and I will spare them as a man spares his son who serves him. Then once more you shall distinguish between the righteous and the wicked, between one who serves God and one who does not serve him. For behold, the day comes, burning like an oven, when all the arrogant and all evildoers will be stubble; the day that comes shall burn them up, says the Lord of hosts, so that it will leave them neither root nor branch. But for you who fear my name the sun of righteousness shall rise, with healing in its wings. Behold, I will send you Eli'jah the prophet before the great and terrible day of the Lord comes. And he will turn the hearts of fathers to their children and the hearts of children to their fathers, lest I come and smite the land with a curse."

Psalm 98 [page 727] or *98:5-10* [page 728]

A Reading (Lesson) from the Second Letter of Paul to the Thessalonians [3:6-13]

Now we command you, brethren, in the name of our Lord Jesus Christ, that you keep away from any brother who is living in idleness and not in accord with the tradition that you received from us. For you yourselves know how you ought to imitate us; we were not idle when we were with you, we did not eat any one's bread without paying, but with toil and labor we worked night and day, that we might not burden any of you. It was not because we have not that right, but to give you in our conduct an example to imitate. For even when we were with you, we gave you this command: If any one will not work, let him not eat. For we hear that some of you are living in idleness, mere busybodies, not doing any work. Now such persons we command and exhort in the Lord Jesus Christ to do their work in quietness and to earn their own living. Brethren, do not be weary in well-doing.

✠ *The Holy Gospel of Our Lord Jesus Christ*
   According to Luke [21:5-19]

As some spoke of the temple, how it was adorned with noble stones and offerings, Jesus said,"As for these things which you see, the days will come when there shall not be left here one stone upon another that will not be thrown down." And they asked him,"Teacher, when will this be, and what will be the sign when this is about to take place?" And he said,"Take heed that you are not led astray; for many will come in my name, saying,'I am he!' and,'The time is at hand!' Do not go after them. And when you hear of wars and tumults, do not be terrified; for this must first take place, but the end will not be at once." Then he said to them,"Nation will rise against nation, and kingdom against kingdom; there will be great earthquakes, and in various places famines and pestilences; and there will be terrors and great signs from heaven. But before all this they will lay their hands on you and persecute you, delivering you up to the synagogues and prisons, and you will be brought before kings and governors for my name's sake. This will be a time for you to bear testimony. Settle it therefore in your minds, not to meditate beforehand how to answer; for I will give you a mouth and wisdom, which none of your adversaries will be able to withstand or contradict. You will be delivered up even by parents and brothers and kinsmen and friends, and some of you they will put to death; you will be hated by all for my name's sake. But not a hair of your head will perish. By your endurance you will gain your lives."

Proper 29   *The Sunday closest to November 23*

A Reading (Lesson) from the Book of Jeremiah [23:1-6]

"Woe to the shepherds who destroy and scatter the sheep of
my pasture!" says the Lord. Therefore thus says the Lord,
the God of Israel, concerning the shepherds who care for
my people: "You have scattered my flock, and have driven
them away, and you have not attended to them. Behold,
I will attend to you for your evil doings, says the Lord.
Then I will gather the remnant of my flock out of all the
countries where I have driven them, and I will bring them
back to their fold, and they shall be fruitful and multiply.
I will set shepherds over them who will care for them, and
they shall fear no more, nor be dismayed, neither shall any
be missing, says the Lord. Behold, the days are coming,
says the Lord, when I will raise up for David a righteous
Branch, and he shall reign as king and deal wisely, and
shall execute justice and righteousness in the land. In his
days Judah will be saved, and Israel will dwell securely.
And this is the name by which he will be called: 'The Lord is
our righteousness.' "

Psalm 46 [page 649]

*A Reading (Lesson) from the Letter of Paul
to the Colossians* [1:11-20]

May you be strengthened with all power, according to his
glorious might, for all endurance and patience with joy,
giving thanks to the Father, who has qualified us to share
in the inheritance of the saints in light. He has delivered us
from the dominion of darkness and transferred us to the
kingdom of his beloved Son, in whom we have
redemption, the forgiveness of sins. He is the image of the
invisible God, the first-born of all creation; for in him all
things were created, in heaven and on earth, visible and

invisible, whether thrones or dominions or principalities or authorities—all things were created through him and for him. He is before all things, and in him all things hold together. He is the head of the body, the church; he is the beginning, the first-born from the dead, that in everything he might be pre-eminent. For in him all the fullness of God was pleased to dwell, and through him to reconcile to himself all things, whether on earth or in heaven, making peace by the blood of his cross.

✝ *The Holy Gospel of Our Lord Jesus Christ According to Luke* [23:35-43]

The people stood by, watching Jesus on the cross; but the rulers scoffed at him, saying,"He saved others; let him save himself, if he is the Christ of God, his Chosen One!" The soldiers also mocked him, coming up and offering him vinegar, and saying,"If you are the King of the Jews, save yourself!" There was also an inscription over him,"This is the King of the Jews." One of the criminals who were hanged railed at him, saying,"Are you not the Christ? Save yourself and us!" But the other rebuked him, saying,"Do you not fear God, since you are under the same sentence of condemnation? And we indeed justly; for we are receiving the due reward of our deeds; but this man has done nothing wrong." And he said,"Jesus, remember me when you come into your kingdom." And he said to him,"Truly I say to you, today you will be with me in Paradise."

or this

✝ *The Holy Gospel of Our Lord Jesus Christ According to Luke* [19:29-38]

When Jesus drew near to Beth'phage and Bethany, at the mount that is called Olivet, he sent two of the disciples, saying,"Go into the village opposite, where on entering you will find a colt tied, on which no one has ever yet sat; untie it and bring it here. If any one asks you, 'Why are you untying it?' you shall say this, 'The Lord has need of it.' " So those who were sent went away and found it as he had told them. And as they were untying the colt, its owners said to them, "Why are you untying the colt?" And they said, "The Lord has need of it." And they brought it to Jesus, and throwing their garments on the colt they set Jesus upon it. And as he rode along, they spread their garments on the road. As he was now drawing near, at the descent of the Mount of Olives, the whole multitude of the disciples began to rejoice and praise God with a loud voice for all the mighty works that they had seen, saying, "Blessed is the King who comes in the name of the Lord! Peace in heaven and glory in the highest!"

Holy Days

Saint Andrew   *November 30*

A Reading (Lesson) from the Book of Deuteronomy
[30:11-14]

Moses summoned all Israel and said to them: "This commandment which I command you this day is not too hard for you, neither is it far off. It is not in heaven, that you should say,'Who will go up for us to heaven, and bring it to us, that we may hear it and do it?' Neither is it beyond the sea, that you should say,'Who will go over the sea for us, and bring it to us, that we may hear it and do it?' But the word is very near you; it is in your mouth and in your heart, so that you can do it."

Psalm 19 [page 606]   or   *19:1-6* [page 606]

*A Reading (Lesson) from the Letter of Paul
to the Romans* [10:8b-18]

The word is near you, on your lips and in your heart (that is, the word of faith which we preach); because, if you confess with your lips that Jesus is Lord and believe in your heart that God raised him from the dead, you will be saved. For man believes with his heart and so is justified, and he confesses with his lips and so is saved. The scripture says,"No one who believes in him will be put to shame."

For there is no distinction between Jew and Greek; the same Lord is Lord of all and bestows his riches upon all who call upon him. For, "every one who calls upon the name of the Lord will be saved." But how are men to call upon him in whom they have not believed? And how are they to believe in him of whom they have never heard? And how are they to hear without a preacher? And how can men preach unless they are sent? As it is written, "How beautiful are the feet of those who preach good news!" But they have not all obeyed the gospel; for Isaiah says, "Lord, who has believed what he has heard from us?" So faith comes from what is heard, and what is heard comes by the preaching of Christ. But I ask, have they not heard? Indeed they have; for "Their voice has gone out to all the earth, and their words to the ends of the world."

✝ *The Holy Gospel of Our Lord Jesus Christ According to Matthew* [4:18-22]

As Jesus walked by the Sea of Galilee, he saw two brothers, Simon who is called Peter and Andrew his brother, casting a net into the sea; for they were fishermen. And he said to them, "Follow me, and I will make you fishers of men." Immediately they left their nets and followed him. And going on from there he saw two other brothers, James the son of Zeb'edee and John his brother, in the boat with Zeb'edee their father, mending their nets, and he called them. Immediately they left the boat and their father, and followed him.

Saint Thomas   *December 21*

A Reading (Lesson) from the Book of Habak'kuk [2:1-4]

I will take my stand to watch, and station myself on the tower, and look forth to see what he will say to me, and what I will answer concerning my complaint. And the

Lord answered me, "Write the vision; make it plain upon tablets, so he may run who reads it. For still the vision awaits its time; it hastens to the end—it will not lie. If it seem slow, wait for it; it will surely come, it will not delay. Behold, he whose soul is not upright in him shall fail, but the righteous shall live by his faith."

Psalm 126 [page 782]

A Reading (Lesson) from the Letter to the Hebrews
[10:35—11:1]

Do not throw away your confidence, which has a great reward. For you have need of endurance, so that you may do the will of God and receive what is promised. "For yet a little while, and the coming one shall come and shall not tarry; but my righteous one shall live by faith, and if he shrinks back, my soul has no pleasure in him." But we are not of those who shrink back and are destroyed, but of those who have faith and keep their souls. Now faith is the assurance of things hoped for, the conviction of things not seen.

✝ *The Holy Gospel of Our Lord Jesus Christ According to John* [20:24-29]

Thomas, one of the twelve, called the Twin, was not with the other disciples when Jesus came. So the other disciples told him, "We have seen the Lord." But he said to them, "Unless I see in his hands the print of the nails, and place my finger in the mark of the nails, and place my hand in his side, I will not believe." Eight days later, his disciples were again in the house, and Thomas was with them. The doors were shut, but Jesus came and stood among them, and said, "Peace be with you." Then he said to Thomas, "Put your finger here, and see my hands; and put out your hand, and place it in my side; do not be faithless, but believing."

Thomas answered him, "My Lord and my God!" Jesus said to him, "Have you believed because you have seen me? Blessed are those who have not seen and yet believe."

Saint Stephen *December 26*

A Reading (Lesson) from the Book of Jeremiah [26:1-9, 12-15]

In the beginning of the reign of Jehoi′akim the son of Josi′ah, king of Judah, this word came from the Lord, "Thus says the Lord: Stand in the court of the Lord's house, and speak to all the cities of Judah which come to worship in the house of the Lord all the words that I command you to speak to them; do not hold back a word. It may be they will listen, and every one turn from his evil way, that I may repent of the evil which I intend to do to them because of their evil doings. You shall say to them, 'Thus says the Lord: If you will not listen to me, to walk in my law which I have set before you, and to heed the words of my servants the prophets whom I send to you urgently, though you have not heeded, then I will make this house like Shiloh, and I will make this city a curse for all the nations of the earth.'" The priests and the prophets and all the people heard Jeremiah speaking these words in the house of the Lord. And when Jeremiah had finished speaking all that the Lord had commanded him to speak to all the people, then the priests and the prophets and all the people laid hold of him, saying, "You shall die! Why have you prophesied in the name of the Lord, saying, 'This house shall be like Shiloh, and this city shall be desolate, without inhabitant'?" And all the people gathered about Jeremiah in the house of the Lord. Then Jeremiah spoke to all the princes and all the people, saying, "The Lord sent me to prophesy against this house and this city all the words you have heard. Now therefore amend your ways and your doings, and obey the voice of the Lord your God and the

Lord will repent of the evil which he has pronounced against you. But as for me, behold, I am in your hands. Do with me as seems good and right to you. Only know for certain that if you put me to death, you will bring innocent blood upon yourselves and upon this city and its inhabitants, for in truth the Lord sent me to you to speak all these words in your ears."

Psalm 31 [page 622] or *31:1-5* [page 622]

A Reading (Lesson) from the Acts of the Apostles
[6:8—7:2a, 51c-60]

Stephen, full of grace and power, did great wonders and signs among the people. Then some of those who belonged to the synagogue of the Freedmen (as it was called), and of the Cyre'nians, and of the Alexandrians, and of those from Cili'cia and Asia, arose and disputed with Stephen. But they could not withstand the wisdom and the Spirit with which he spoke. Then they secretly instigated men, who said,"We have heard him speak blasphemous words against Moses and God." And they stirred up the people and the elders and the scribes, and they came upon him and seized him and brought him before the council, and set up false witnesses who said,"This man never ceases to speak words against this holy place and the law; for we have heard him say that this Jesus of Nazareth will destroy this place, and will change the customs which Moses delivered to us." And gazing at him, all who sat in the council saw that his face was like the face of an angel. And the high priest said,"Is this so?" And Stephen said, "Brethren and fathers, hear me. As your fathers did, so do you. Which of the prophets did not your fathers persecute? And they killed those who announced beforehand the coming of the Righteous One, whom you have now betrayed and murdered, you who received the law as delivered by angels and did not keep it." Now when they heard these things they were enraged, and they ground their teeth against him. But he, full of the Holy Spirit, gazed into heaven and saw the glory of God, and Jesus standing at the right hand of God; and he said, "Behold, I see the heavens opened, and the Son of man standing at the right hand of God." But they cried out with a loud voice and stopped their ears and rushed together upon him. Then they cast him out of the city and stoned him; and the witnesses laid down their garments at the feet of a young man named Saul. And as they were stoning Stephen, he prayed, "Lord Jesus, receive my spirit." And he knelt down and cried with a loud voice, "Lord, do not hold this sin against them." And when he had said this, he fell asleep.

✝ *The Holy Gospel of Our Lord Jesus Christ According to Matthew* [23:34-39]

Jesus said, "I will send you prophets and wise men and scribes, some of whom you will kill and crucify, and some you will scourge in your synagogues and persecute from town to town, that upon you may come all the righteous blood shed on earth, from the blood of innocent Abel to the blood of Zechari'ah the son of Barachi'ah, whom you murdered between the sanctuary and the altar. Truly, I say to you, all this will come upon this generation. O Jerusalem, Jerusalem, killing the prophets and stoning those who are sent to you! How often would I have gathered your children together as a hen gathers her brood under her wings, and you would not! Behold, your house is forsaken and desolate. For I tell you, you will not see me again, until you say, 'Blessed is he who comes in the name of the Lord.'"

Saint John *December 27*

A Reading (Lesson) from the Book of Exodus [33:18-23]

Moses said to God, "I pray thee, show me thy glory." And he said, "I will make all my goodness pass before you, and will proclaim before you my name 'The Lord'; and I will be gracious to whom I will be gracious, and will show mercy on whom I will show mercy. But," he said, "you cannot see my face; for man shall not see me and live." And the Lord said, "Behold, there is a place by me where you shall stand upon the rock; and while my glory passes by I will put you in a cleft of the rock, and I will cover you with my hand until I have passed by; then I will take away my hand, and you shall see my back; but my face shall not be seen."

Psalm 92 [page 720]   or   *92: 1-4, 11-14* [page 720]

A Reading (Lesson) from the First Letter of John [1:1-9]

That which was from the beginning, which we have heard, which we have seen with our eyes, which we have looked upon and touched with our hands, concerning the word of life—the life was made manifest, and we saw it, and testify to it, and proclaim to you the eternal life which was with the Father and was made manifest to us—that which we have seen and heard we proclaim also to you, so that you may have fellowship with us; and our fellowship is with the Father and with his Son Jesus Christ. And we are writing this that our joy may be complete. This is the message we have heard from him and proclaim to you, that God is light and in him is no darkness at all. If we say we have fellowship with him while we walk in darkness, we lie and do not live according to the truth; but if we walk in the light, as he is in the light, we have fellowship with one another, and the blood of Jesus his Son cleanses us from all sin. If we say we have no sin we deceive ourselves, and the truth is not in us. If we confess our sins, he is faithful and just, and will forgive our sins and cleanse us from all unrighteousness.

✝ *The Holy Gospel of Our Lord Jesus Christ*
According to John [21:19b-24]

Jesus said to Peter, "Follow me." Peter turned and saw following them the disciple whom Jesus loved, who had lain close to his breast at the supper and had said, "Lord, who is it that is going to betray you?" When Peter saw him, he said to Jesus, "Lord, what about this man?" Jesus said to him, "If it is my will that he remain until I come, what is that to you? Follow me!" The saying spread abroad among the brethren that this disciple was not to die; yet Jesus did not say to him that he was not to die, but, "If it is my will that he remain until I come, what is that to you?" This is the disciple who is bearing witness to these things, and who has written these things; and we know that his testimony is true.

The Holy Innocents   *December 28*

A Reading (Lesson) from the Book of Jeremiah [31:15-17]

Thus says the Lord: "A voice is heard in Ramah, lamentation and bitter weeping. Rachel is weeping for her children; she refuses to be comforted for her children, because they are not." Thus says the Lord: "Keep your voice from weeping, and your eyes from tears; for your work shall be rewarded, says the Lord, and they shall come back from the land of the enemy. There is hope for your future, says the Lord, and your children shall come back to their own country."

Psalm 124 [page 781]

A Reading (Lesson) from the Revelation to John [21:1-7]

I saw a new heaven and a new earth; for the first heaven
and the first earth had passed away, and the sea was no
more. And I saw the holy city, new Jerusalem, coming
down out of heaven from God, prepared as a bride
adorned for her husband; and I heard a loud voice from
the throne saying,"Behold, the dwelling of God is with men.
He will dwell with them, and they shall be his people, and
God himself will be with them; he will wipe away every
tear from their eyes, and death shall be no more, neither
shall there be mourning nor crying nor pain any more, for
the former things have passed away." And he who sat upon
the throne said,"Behold, I make all things new." Also he
said,"Write this, for these words are trustworthy and
true." And he said to me,"It is done! I am the Alpha and
the Omega, the beginning and the end. To the thirsty I will
give from the fountain of the water of life without
payment. He who conquers shall have this heritage,
and I will be his God and he shall be my son."

✝ *The Holy Gospel of Our Lord Jesus Christ*
According to Matthew [2:13-18]

When the wise men had departed, behold, an angel of the
Lord appeared to Joseph in a dream and said,"Rise, take
the child and his mother, and flee to Egypt, and remain
there till I tell you; for Herod is about to search for the
child, to destroy him." And he rose and took the child and
his mother by night, and departed to Egypt, and remained
there until the death of Herod. This was to fulfill what the
Lord had spoken by the prophet,"Out of Egypt have I
called my son." Then Herod, when he saw that he had been
tricked by the wise men, was in a furious rage, and he sent
and killed all the male children in Bethlehem and in all that
region who were two years old or under, according to the
time which he had ascertained from the wise men. Then

was fulfilled what was spoken by the prophet Jeremiah: "A voice was heard in Ramah, wailing and loud lamentation, Rachel weeping for her children; she refused to be consoled, because they were no more."

Confession of Saint Peter   *January 18*

A Reading (Lesson) from the Acts of the Apostles [4:8-13]

Peter, filled with the Holy Spirit, said, "Rulers of the people and elders, if we are being examined today concerning a good deed done to a cripple, by what means this man has been healed, be it known to you all, and to all the people of Israel, that by the name of Jesus Christ of Nazareth, whom you crucified, whom God raised from the dead, by him this man is standing before you well. This is the stone which was rejected by you builders, but which has become the head of the corner. And there is salvation in no one else, for there is no other name under heaven given among men by which we must be saved." Now when they saw the boldness of Peter and John, and perceived that they were uneducated, common men, they wondered; and they recognized that they had been with Jesus.

Psalm 23 [page 612]

A Reading (Lesson) from the First Letter of Peter [5:1-4]

I exhort the elders among you, as a fellow elder and a witness of the sufferings of Christ as well as a partaker in the glory that is to be revealed. Tend the flock of God that is your charge, not by constraint but willingly, not for shameful gain but eagerly, not as domineering over those in your charge but being examples to the flock. And when the chief Shepherd is manifested you will obtain the unfading crown of glory.

✝ *The Holy Gospel of Our Lord Jesus Christ*
According to Matthew [16:13-19]

When Jesus came into the district of Caesare'a Philippi, he asked his disciples,"Who do men say that the Son of man is?" And they said,"Some say John the Baptist, others say Eli'jah, and others Jeremiah or one of the prophets." He said to them,"But who do you say that I am?" Simon Peter replied,"You are the Christ, the Son of the living God." And Jesus answered him."Blessed are you, Simon Bar-Jona! For flesh and blood has not revealed this to you, but my Father who is in heaven. And I tell you, you are Peter, and on this rock I will build my church, and the powers of death shall not prevail against it. I will give you the keys of the kingdom of heaven, and whatever you bind on earth shall be bound in heaven, and whatever you loose on earth shall be loosed in heaven."

Conversion of Saint Paul   *January 25*

A Reading (Lesson) from the Acts of the Apostles [26:9-21]

Paul said to King Agrippa,"I myself was convinced that I ought to do many things in opposing the name of Jesus of Nazareth. And I did so in Jerusalem; I not only shut up many of the saints in prison, by authority from the chief priests, but when they were put to death I cast my vote against them. And I punished them often in all the synagogues and tried to make them blaspheme; and in raging fury against them, I persecuted them even to foreign cities. Thus I journeyed to Damascus with the authority and commission of the chief priests. At midday, O king, I saw on the way a light from heaven, brighter than the sun, shining round me and those who journeyed with me. And when we had all fallen to the ground, I heard a voice saying to me in the Hebrew language,'Saul, Saul, why do you persecute me? It hurts you to kick against the goads.' And I said,'Who are you, Lord?' And the Lord said,'I am Jesus whom you are persecuting. But rise and stand upon your feet; for I have appeared to you for this purpose, to appoint you to serve and bear witness to the things in which you have seen me and to those in which I will appear to you, delivering you from the people and from the Gentiles—to whom I send you to open their eyes, that they may turn from darkness to light and from the power of Satan to God, that they may receive forgiveness of sins and a place among those who are sanctified by faith in me.' Wherefore, O King Agrippa, I was not disobedient to the heavenly vision, but declared first to those at Damascus, then at Jerusalem and throughout all the country of Judea, and also to the Gentiles, that they should repent and turn to God and perform deeds worthy of their repentance. For this reason the Jews seized me in the temple and tried to kill me."

Psalm 67 [page 675]

A Reading (Lesson) from the Letter of Paul to the Galatians [1:11-24]

I would have you know, brethren, that the gospel which was preached by me is not man's gospel. For I did not receive it from man, nor was I taught it, but it came through a revelation of Jesus Christ. For you have heard of my former life in Judaism, how I persecuted the church of God violently and tried to destroy it; and I advanced in Judaism beyond many of my own age among my people, so extremely zealous was I for the traditions of my fathers. But when he who had set me apart before I was born, and had called me through his grace, was pleased to reveal his Son to me, in order that I might preach him among the Gentiles, I did not confer with flesh and blood, nor did I go up to Jerusalem to those who were apostles before me, but

I went away into Arabia; and again I returned to Damascus. Then after three years I went up to Jerusalem to visit Cephas, and remained with him fifteen days. But I saw none of the other apostles except James the Lord's brother. (In what I am writing to you, before God, I do not lie!) Then I went into the regions of Syria and Cilicia. And I was still not known by sight to the churches of Christ in Judea; they only heard it said, "He who once persecuted us is now preaching the faith he once tried to destroy." And they glorified God because of me.

✝ The Holy Gospel of Our Lord Jesus Christ
  According to Matthew [10:16-22]

Jesus said, "Behold, I send you out as sheep in the midst of wolves; so be wise as serpents and innocent as doves. Beware of men; for they will deliver you up to councils, and flog you in their synagogues, and you will be dragged before governors and kings for my sake, to bear testimony before them and the Gentiles. When they deliver you up, do not be anxious how you are to speak or what you are to say; for what you are to say will be given to you in that hour; for it is not you who speak, but the Spirit of your Father speaking through you. Brother will deliver up brother to death, and the father his child, and children will rise against parents and have them put to death; and you will be hated by all for my name's sake. But he who endures to the end will be saved."

The Presentation   *February 2*

A Reading (Lesson) from the Book of Malachi [3:1-4]

Thus says the Lord, "Behold, I send my messenger to prepare the way before me, and the Lord whom you seek will suddenly come to his temple; the messenger of the covenant in whom you delight, behold, he is coming, says the Lord of hosts. But who can endure the day of his coming, and who can stand when he appears? For he is like a refiner's fire and like fullers' soap; he will sit as a refiner and purifier of silver, and he will purify the sons of Levi and refine them like gold and silver, till they present right offerings to the Lord. Then the offering of Judah and Jerusalem will be pleasing to the Lord as in the days of old and as in former years."

Psalm 84 [page 707]   or   *84:1-6* [page 707]

A Reading (Lesson) from the Letter to the Hebrews [2:14-18]

Since God's children share in flesh and blood, Jesus himself likewise partook of the same nature, that through death he might destroy him who has the power of death, that is, the devil, and deliver all those who through fear of death were subject to lifelong bondage. For surely it is not with angels that he is concerned but with the descendants of Abraham. Therefore he had to be made like his brethren in every respect, so that he might become a merciful and faithful high priest in the service of God, to make expiation for the sins of the people. For because he himself has suffered and been tempted, he is able to help those who are tempted.

✝ *The Holy Gospel of Our Lord Jesus Christ According to Luke* [2:22-40]

When the time came for their purification according to the law of Moses, the parents of Jesus brought him up to Jerusalem to present him to the Lord (as it is written in the law of the Lord, "Every male that opens the womb shall be called holy to the Lord") and to offer a sacrifice according to what is said in the law of the Lord, "a pair of turtledoves, or two young pigeons." Now there was a man in Jerusalem, whose name was Simeon, and this man was righteous and devout, looking for the consolation of Israel, and the Holy Spirit was upon him. And it had been revealed to him by the Holy Spirit that he should not see death before he had seen the Lord's Christ. And inspired by the Spirit he came into the temple; and when the parents brought in the child Jesus, to do for him according to the custom of the law, he took him up in his arms and blessed God and said,"Lord, now lettest thou thy servant depart in peace, according to thy word; for mine eyes have seen thy salvation which thou hast prepared in the presence of all peoples, a light for revelation to the Gentiles, and for glory to thy people Israel." And his father and his mother marveled at what was said about him; and Simeon blessed them and said to Mary his mother,"Behold, this child is set for the fall and rising of many in Israel, and for a sign that is spoken against (and a sword will pierce through your own soul also), that thoughts out of many hearts may be revealed." And there was a prophetess, Anna, the daughter of Pha'nu-el, of the tribe of Asher; she was of great age, having lived with her husband seven years from her virginity, and as a widow till she was eighty-four. She did not depart from the temple, worshiping with fasting and prayer night and day. And coming up at that very hour she gave thanks to God, and spoke of him to all who were looking for the redemption of Jerusalem. And when they had performed everything according to the law of the Lord, they returned into Galilee, to their own city, Nazareth. And the child grew and became strong, filled with wisdom; and the favor of God was upon him.

Saint Matthias *February 24*

A Reading (Lesson) from the Acts of the Apostles [1:15-26]

Peter stood up among the brethren (the company of persons was in all about a hundred and twenty), and said,"Brethren, the scripture had to be fulfilled, which the

Holy Spirit spoke beforehand by the mouth of David, concerning Judas who was guide to those who arrested Jesus. For he was numbered among us, and was allotted his share in this ministry. (Now this man bought a field with the reward of his wickedness; and falling headlong he burst open in the middle and all his bowels gushed out. And it became known to all the inhabitants of Jerusalem, so that the field was called in their language Akel'dama, that is, Field of Blood.) For it is written in the book of Psalms, 'Let his habitation become desolate, and let there be no one to live in it; and 'His office let another take.' So one of the men who have accompanied us during all the time that the Lord Jesus went in and out among us, beginning from the baptism of John until the day when he was taken up from us—one of these men must become with us a witness to his resurrection." And they put forward two, Joseph called Barsab'bas, who was surnamed Justus, and Matthi'as. And they prayed and said, "Lord, who knowest the hearts of all men, show which one of these two thou hast chosen to take the place in this ministry and apostleship from which Judas turned aside, to go to his own place." And they cast lots for them, and the lot fell on Matthi'as; and he was enrolled with the eleven apostles.

Psalm 15 [page 599]

A Reading (Lesson) from the Letter of Paul to the Philippians [3:13b-21]

One thing I do, forgetting what lies behind and straining forward to what lies ahead, I press on toward the goal for the prize of the upward call of God in Christ Jesus. Let those of us who are mature be thus minded; and if in anything you are otherwise minded, God will reveal that also to you. Only let us hold true to what we have attained. Brethren, join in imitating me, and mark those who so live as you have an example in us. For many, of whom I have often told you and now tell you even with tears, live as enemies of the cross of Christ. Their end is destruction, their god is the belly, and they glory in their shame, with minds set on earthly things. But our commonwealth is in heaven, and from it we await a Savior, the Lord Jesus Christ, who will change our lowly body to be like his glorious body, by the power which enables him even to subject all things to himself.

✝ *The Holy Gospel of Our Lord Jesus Christ
According to John* [15:1, 6-16]

Jesus said, "I am the true vine, and my Father is the vinedresser. If a man does not abide in me, he is cast forth as a branch and withers; and the branches are gathered, thrown into the fire and burned. If you abide in me, and my words abide in you, ask whatever you will, and it shall be done for you. By this my Father is glorified, that you bear much fruit, and so prove to be my disciples. As the Father has loved me, so have I loved you; abide in my love. If you keep my commandments, you will abide in my love, just as I have kept my Father's commandments and abide in his love. These things I have spoken to you, that my joy may be in you, and that your joy may be full. This is my commandment, that you love one another as I have loved you. Greater love has no man than this, that a man lay down his life for his friends. You are my friends if you do what I command you. No longer do I call you servants, for the servant does not know what his master is doing; but I have called you friends, for all that I have heard from my Father I have made known to you. You did not choose me, but I chose you and appointed you that you should go and bear fruit and that your fruit should abide; so that whatever you ask the Father in my name, he may give it to you."

Saint Joseph   *March 19*

A Reading (Lesson) from the Second Book of Samuel
[7:4, 8-16]

The word of the Lord came to Nathan,"Thus you shall say to my servant David: 'Thus says the Lord of hosts, I took you from the pasture, from following the sheep, that you should be prince over my people Israel; and I have been with you wherever you went, and have cut off all your enemies from before you; and I will make for you a great name, like the name of the great ones of the earth. And I will appoint a place for my people Israel, and will plant them, that they may dwell in their own place, and be disturbed no more; and violent men shall afflict them no more, as formerly, from the time that I appointed judges over my people Israel; and I will give you rest from all your enemies. Moreover the Lord declares to you that the Lord will make you a house. When your days are fulfilled and you lie down with your fathers, I will raise up your offspring after you, who shall come forth from your body, and I will establish his kingdom. He shall build a house for my name, and I will establish the throne of his kingdom for ever. I will be his father, and he shall be my son. When he commits iniquity, I will chasten him with the rod of men, with the stripes of the sons of men; but I will not take my steadfast love from him, as I took it from Saul, whom I put away from before you. And your house and your kingdom shall be made sure for ever before me; your throne shall be established for ever."

Psalm 89:1-29 [page 713]   or

Psalm 89:1-4, 26-29 [page 713]

A Reading (Lesson) from the Letter of Paul to the Romans
[4:13-18]

The promise to Abraham and his descendants, that they should inherit the world, did not come through the law but through the righteousness of faith. If it is the adherents of the law who are to be the heirs, faith is null and the promise is void. For the law brings wrath, but where there is no law there is no transgression. That is why it depends on faith, in order that the promise may rest on grace and be guaranteed to all his descendants—not only to the adherents of the law but also to those who share the faith of Abraham, for he is the father of us all, as it is written, "I have made you the father of many nations"—in the presence of the God in whom he believed, who gives life to the dead and calls into existence the things that do not exist. In hope he believed against hope, that he should become the father of many nations; as he had been told, "So shall your descendants be."

✝ *The Holy Gospel of Our Lord Jesus Christ According to Luke* [2:41-52]

Jesus' parents went to Jerusalem every year at the feast of the Passover. And when he was twelve years old, they went up according to custom; and when the feast was ended, as they were returning, the boy Jesus stayed behind in Jerusalem. His parents did not know it, but supposing him to be in the company they went a day's journey, and they sought him among their kinsfolk and acquaintances; and when they did not find him, they returned to Jerusalem, seeking him. After three days they found him in the temple, sitting among the teachers, listening to them and asking them questions; and all who heard him were amazed at his understanding and his answers. And when they saw him they were astonished; and his mother said to him, "Son, why have you treated us so? Behold, your father and I have

been looking for you anxiously." And he said to them,
"How is it that you sought me? Did you not know that
I must be in my Father's house?" And they did not
understand the saying which he spoke to them. And he
went down with them and came to Nazareth, and was
obedient to them; and his mother kept all these things in
her heart. And Jesus increased in wisdom and in stature,
and in favor with God and man.

The Annunciation   *March 25*

A Reading (Lesson) from the Book of Isaiah [7:10-14]

The Lord spoke to Ahaz,"Ask a sign of the Lord your God;
let it be deep as Sheol or high as heaven." But Ahaz said,
"I will not ask, and I will not put the Lord to the test." And
he said,"Hear then, O house of David! Is it too little for you
to weary men, that you weary my God also? Therefore the
Lord himself will give you a sign. Behold, a young woman
shall conceive and bear a son, and shall call his name
Imman'u-el."

Psalm 40:1-11 [page 640]   or   *40:5-10* [page 640]   or

The Magnificat, Canticle 3 or 15 [page 50 or 91]

A Reading (Lesson) from the Letter to the Hebrews [10:5-10]

When Christ came into the world, he said,"Sacrifices and
offerings thou hast not desired, but a body hast thou
prepared for me; in burnt offerings and sin offerings thou
hast taken no pleasure. Then I said,'Lo, I have come to do
thy will, O God,' as it is written of me in the roll of the
book." When he said above,"Thou hast neither desired nor
taken pleasure in sacrifices and offerings and burnt
offerings and sin offerings" (these are offered according to
the law), then he added,"Lo, I have come to do thy will."

He abolishes the first in order to establish the second. And by that will we have been sanctified through the offering of the body of Jesus Christ once for all.

✝ *The Holy Gospel of Our Lord Jesus Christ According to Luke* [1:26-38]

In the sixth month the angel Gabriel was sent from God to a city of Galilee named Nazareth, to a virgin betrothed to a man whose name was Joseph, of the house of David; and the virgin's name was Mary. And he came to her and said, "Hail, O favored one, the Lord is with you!" But she was greatly troubled at the saying, and considered in her mind what sort of greeting this might be. And the angel said to her, "Do not be afraid, Mary, for you have found favor with God. And behold, you will conceive in your womb and bear a son, and you shall call his name Jesus. He will be great, and will be called the Son of the Most High; and the Lord God will give to him the throne of his father David, and he will reign over the house of Jacob for ever; and of his kingdom there will be no end." And Mary said to the angel, "How shall this be, since I have no husband?" And the angel said to her, "The Holy Spirit will come upon you, and the power of the Most High will overshadow you; therefore the child to be born will be called holy, the Son of God. And behold, your kinswoman Elizabeth in her old age has also conceived a son; and this is the sixth month with her who was called barren. For with God nothing will be impossible." And Mary said, "Behold, I am the handmaid of the Lord; let it be to me according to your word." And the angel departed from her.

Saint Mark   *April 25*

A Reading (Lesson) from the Book of Isaiah [52:7-10]

How beautiful upon the mountains are the feet of him who
brings good tidings, who publishes peace, who brings good
tidings of good, who publishes salvation, who says to
Zion, "Your God reigns." Hark, your watchmen lift up
their voice, together they sing for joy; for eye to eye they
see the return of the Lord to Zion. Break forth together
into singing, you waste places of Jerusalem; for the Lord
has comforted his people, he has redeemed Jerusalem. The
Lord has bared his holy arm before the eyes of all the
nations; and all the ends of the earth shall see the salvation
of our God.

Psalm 2 [page 586]   or   *2:7-10* [page 586]

*A Reading (Lesson) from the Letter of Paul
to the Ephesians* [4:7-8, 11-16]

Grace was given to each of us according to the measure of
Christ's gift. Therefore it is said, "When he ascended on
high he led a host of captives, and he gave gifts to men."
And his gifts were that some should be apostles, some
prophets, some evangelists, some pastors and teachers, to
equip the saints for the work of ministry, for building up
the body of Christ, until we all attain to the unity of the
faith and of the knowledge of the Son of God, to mature
manhood, to the measure of the stature of the fullness of
Christ; so that we may no longer be children, tossed to and
fro and carried about with every wind of doctrine, by the
cunning of men, by their craftiness in deceitful wiles.
Rather, speaking the truth in love, we are to grow up in
every way into him who is the head, into Christ, from
whom the whole body, joined and knit together by every
joint with which it is supplied, when each part is working
properly, makes bodily growth and upbuilds itself in love.

✝ *The Holy Gospel of Our Lord Jesus Christ*
According to Mark [1:1-15]

The beginning of the gospel of Jesus Christ, the Son of God. As it is written in Isaiah the prophet, "Behold, I send my messenger before thy face, who shall prepare thy way; the voice of one crying in the wilderness: Prepare the way of the Lord, make his paths straight." John the baptizer appeared in the wilderness, preaching a baptism of repentance for the forgiveness of sins. And there went out to him all the country of Judea, and all the people of Jerusalem; and they were baptized by him in the river Jordan, confessing their sins. Now John was clothed with camel's hair, and had a leather girdle around his waist, and ate locusts and wild honey. And he preached, saying, "After me comes he who is mightier than I, the thong of whose sandals I am not worthy to stoop down and untie. I have baptized you with water; but he will baptize you with the Holy Spirit." In those days Jesus came from Nazareth of Galilee and was baptized by John in the Jordan. And when he came up out of the water, immediately he saw the heavens opened and the Spirit descending upon him like a dove; and a voice came from heaven, "Thou art my beloved Son; with thee I am well pleased." The Spirit immediately drove him out into the wilderness. And he was in the wilderness forty days, tempted by Satan; and he was with the wild beasts; and the angels ministered to him. Now after John was arrested, Jesus came into Galilee, preaching the gospel of God, and saying, "The time is fulfilled, and the kingdom of God is at hand; repent, and believe in the gospel."

or the following

✝ *The Holy Gospel of Our Lord Jesus Christ*
According to Mark [16:15-20]

Jesus said to the apostles, "Go into all the world and preach the gospel to the whole creation. He who believes and is baptized will be saved; but he who does not believe will be condemned. And these signs will accompany those who believe: in my name they will cast out demons; they will speak in new tongues; they will pick up serpents, and if they drink any deadly thing, it will not hurt them; they will lay their hands on the sick, and they will recover." So then the Lord Jesus, after he had spoken to them, was taken up into heaven, and sat down at the right hand of God. And they went forth and preached everywhere, while the Lord worked with them and confirmed the message by the signs that attended it.

Saint Philip and Saint James   *May 1*

A Reading (Lesson) from the Book of Isaiah [30:18-21]

The Lord waits to be gracious to you; therefore he exalts himself to show mercy to you. For the Lord is a God of justice; blessed are all those who wait for him. Yea, O people in Zion who dwell at Jerusalem; you shall weep no more. He will surely be gracious to you at the sound of your cry; when he hears it, he will answer you. And though the Lord give you the bread of adversity and the water of affliction, yet your Teacher will not hide himself any more, but your eyes shall see your Teacher. And your ears shall hear a word behind you, saying, "This is the way, walk in it," when you turn to the right or when you turn to the left.

Psalm 119:33-40 [page 766]

*A Reading (Lesson) from the Second Letter of Paul
to the Corinthians* [4:1-6]

Having this ministry by the mercy of God, we do not lose
heart. We have renounced disgraceful, underhanded ways;
we refuse to practice cunning or to tamper with God's
word, but by the open statement of the truth we would
commend ourselves to every man's conscience in the sight
of God. And even if our gospel is veiled, it is veiled only to
those who are perishing. In their case the god of this world
has blinded the minds of the unbelievers, to keep them
from seeing the light of the gospel of the glory of Christ,
who is the likeness of God. For what we preach is not
ourselves, but Jesus Christ as Lord, with ourselves as your
servants for Jesus' sake. For it is the God who said, "Let
light shine out of darkness," who has shone in our hearts to
give the light of the knowledge of the glory of God in the
face of Christ.

✝ *The Holy Gospel of Our Lord Jesus Christ
According to John* [14:6-14]

Jesus said to Thomas, "I am the way, and the truth, and the
life; no one comes to the Father, but by me. If you had
known me, you would have known my Father also;
henceforth you know him and have seen him." Philip said
to him, "Lord, show us the Father, and we shall be
satisfied." Jesus said to him, "Have I been with you so long,
and yet you do not know me, Philip? He who has seen me
has seen the Father; how can you say, 'Show us the Father'?
Do you not believe that I am in the Father and the Father in
me? The words that I say to you I do not speak on my own
authority; but the Father who dwells in me does his works.
Believe me that I am in the Father and the Father in me; or
else believe me for the sake of the works themselves. Truly,
truly, I say to you, he who believes in me will also do the
works that I do; and greater works than these will he do,

because I go to the Father. Whatever you ask in my name, I will do it, that the Father may be glorified in the Son; if you ask anything in my name, I will do it."

The Visitation *May 31*

A Reading (Lesson) from the Book of Zephaniah [3:14-18a]

Sing aloud, O daughter of Zion; shout, O Israel! Rejoice and exult with all your heart, O daughter of Jerusalem! The Lord has taken away the judgments against you, he has cast out your enemies. The King of Israel, the Lord, is in your midst; you shall fear evil no more. On that day it shall be said to Jerusalem,"Do not fear, O Zion; let not your hands grow weak. The Lord, your God, is in your midst, a warrior who gives victory; he will rejoice over you with gladness, he will renew you in his love; he will exult over you with loud singing as on a day of festival."

Psalm 113 [page 756] or

The First Song of Isaiah, Canticle 9 [page 86]

A Reading (Lesson) from the Letter of Paul to the Colossians [3:12-17]

Put on, as God's chosen ones, holy and beloved, compassion, kindness, lowliness, meekness, and patience, forbearing one another and, if one has a complaint against another, forgiving each other; as the Lord has forgiven you, so you also must forgive. And above all these put on love, which binds everything together in perfect harmony. And let the peace of Christ rule in your hearts, to which indeed you were called in the one body. And be thankful. Let the word of Christ dwell in you richly, teach and admonish one another in all wisdom, and sing psalms and hymns and spiritual songs with thankfulness in your hearts to God. And whatever you do, in word or deed, do everything in the name of the Lord Jesus, giving thanks to God the Father through him.

✝ *The Holy Gospel of Our Lord Jesus Christ According to Luke* [1:39-49]

Mary arose and went with haste into the hill country, to a city of Judah, and she entered the house of Zechari'ah and greeted Elizabeth. And when Elizabeth heard the greeting of Mary, the babe leaped in her womb; and Elizabeth was filled with the Holy Spirit and she exclaimed with a loud cry,"Blessed are you among women, and blessed is the fruit of your womb! And why is this granted me, that the mother of my Lord should come to me? For behold, when the voice of your greeting came to my ears, the babe in my womb leaped for joy. And blessed is she who believed that there would be a fulfillment of what was spoken to her from the Lord." And Mary said,"My soul magnifies the Lord, and my spirit rejoices in God my Savior, for he has regarded the low estate of his handmaiden. For behold, henceforth all generations will call me blessed; for he who is mighty has done great things for me, and holy is his name."

Saint Barnabas *June 11*

A Reading (Lesson) from the Book of Isaiah [42:5-12]

Thus says God, the Lord, who created the heavens and stretched them out, who spread forth the earth and what comes from it, who gives breath to the people upon it and spirit to those who walk in it: "I am the Lord, I have called you in righteousness, I have taken you by the hand and kept you; I have given you as a covenant to the people, a light to the nations, to open the eyes that are blind, to bring out the prisoners from the dungeon, from the prison those who sit in darkness. I am the Lord, that is my name; my glory I give to no other, nor my praise to graven images. Behold, the former things have come to pass, and new things I now declare; before they spring forth I tell you of them." Sing to the Lord a new song, his praise from the end of the earth! Let the sea roar and all that fills it, the coastlands and their inhabitants. Let the desert and its cities lift up their voice, the villages that Kedar inhabits; let the inhabitants of Sela sing for joy, let them shout from the top of the mountains. Let them give glory to the Lord, and declare his praise in the coastlands.

Psalm 112 [page 755]

A Reading (Lesson) from the Acts of the Apostles
[11:19-30; 13:1-3]

Those who were scattered because of the persecution that arose over Stephen traveled as far as Phoeni'cia and Cyprus and Antioch, speaking the word to none except Jews. But there were some of them, men of Cyprus and Cyre'ne, who on coming to Antioch spoke to the Greeks also, preaching the Lord Jesus. And the hand of the Lord was with them, and a great number that believed turned to the Lord. News of this came to the ears of the church in Jerusalem, and they sent Barnabas to Antioch. When he came and saw the grace of God, he was glad; and he exhorted them all to remain faithful to the Lord with steadfast purpose; for he was a good man, full of the Holy Spirit and of faith. And a large company was added to the Lord. So Barnabas went to Tarsus to look for Saul; and when he had found him, he brought him to Antioch. For a whole year they met with the church, and taught a large company of people; and in Antioch the disciples were for the first time called Christians. Now in these days prophets came down from Jerusalem to Antioch. And one of them named Ag'abus stood up and foretold by the Spirit that there would be a great famine over all the world; and this took place in the days of Claudius. And the disciples determined, every one according to his ability, to send relief to the brethren who lived in Judea; and they did so, sending it to the elders by the hand of Barnabas and Saul. Now in the church at Antioch there were prophets and teachers, Barnabas, Simeon who was called Niger, Lucius of Cyre′ne, Man′a-en a member of the court of Herod the tetrarch, and Saul. While they were worshiping the Lord and fasting, the Holy Spirit said,"Set apart for me Barnabas and Saul for the work to which I have called them." Then after fasting and praying they laid their hands on them and sent them off.

✝ *The Holy Gospel of Our Lord Jesus Christ*
According to Matthew [10:7-16]

Jesus said to the twelve,"Preach as you go, saying, 'The kingdom of heaven is at hand.' Heal the sick, raise the dead, cleanse lepers, cast out demons. You received without paying, give without pay. Take no gold, nor silver, nor copper in your belts, no bag for your journey, nor two tunics, nor sandals, nor a staff; for the laborer deserves his food. And whatever town or village you enter, find out who is worthy in it, and stay with him until you depart. As you enter the house, salute it. And if the house is worthy, let your peace come upon it; but if it is not worthy, let your peace return to you. And if any one will not receive you or listen to your words, shake off the dust from your feet as you leave that house or town. Truly, I say to you, it shall be more tolerable on the day of judgment for the land of Sodom and Gomor′rah than for that town. Behold, I send you out as sheep in the midst of wolves; so be wise as serpents and innocent as doves."

Nativity of Saint John the Baptist   *June 24*

A Reading (Lesson) from the Book of Isaiah   [40:1-11]

Comfort, comfort my people, says your God. Speak
tenderly to Jerusalem, and cry to her that her warfare is
ended, that her iniquity is pardoned, that she has received
from the Lord's hand double for all her sins. A voice cries:
"In the wilderness prepare the way of the Lord, make
straight in the desert a highway for our God. Every valley
shall be lifted up, and every mountain and hill be made
low; the uneven ground shall become level, and the rough
places a plain. And the glory of the Lord shall be revealed,
and all flesh shall see it together, for the mouth of the Lord
has spoken." A voice says, "Cry!" and I said, "What shall I
cry?" All flesh is grass, and all its beauty is like the flower of
the field. The grass withers, the flower fades, when the
breath of the Lord blows upon it; surely the people is grass.
The grass withers, the flower fades; but the word of our
God will stand for ever. Get you up to a high mountain,
O Zion, herald of good tidings; lift up your voice with
strength, O Jerusalem, herald of good tidings, lift it up,
fear not; say to the cities of Judah, "Behold your God!"
Behold, the Lord God comes with might, and his arm rules
for him; behold, his reward is with him, and his recompense
before him. He will feed his flock like a shepherd,
he will gather the lambs in his arms, he will carry them in
his bosom, and gently lead those that are with young.

Psalm 85   [page 708]   or   *85:7-13*   [page 709]

A Reading (Lesson) from the Acts of the Apostles
[13:14b-26]

On the sabbath day Paul and his company went into the
synagogue and sat down. After the reading of the law and
the prophets, the rulers of the synagogue sent to them,

saying, "Brethren, if you have any word of exhortation for the people, say it." So Paul stood up, and motioning with his hands said: "Men of Israel, and you that fear God, listen. The God of this people Israel chose our fathers and made the people great during their stay in the land of Egypt, and with uplifted arm he led them out of it. And when he had destroyed seven nations in the land of Canaan, he gave them their land as an inheritance, for about four hundred and fifty years. And after that he gave them judges until Samuel the prophet. Then they asked for a king; and God gave them Saul the son of Kish, a man of the tribe of Benjamin, for forty years. And when he had removed him, he raised up David to be their king; of whom he testified and said,'I have found in David the son of Jesse a man after my heart, who will do all my will.' Of this man's posterity God has brought to Israel a Savior, Jesus, as he promised. Before his coming John had preached a baptism of repentance to all the people of Israel. And as John was finishing his course, he said,'What do you suppose that I am? I am not he. No, but after me one is coming, the sandals of whose feet I am not worthy to untie.' Brethren, sons of the family of Abraham, and those among you that fear God, to us has been sent the message of this salvation."

✝ *The Holy Gospel of Our Lord Jesus Christ According to Luke* [1:57-80]

The time came for Elizabeth to be delivered, and she gave birth to a son. And her neighbors and kinsfolk heard that the Lord had shown great mercy to her, and they rejoiced with her. And on the eighth day they came to circumcise the child; and they would have named him Zechari'ah after his father, but his mother said, "Not so; he shall be called John." And they said to her, "None of your kindred is called by this name." And they made signs to his father, inquiring what he would have him called. And he asked for a writing tablet, and wrote,"His name is John." And they all marveled. And immediately his mouth was opened and his tongue loosed, and he spoke, blessing God. And fear came on all their neighbors. And all these things were talked about through all the hill country of Judea; and all who heard them laid them up in their hearts, saying,"What then will this child be?" For the hand of the Lord was with him. And his father Zechari'ah was filled with the Holy Spirit, and prophesied, saying,"Blessed be the Lord God of Israel, for he has visited and redeemed his people, and has raised up a horn of salvation for us in the house of his servant David, as he spoke by the mouth of his holy prophets from of old, that we should be saved from our enemies, and from the hand of all who hate us; to perform the mercy promised to our fathers, and to remember his holy covenant, the oath which he swore to our father Abraham, to grant us that we, being delivered from the hand of our enemies, might serve him without fear, in holiness and righteousness before him all the days of our life. And you, child, will be called the prophet of the Most High; for you will go before the Lord to prepare his ways, to give knowledge of salvation to his people in the forgiveness of their sins, through the tender mercy of our God, when the day shall dawn upon us from on high to give light to those who sit in darkness and in the shadow of death, to guide our feet into the way of peace." And the child grew and became strong in spirit, and he was in the wilderness till the day of his manifestation to Israel.

Saint Peter and Saint Paul   *June 29*

A Reading (Lesson) from the Book of Ezekiel   [34:11-16]

Thus says the Lord God: Behold, I, I myself will search for my sheep, and will seek them out. As a shepherd seeks out his flock when some of his sheep have been scattered abroad, so will I seek out my sheep; and I will rescue them from all places where they have been scattered on a day of clouds and thick darkness. And I will bring them out from the peoples, and gather them from the countries, and will bring them into their own land; and I will feed them on the mountains of Israel, by the fountains, and in all the inhabited places of the country. I will feed them with good pasture, and upon the mountain heights of Israel shall be their pasture; there they shall lie down in good grazing land, and on fat pasture they shall feed on the mountains of Israel. I myself will be the shepherd of my sheep, and I will make them lie down, says the Lord God. I will seek the lost, and I will bring back the strayed, and I will bind up the crippled, and I will strengthen the weak, and the fat and the strong I will watch over; I will feed them in justice."

Psalm 87 [page 711]

A Reading (Lesson) from the Second Letter of Paul to Timothy [4:1-8]

I charge you in the presence of God and of Christ Jesus who is to judge the living and the dead, and by his appearing and his kingdom: preach the word, be urgent in season and out of season, convince, rebuke, and exhort, be unfailing in patience and in teaching. For the time is coming when people will not endure sound teaching, but having itching ears they will accumulate for themselves teachers to suit their own likings, and will turn away from listening to the truth and wander into myths. As for you, always be steady, endure suffering, do the work of an evangelist, fulfill your ministry. For I am already on the point of being sacrificed; the time of my departure has come. I have fought the good fight, I have finished the race, I have kept the faith. Henceforth there is laid up for me the crown of righteousness, which the Lord, the righteous

judge, will award to me on that Day, and not only to me
but also to all who have loved his appearing.

✝ *The Holy Gospel of Our Lord Jesus Christ*
According to John [21:15-19]

When they had finished breakfast, Jesus said to Simon
Peter,"Simon, son of John, do you love me more than
these?" He said to him,"Yes, Lord; you know that I love
you." He said to him,"Feed my lambs." A second time he
said to him,"Simon, son of John, do you love me?" He said
to him,"Yes, Lord; you know that I love you." He said to
him,"Tend my sheep." He said to him the third time,
"Simon, son of John, do you love me?" Peter was grieved
because he said to him the third time,"Do you love me?"
And he said to him,"Lord, you know everything; you
know that I love you." Jesus said to him,"Feed my sheep.
Truly, truly, I say to you, when you were young, you girded
yourself and walked where you would; but when you are
old, you will stretch out your hands, and another will gird
you and carry you where you do not wish to go." (This he
said to show by what death he was to glorify God.) And
after this he said to him,"Follow me."

Independence Day   *July 4*

The Lessons and Psalm "For the Nation," may be used in place of
the following. [See texts and citations on pages 257-259 below]

A Reading (Lesson) from the Book of Deuteronomy
[10:17-21]

The Lord your God is God of gods and Lord of lords, the
great, the mighty, and the terrible God, who is not partial
and takes no bribe. He executes justice for the fatherless
and the widow, and loves the sojourner, giving him food
and clothing. Love the sojourner therefore; for you were

sojourners in the land of Egypt. You shall fear the Lord your God; you shall serve him and cleave to him, and by his name you shall swear. He is your praise; he is your God, who has done for you these great and terrible things which your eyes have seen.

Psalm 145 [page 801] or *145:1-9* [page 801]

A Reading (Lesson) from the Letter to the Hebrews [11:8-16]

By faith Abraham obeyed when he was called to go out to a place which he was to receive as an inheritance; and he went out, not knowing where he was to go. By faith he sojourned in the land of promise, as in a foreign land, living in tents with Isaac and Jacob, heirs with him of the same promise. For he looked forward to the city which has foundations, whose builder and maker is God. By faith Sarah herself received power to conceive, even when she was past the age, since she considered him faithful who had promised. Therefore from one man, and him as good as dead, were born descendants as many as the stars of heaven and as the innumerable grains of sand by the seashore. These all died in faith, not having received what was promised, but having seen it and greeted it from afar, and having acknowledged that they were strangers and exiles on the earth. For people who speak thus make it clear that they are seeking a homeland. If they had been thinking of that land from which they had gone out, they would have had opportunity to return. But as it is, they desire a better country, that is, a heavenly one. Therefore God is not ashamed to be called their God, for he has prepared for them a city.

✠ *The Holy Gospel of Our Lord Jesus Christ According to Matthew* [5:43-48]

Jesus said, "You have heard that it was said, 'You shall love your neighbor and hate your enemy.' But I say to you, Love your enemies and pray for those who persecute you, so that you may be sons of your Father who is in heaven; for he makes his sun rise on the evil and on the good, and sends rain on the just and on the unjust. For if you love those who love you, what reward have you? Do not even the tax collectors do the same? And if you salute only your brethren, what more are you doing than others? Do not even the Gentiles do the same? You, therefore, must be perfect, as your heavenly Father is perfect."

For the Nation   *July 4*

Alternative for Independence Day above.

A Reading (Lesson) from the Book of Isaiah [26:1-8]

In that day this song will be sung in the land of Judah: "We have a strong city; he sets up salvation as walls and bulwarks. Open the gates, that the righteous nation which keeps faith may enter in. Thou dost keep him in perfect peace, whose mind is stayed on thee, because he trusts in thee. Trust in the Lord for ever, for the Lord God is an everlasting rock. For he has brought low the inhabitants of the height, the lofty city. He lays it low, lays it low to the ground, casts it to the dust. The foot tramples it, the feet of the poor, the steps of the needy." The way of the righteous is level; thou dost make smooth the path of the righteous. In the path of thy judgments, O Lord, we wait for thee; thy memorial name is the desire of our soul.

Psalm 47 [page 650]

*A Reading (Lesson) from the Letter of Paul
to the Romans* [13:1-10]

Let every person be subject to the governing authorities. For there is no authority except from God, and those that exist have been instituted by God. Therefore he who resists the authorities resists what God has appointed, and those who resist will incur judgment. For rulers are not a terror to good conduct, but to bad. Would you have no fear of him who is in authority? Then do what is good, and you will receive his approval, for he is God's servant for your good. But if you do wrong, be afraid, for he does not bear the sword in vain; he is the servant of God to execute his wrath on the wrongdoer. Therefore one must be subject, not only to avoid God's wrath but also for the sake of conscience. For the same reason you also pay taxes, for the authorities are ministers of God, attending to this very thing. Pay all of them their dues, taxes to whom taxes are due, revenue to whom revenue is due, respect to whom respect is due, honor to whom honor is due. Owe no one anything, except to love one another; for he who loves his neighbor has fulfilled the law. The commandments, "You shall not commit adultery, You shall not kill, You shall not steal, You shall not covet," and any other commandment, are summed in this sentence, "You shall love your neighbor as yourself." Love does no wrong to a neighbor; therefore love is the fulfilling of the law.

✝ *The Holy Gospel of Our Lord Jesus Christ According to Mark* [12:13-17]

Some of the Pharisees and some of the Herodians were sent to Jesus to entrap him in his talk. And they came and said to him, "Teacher, we know that you are true, and care for no man; for you do not regard the position of men, but truly teach the way of God. Is it lawful to pay taxes to Caesar, or not? Should we pay them, or should we not?" But knowing their hypocrisy, he said to them, "Why put me to the test? Bring me a coin, and let me look at it." And they brought one. And he said to them, "Whose likeness and inscription is this?" They said to him, "Caesar's." Jesus said to them, "Render to Caesar the things that are Caesar's,

and to God the things that are God's." And they were
amazed at him.

Saint Mary Magdalene   *July 22*

A Reading (Lesson) from the Book of Judith   [9:1,11-14]

Judith fell upon her face, and put ashes on her head, and
uncovered the sackcloth she was wearing; and at the very
time when that evening's incense was being offered in the
house of God in Jerusalem, Judith cried out to the Lord
with a loud voice, and said, "O God my God, hear me. Thy
power depends not upon numbers, nor thy might upon
men of strength; for thou art God of the lowly, helper of
the oppressed, upholder of the weak, protector of the
forlorn, savior of those without hope. Hear, O hear me,
God of my father, God of the inheritance of Israel, Lord of
heaven and earth, Creator of the waters, King of all thy
creation, hear my prayer! Make my deceitful words to be
their wound and stripe, for they have planned cruel things
against thy covenant, and against thy consecrated house,
and against the top of Zion, and against the house
possessed by thy children. And cause thy whole nation and
every tribe to know and understand that thou art God, the
God of all power and might, and that there is no other who
protects the people of Israel but thou alone!"

Psalm 42:1-7 [page 643]

*A Reading (Lesson) from the Second Letter of Paul
to the Corinthians* [5:14-18]

The love of Christ controls us, because we are convinced
that one has died for all; therefore all have died. And he
died for all, that those who live might live no longer for
themselves but for him who for their sake died and was
raised. From now on, therefore, we regard no one from a

human point of view; even though we once regarded Christ from a human point of view, we regard him thus no longer. Therefore, if any one is in Christ, he is a new creation; the old has passed away, behold, the new has come. All this is from God, who through Christ reconciled us to himself and gave us the ministry of reconciliation.

✝ *The Holy Gospel of Our Lord Jesus Christ According to John* [20:11-18]

Mary stood weeping outside the tomb, and as she wept she stooped to look into the tomb; and she saw two angels in white, sitting where the body of Jesus had lain, one at the head and one at the feet. They said to her, "Woman, why are you weeping?" She said to them, "Because they have taken away my Lord, and I do not know where they have laid him." Saying this, she turned around and saw Jesus standing, but she did not know that it was Jesus. Jesus said to her, "Woman, why are you weeping? Whom do you seek?" Supposing him to be the gardener, she said to him, "Sir, if you have carried him away, tell me where you have laid him, and I will take him away." Jesus said to her, "Mary." She turned and said to him in Hebrew, "Rab-bo'ni!" (which means Teacher). Jesus said to her, "Do not hold me, for I have not yet ascended to the Father; but go to my brethren and say to them, I am ascending to my Father and your Father, to my God and your God." Mary Mag'dalene went and said to the disciples, "I have seen the Lord"; and she told them that he had said these things to her.

Saint James *July 25*

A Reading (Lesson) from the Book of Jeremiah [45:1-5]

The word that Jeremiah the prophet spoke to Baruch the son of Neri'ah, when he wrote these words in a book at the dictation of Jeremiah, in the fourth year of Jehoi'akim the son of Josi'ah, king of Judah: "Thus says the Lord, the God of Israel, to you, O Baruch: You said, 'Woe is me! For the Lord has added sorrow to my pain; I am weary with my groaning, and I find no rest.' Thus shall you say to him, Thus says the Lord: Behold, what I have built I am breaking down, and what I have planted I am plucking up—that is, the whole land. And do you seek great things for yourself? Seek them not; for, behold, I am bringing evil upon all flesh, says the Lord; but I will give you your life as a prize of war in all places to which you may go."

Psalm 7:1-10 [page 590]

A Reading (Lesson) from the Acts of the Apostles
[11:27—12:3]

In these days prophets came down from Jerusalem to Antioch. And one of them named Ag'abus stood up and foretold by the Spirit that there would be a great famine over all the world; and this took place in the days of Claudius. And the disciples determined, every one according to his ability, to send relief to the brethren who lived in Judea; and they did so, sending it to the elders by the hand of Barnabas and Saul. About that time Herod the king laid violent hands upon some who belonged to the church. He killed James the brother of John with the sword; and when he saw that it pleased the Jews, he proceeded to arrest Peter also. This was during the days of Unleavened Bread.

✝ *The Holy Gospel of Our Lord Jesus Christ*
According to Matthew [20:20-28]

The mother of the sons of Zeb'edee came up to Jesus with her sons, and kneeling before him she asked him for something. And he said to her, "What do you want?" She said to him, "Command that these two sons of mine may sit, one at your right hand and one at your left, in your kingdom." But Jesus answered, "You do not know what you are asking. Are you able to drink the cup that I am to drink?" They said to him, "We are able." He said to them, "You will drink my cup, but to sit at my right hand and at my left is not mine to grant, but it is for those for whom it has been prepared by my Father." And when the ten heard it, they were indignant at the two brothers. But Jesus called them to him and said, "You know that the rulers of the Gentiles lord it over them, and their great men exercise authority over them. It shall not be so among you; but whoever would be great among you must be your servant, and whoever would be first among you must be your slave; even as the Son of man came not to be served but to serve, and to give his life as a ransom for many."

The Transfiguration   *August 6*

A Reading (Lesson) from the Book of Exodus [34:29-35]

When Moses came down from Mount Sinai, with the two tables of the testimony in his hand as he came down from the mountain, Moses did not know that the skin of his face shone because he had been talking with God. And when Aaron and all the people of Israel saw Moses, behold, the skin of his face shone, and they were afraid to come near him. But Moses called to them; and Aaron and all the leaders of the congregation returned to him, and Moses talked with them. And afterward all the people of Israel came near, and he gave them in commandment all that the Lord had spoken with him in Mount Sinai. And when Moses had finished speaking with them, he put a veil on his face; but whenever Moses went in before the Lord to speak with him, he took the veil off, until he came out; and when he came out, and told the people of Israel what he was commanded, the people of Israel saw the face of Moses, that the skin of Moses' face shone; and Moses would put the veil upon his face again, until he went in to speak with him.

Psalm 99 [page 728]   or   *99:5-9* [page 729]

A Reading (Lesson) from the Second Letter of Peter
[1:13-21]

I think it right, as long as I am in this body, to arouse you by way of reminder, since I know that the putting off of my body will be soon, as our Lord Jesus Christ showed me. And I will see to it that after my departure you may be able at any time to recall these things. For we did not follow cleverly devised myths when we made known to you the power and coming of our Lord Jesus Christ, but we were eyewitnesses of his majesty. For when he received honor and glory from God the Father and the voice was borne to him by the Majestic Glory, "This is my beloved Son, with whom I am well pleased," we heard this voice borne from heaven, for we were with him on the holy mountain. And we have the prophetic word made more sure. You will do well to pay attention to this as to a lamp shining in a dark place, until the day dawns and the morning star rises in your hearts. First of all you must understand this, that no prophecy of scripture is a matter of one's own interpretation, because no prophecy ever came by the impulse of man, but men moved by the Holy Spirit spoke from God.

✝ *The Holy Gospel of Our Lord Jesus Christ*
According to Luke [9:28-36]

Now about eight days after Jesus had foretold his death and resurrection, he took with him Peter and John and James, and went up on the mountain to pray. And as he was praying, the appearance of his countenance was altered, and his raiment became dazzling white. And behold, two men talked with him, Moses and Eli'jah, who appeared in glory and spoke of his departure, which he was to accomplish at Jerusalem. Now Peter and those who were with him were heavy with sleep, and when they wakened they saw his glory and the two men who stood with him. And as the men were parting from him, Peter said to Jesus, "Master, it is well that we are here; let us make three booths, one for you and one for Moses and one for Eli'jah"—not knowing what he said. As he said this, a cloud came and overshadowed them; and they were afraid as they entered the cloud. And a voice came out of the cloud, saying, "This is my Son, my Chosen; listen to him!" And when the voice had spoken, Jesus was found alone. And they kept silence and told no one in those days anything of what they had seen.

Saint Mary the Virgin   *August 15*

A Reading (Lesson) from the Book of Isaiah [61:10-11]

I will greatly rejoice in the Lord, my soul shall exult in my God; for he has clothed me with the garments of salvation, he has covered me with the robe of righteousness, as a bridegroom decks himself with a garland, and as a bride adorns herself with her jewels. For as the earth brings forth its shoots, and as a garden causes what is sown in it to spring up, so the Lord God will cause righteousness and praise to spring forth before all the nations.

Psalm 34 [page 627]   or   *34:1-9* [page 627]

A Reading (Lesson) from the Letter of Paul to the Galatians [4:4-7]

When the time had fully come, God sent forth his Son, born of woman, born under the law, to redeem those who were under the law, so that we might receive adoption as sons. And because you are sons, God has sent the Spirit of his Son into our hearts, crying, "Abba! Father!" So through God you are no longer a slave but a son, and if a son then an heir.

✝ *The Holy Gospel of Our Lord Jesus Christ*
According to Luke [1:46-55]

Mary said, "My soul magnifies the Lord, and my spirit rejoices in God my Savior, for he has regarded the low estate of his handmaiden. For behold, henceforth all generations will call me blessed; for he who is mighty has done great things for me, and holy is his name. And his mercy is on those who fear him from generation to generation. He has shown strength with his arm, he has scattered the proud in the imagination of their hearts, he has put down the mighty from their thrones, and exalted those of low degree; he has filled the hungry with good things, and the rich he has sent empty away. He has helped his servant Israel, in remembrance of his mercy, as he spoke to our fathers, to Abraham and to his posterity for ever."

Saint Bartholomew *August 24*

A Reading (Lesson) from the Book of Deuteronomy [18:15-18]

Moses said to the people, "The Lord your God will raise up for you a prophet like me from among you, from your brethren—him you shall heed—just as you desired of the Lord your God at Horeb on the day of the assembly, when you said, 'Let me not hear again the voice of the Lord my God, or see this great fire any more, lest I die.' And the Lord said to me, 'They have rightly said all that they have spoken. I will raise up for them a prophet like you from

among their brethren; and I will put my words in his
mouth, and he shall speak to them all that I command him.' "

Psalm 91 [page 719]   or   *91:1-4* [page 719]

*A Reading (Lesson) from the First Letter of Paul
to the Corinthians* [4:9-15]

I think that God has exhibited us apostles as last of all, like
men sentenced to death; because we have become a
spectacle to the world, to angels and to men. We are fools
for Christ's sake, but you are wise in Christ. We are weak,
but you are strong. You are held in honor, but we in
disrepute. To the present hour we hunger and thirst, we are
ill-clad and buffeted and homeless, and we labor, working
with our own hands. When reviled, we bless; when
persecuted, we endure; when slandered, we try to
conciliate; we have become, and are now, as the refuse of
the world, the offscouring of all things. I do not write this
to make you ashamed, but to admonish you as my beloved
children. For though you have countless guides in Christ,
you do not have many fathers. For I became your father in
Christ Jesus through the gospel.

✝ *The Holy Gospel of Our Lord Jesus Christ
According to Luke* [22:24-30]

A dispute arose among the apostles, which of them was to
be regarded as the greatest. And Jesus said to them, "The
kings of the Gentiles exercise lordship over them; and
those in authority over them are called benefactors. But
not so with you; rather let the greatest among you become
as the youngest, and the leader as one who serves. For
which is the greater, one who sits at table, or one who
serves? Is it not the one who sits at table? But I am among
you as one who serves. You are those who have continued
with me in my trials; and I assign to you, as my Father

assigned to me, a kingdom, that you may eat and drink at my table in my kingdom, and sit on thrones judging the twelve tribes of Israel."

Holy Cross Day *September 14*

A Reading (Lesson) from the Book of Isaiah [45:21-25]

Thus says the Lord: "Declare and present your case; let them take counsel together! Who told this long ago? Who declared it of old? Was it not I, the Lord? And there is no other god besides me, a righteous God and a Savior; there is none besides me. Turn to me and be saved, all the ends of the earth! For I am God, and there is no other. By myself I have sworn, from my mouth has gone forth in righteousness a word that shall not return: 'To me every knee shall bow, every tongue shall swear.' Only in the Lord, it shall be said of me, are righteousness and strength; to him shall come and be ashamed, all who were incensed against him. In the Lord all the offspring of Israel shall triumph and glory."

Psalm 98 [page 727]   or   *98:1-4* [page 727]

A Reading (Lesson) from the Letter of Paul to the Philippians [2:5-11]

Have this mind among yourselves, which is yours in Christ Jesus, who, though he was in the form of God, did not count equality with God a thing to be grasped, but emptied himself, taking the form of a servant, being born in the likeness of men. And being found in human form he humbled himself and became obedient unto death, even death on a cross. Therefore God has highly exalted him and bestowed on him the name which is above every name, that at the name of Jesus every knee should bow, in heaven and on earth and under the earth, and every tongue confess that Jesus Christ is Lord, to the glory of God the Father.

or this

A Reading (Lesson) from the Letter of Paul to the Galatians [6:14-18]

Far be it from me to glory except in the cross of our Lord Jesus Christ, by which the world has been crucified to me, and I to the world. For neither circumcision counts for anything, nor uncircumcision, but a new creation. Peace and mercy be upon all who walk by this rule, upon the Israel of God. Henceforth let no man trouble me; for I bear on my body the marks of Jesus. The grace of our Lord Jesus Christ be with your spirit, brethren. Amen.

✝ *The Holy Gospel of Our Lord Jesus Christ According to John* [12:31-36a]

Jesus said, "Now is the judgment of this world, now shall the ruler of this world be cast out; and I, when I am lifted up from the earth, will draw all men to myself." He said this to show by what death he was to die. The crowd answered him, "We have heard from the law that the Christ remains for ever. How can you say that the Son of man must be lifted up? Who is this Son of man?" Jesus said to them, "The light is with you for a little longer. Walk while you have the light, lest the darkness overtake you; he who walks in the darkness does not know where he goes. While you have the light, believe in the light, that you may become sons of light."

Saint Matthew *September 21*

A Reading (Lesson) from the Book of Proverbs [3:1-6]

My son, do not forget my teaching, but let your heart keep my commandments; for length of days and years of life and abundant welfare will they give you. Let not loyalty and faithfulness forsake you; bind them about your neck, write them on the tablet of your heart. So you will find favor and good repute in the sight of God and man. Trust in the Lord with all your heart, and do not rely on your own insight. In all your ways acknowledge him, and he will make straight your paths.

Psalm 119:33-40 [page 766]

A Reading (Lesson) from the Second Letter of Paul to Timothy [3:14-17]

As for you, continue in what you have learned and have firmly believed, knowing from whom you learned it and how from childhood you have been acquainted with the sacred writings which are able to instruct you for salvation through faith in Christ Jesus. All scripture is inspired by God and profitable for teaching, for reproof, for correction, and for training in righteousness, that the man of God may be complete, equipped for every good work.

✝ *The Holy Gospel of Our Lord Jesus Christ According to Matthew* [9:9-13]

Jesus saw a man called Matthew sitting at the tax office; and he said to him, "Follow me." And he rose and followed him. And as he sat at table in the house, behold, many tax collectors and sinners came and sat down with Jesus and his disciples. And when the Pharisees saw this, they said to his disciples, "Why does your teacher eat with tax collectors and sinners?" But when he heard it, he said, "Those who are well have no need of a physician, but those who are sick. Go and learn what this means,'I desire mercy, and not sacrifice.' For I came not to call the righteous, but sinners."

Saint Michael and All Angels *September 29*

A Reading (Lesson) from the Book of Genesis [28:10-17]

Jacob left Beer-sheba, and went toward Haran. And he
came to a certain place, and stayed there that night,
because the sun had set. Taking one of the stones of the
place, he put it under his head and lay down in that place
to sleep. And he dreamed that there was a ladder set up on
the earth, and the top of it reached to heaven; and behold,
the angels of God were ascending and descending on it!
And behold, the Lord stood above it and said,"I am the
Lord, the God of Abraham your father and the God of
Isaac; the land on which you lie I will give to you and to
your descendants; and your descendants shall be like the
dust of the earth, and you shall spread abroad to the west
and to the east and to the north and to the south; and by
you and your descendants shall all the families of the earth
bless themselves. Behold, I am with you and will keep you
wherever you go, and will bring you back to this land; for
I will not leave you until I have done that of which I have
spoken to you." Then Jacob awoke from his sleep and
said,"Surely the Lord is in this place; and I did not know
it." And he was afraid, and said,"How awesome is this
place! This is none other than the house of God, and this is
the gate of heaven."

Psalm 103 [page 733]   or   *103:19-22* [page 734]

A Reading (Lesson) from the Revelation to John [12:7-12]

Now war arose in heaven, Michael and his angels fighting
against the dragon; and the dragon and his angels fought,
but they were defeated and there was no longer any place
for them in heaven. And the great dragon was thrown
down, that ancient serpent, who is called the Devil and
Satan, the deceiver of the whole world—he was thrown

down to the earth, and his angels were thrown down with him. And I heard a loud voice in heaven, saying, "Now the salvation and the power and the kingdom of our God and the authority of his Christ have come, for the accuser of our brethren has been thrown down, who accuses them day and night before our God. And they have conquered him by the blood of the Lamb and by the word of their testimony; for they loved not their lives even unto death. Rejoice then, O heaven and you that dwell therein! But woe to you, O earth and sea, for the devil has come down to you in great wrath, because he knows that his time is short!"

✝ *The Holy Gospel of Our Lord Jesus Christ According to John* [1:47-51]

Jesus saw Nathan'a-el coming to him, and said of him, "Behold, an Israelite indeed, in whom is no guile!" Nathan'a-el said to him, "How do you know me?" Jesus answered him, "Before Philip called you, when you were under the fig tree, I saw you." Nathan'a-el answered him, "Rabbi, you are the son of God! You are the King of Israel!" Jesus answered him, "Because I said to you, I saw you under the fig tree, do you believe? You shall see greater things than these." And he said to him, "Truly, truly, I say to you, you will see heaven opened, and the angels of God ascending and descending upon the Son of man."

Saint Luke *October 18*

A Reading (Lesson) from the Book of Ecclesiasticus [38:1-4, 6-10, 12-14]

Honor the physician with the honor due him, according to your need of him, for the Lord created him; for healing comes from the Most High, and he will receive a gift from the king. The skill of the physician lifts up his head, and in the presence of great men he is admired. The Lord created medicines from the earth, and a sensible man will not despise them. And he gave skill to men that he might be glorified in his marvelous works. By them he heals and takes away pain; the pharmacist makes of them a compound. His works will never be finished; and from him health is upon the face of the earth. My son, when you are sick do not be negligent, but pray to the Lord, and he will heal you. Give up your faults and direct your hands aright, and cleanse your heart from all sin. And give the physician his place, for the Lord created him; let him not leave you, for there is need of him. There is a time when success lies in the hands of physicians, for they too will pray to the Lord that he should grant them success in diagnosis and in healing, for the sake of preserving life.

Psalm 147 [page 804]   or   *147:1-7* [page 804]

A Reading (Lesson) from the Second Letter of Paul to Timothy [4:5-13]

As for you, always be steady, endure suffering, do the work of an evangelist, fulfill your ministry. For I am already on the point of being sacrificed; the time of my departure has come. I have fought the good fight, I have finished the race, I have kept the faith. Henceforth there is laid up for me the crown of righteousness, which the Lord, the righteous judge, will award to me on that Day, and not only to me but also to all who have loved his appearing. Do your best to come to me soon. For Demas, in love with this present world, has deserted me and gone to Thessaloni'ca; Crescens has gone to Galatia, Titus to Dalmatia. Luke alone is with me. Get Mark and bring him with you; for he is very useful in serving me. Tych'icus I have sent to Ephesus. When you come, bring the cloak that I left with Carpus at Tro'as, also the books, and above all the parchments.

✝ *The Holy Gospel of Our Lord Jesus Christ*
According to Luke [4:14-21]

Jesus returned in the power of the Spirit into Galilee, and a report concerning him went out through all the surrounding country. And he taught in their synagogues, being glorified by all. And he came to Nazareth, where he had been brought up; and went to the synagogue, as his custom was, on the sabbath day. And he stood up to read; and there was given to him the book of the prophet Isaiah. He opened the book and found the place where it was written, "The Spirit of the Lord is upon me, because he has anointed me to preach good news to the poor. He has sent me to proclaim release to the captives and recovering of sight to the blind, to set at liberty those who are oppressed, to proclaim the acceptable year of the Lord." And he closed the book, and gave it back to the attendant, and sat down; and the eyes of all in the synagogue were fixed on him. And he began to say to them, "Today this scripture has been fulfilled in your hearing."

Saint James of Jerusalem   *October 23*

A Reading (Lesson) from the Acts of the Apostles [15:12-22a]

All the apostles and elders kept silence; and they listened to Barnabas and Paul as they related what signs and wonders God had done through them among the Gentiles. After they finished speaking, James replied, "Brethren, listen to me. Simeon has related how God first visited the Gentiles, to take out of them a people for his name. And with this the words of the prophets agree, as it is written, 'After this I will return, and I will rebuild the dwelling of David, which has fallen; I will rebuild its ruins, and I will set it up, that the rest of men may seek the Lord, and all the Gentiles who are called by my name, says the Lord, who has made these things known from of old.' Therefore my judgment is that we should not trouble those of the Gentiles who turn to God, but should write to them to abstain from the pollutions of idols and from unchastity and from what is strangled and from blood. For from early generations Moses has had in every city those who preach him, for he is read every sabbath in the synagogues." Then it seemed good to the apostles and the elders, with the whole church, to choose men from among them and send them to Antioch with Paul and Barnabas.

Psalm 1 [page 585]

A Reading (Lesson) from the First Letter of Paul to the Corinthians [15:1-11]

I would remind you, brethren, in what terms I preached to you the gospel, which you received, in which you stand, by which you are saved, if you hold it fast—unless you believed in vain. For I delivered to you as of first importance what I also received, that Christ died for our sins in accordance with the scriptures, that he was buried, that he was raised on the third day in accordance with the scriptures, and that he appeared to Cephas, then to the twelve. Then he appeared to more than five hundred brethren at one time, most of whom are still alive, though some have fallen asleep. Then he appeared to James, then to all the apostles. Last of all, as to one untimely born, he appeared also to me. For I am the least of the apostles, unfit to be called an apostle, because I persecuted the church of God. But by the grace of God I am what I am, and his grace toward me was not in vain. On the contrary, I worked harder than any of them, though it was not I, but the grace of God which is with me. Whether then it was I or they, so we preach and so you believed.

✝ *The Holy Gospel of Our Lord Jesus Christ*
According to Matthew [13:54-58]

Coming to his own country, Jesus taught them in their synagogue, so that they were astonished, and said,"Where did this man get this wisdom and these mighty works? Is not this the carpenter's son? Is not his mother called Mary? And are not his brothers James and Joseph and Simon and Judas? And are not all his sisters with us? Where then did this man get all this?" And they took offense at him. But Jesus said to them,"A prophet is not without honor except in his own country and in his own house." And he did not do many mighty works there, because of their unbelief.

Saint Simon and Saint Jude   *October 28*

A Reading (Lesson) from the Book of Deuteronomy [32:1-4]

Moses spoke the words of this song,"Give ear, O heavens, and I will speak; and let the earth hear the words of my mouth. May my teaching drop as the rain, my speech distill as the dew, as the gentle rain upon the tender grass, and as the showers upon the herb. For I will proclaim the name of the Lord. Ascribe greatness to our God! The Rock, his work is perfect; for all his ways are justice. A God of faithfulness and without iniquity, just and right is he."

Psalm 119:89-96 [page 770]

A Reading (Lesson) from the Letter of Paul to the Ephesians [2:13-22]

Now in Christ Jesus you Gentiles, who once were far off have been brought near in the blood of Christ. For he is our peace, who has made us both one, and has broken down the dividing wall of hostility, by abolishing in his flesh the law of commandments and ordinances, that he might create in himself one new man in place of the two, so making peace, and might reconcile us both to God in one body through the cross, thereby bringing the hostility to an end. And he came and preached peace to you who were far off and peace to those who were near; for through him we both have access in one Spirit to the Father. So then you are no longer strangers and sojourners, but you are fellow citizens with the saints and members of the household of God, built upon the foundation of the apostles and prophets, Christ Jesus himself being the cornerstone, in whom the whole structure is joined together and grows into a holy temple in the Lord; in whom you also are built into it for a dwelling place of God in the Spirit.

✝ *The Holy Gospel of Our Lord Jesus Christ*
According to John [15:17-27]

Jesus said to his disciples, "This I command you, to love one another. If the world hates you, know that it has hated me before it hated you. If you were of the world, the world would love its own; but because you are not of the world, but I chose you out of the world, therefore the world hates you. Remember the word that I said to you, 'A servant is not greater than his master.' If they persecuted me, they will persecute you; if they kept my word, they will keep yours also. But all this they will do to you on my account, because they do not know him who sent me. If I had not come and spoken to them, they would not have sin; but now they have no excuse for their sin. He who hates me hates my Father also. If I had not done among them the works which no one else did, they would not have sin; but now they have seen and hated both me and my Father. It is to fulfill the word that is written in their law, 'They hated me without a cause.' But when the Counselor comes, whom I shall send to you from the Father, even the Spirit of truth, who proceeds from the Father, he will bear witness to me; and you also are witnesses, because you have been with me from the beginning."

All Saints' Day I *November 1*

A Reading (Lesson) from the Book of Ecclesiasticus
[44:1-10, 13-14]

Let us now praise famous men, and our fathers in their generations. The Lord apportioned to them great glory, his majesty from the beginning. There were those who ruled in their kingdoms, and were men renowned for their power, giving counsel by their understanding, and proclaiming prophecies; leaders of the people in their deliberations and in understanding of learning for the people, wise in their words of instruction; those who composed musical tunes, and set forth verses in writing; rich men furnished with resources, living peaceably in their habitations—all these were honored in their generations, and were the glory of their times. There are some of them who have left a name, so that men declare their praise. And there are some who have no memorial, who have perished as though they had not lived; they have become as though they had not been born, and so have their children after them. But these were men of mercy, whose righteous deeds have not been forgotten. Their posterity will continue for ever, and their glory will not be blotted out. Their bodies were buried in peace, and their name lives to all generations.

Psalm 149 [page 807]

A Reading (Lesson) from the Revelation to John [7:2-4, 9-17]

I saw another angel ascend from the rising of the sun, with the seal of the living God, and he called with a loud voice to the four angels who had been given power to harm earth and sea, saying, "Do not harm the earth or the sea or the trees, till we have sealed the servants of our God upon their foreheads." And I heard the number of the sealed, a hundred and forty-four thousand sealed, out of every tribe of the sons of Israel. After this I looked, and behold, a great multitude which no man could number, from every nation, from all tribes and peoples and tongues, standing before the throne and before the Lamb, clothed in white robes, with palm branches in their hands, and crying out with a loud voice, "Salvation belongs to our God who sits upon the throne, and to the Lamb!" And all the angels stood round the throne and round the elders and the four living creatures, and they fell on their faces before the throne and worshiped God, saying, "Amen! Blessing and glory and wisdom and thanksgiving and honor and power and might be to our God for ever and ever! Amen." Then one of the elders addressed me, saying, "Who are these, clothed in white robes, and whence have they come?" I said to him, "Sir, you know." And he said to me, "These are they who have come out of the great tribulation; they have washed their robes and made them white in the blood of the Lamb. Therefore are they before the throne of God, and serve him day and night within his temple; and he who sits upon the throne will shelter them with his presence. They shall hunger no more, neither thirst any more; the sun shall not strike them, nor any scorching heat. For the Lamb in the midst of the throne will be their shepherd, and he will guide them to springs of living water; and God will wipe away every tear from their eyes."

✝ *The Holy Gospel of Our Lord Jesus Christ According to Matthew* [5:1-12]

Seeing the crowds, Jesus went up on the mountain, and when he sat down his disciples came to him. And he opened his mouth and taught them, saying: "Blessed are the poor in spirit, for theirs is the kingdom of heaven. Blessed are those who mourn, for they shall be comforted. Blessed are the meek, for they shall inherit the earth. Blessed are those who hunger and thirst for righteousness, for they shall be satisfied. Blessed are the merciful, for they shall obtain mercy. Blessed are the pure in heart, for they shall see God. Blessed are the peacemakers, for they shall be called sons of God. Blessed are those who are persecuted for righteousness' sake, for theirs is the kingdom of heaven. Blessed are you when men revile you and persecute you and utter all kinds of evil against you falsely on my account. Rejoice and be glad, for your reward is great in heaven, for so men persecuted the prophets who were before you."

All Saints' Day II   *November 1 (or the Sunday following)*

A Reading (Lesson) from the Book of Ecclesiasticus [2:(1-6)7-11]

> My son, if you come forward to serve the Lord, prepare yourself for temptation. Set your heart right and be steadfast, and do not be hasty in time of calamity. Cleave to him and do not depart, that you may be honored at the end of your life. Accept whatever is brought upon you, and in changes that humble you be patient. For gold is tested in the fire, and acceptable men in the furnace of humiliation. Trust in him, and he will help you; make your ways straight, and hope in him.

You who fear the Lord, wait for his mercy; and turn not aside, lest you fall. You who fear the Lord, trust in him, and your reward will not fail; you who fear the Lord, hope for good things, for everlasting joy and mercy. Consider the ancient generations and see: who ever trusted in the Lord and was put to shame? Or who ever persevered in the fear of the Lord and was forsaken? Or who ever called upon him and was overlooked? For the Lord is compassionate and merciful; he forgives sins and saves in time of affliction.

Psalm 149 [page 807]

A Reading (Lesson) from the Letter of Paul to the Ephesians [1:(11-14) 15-23]

> In Christ, according to the purpose of him who accomplishes all things according to the counsel of his will, we who first hoped in Christ have been destined and appointed to live for the praise of his glory. In him you also, who have heard the word of truth, the gospel of your salvation, and have believed in him, were sealed with the promised Holy Spirit, which is the guarantee of our inheritance until we acquire possession of it, to the praise of his glory.

For this reason, because I have heard of your faith in the Lord Jesus and your love toward all the saints, I do not cease to give thanks for you, remembering you in my prayers, that the God of our Lord Jesus Christ, the Father of glory, may give you a spirit of wisdom and of revelation in the knowledge of him, having the eyes of your hearts enlightened, that you may know what is the hope to which he has called you, what are the riches of his glorious inheritance in the saints, and what is the immeasurable greatness of his power in us who believe, according to the working of his great might which he accomplished in Christ when he raised him from the dead and made him sit at his right hand in the heavenly places, far above all rule and authority and power and dominion, and above every name that is named, not only in this age but also in that which is to come; and he has put all things under his feet and has made him the head over all things for the church, which is his body, the fullness of him who fills all in all.

✝ *The Holy Gospel of Our Lord Jesus Christ*
According to Luke [6:20-26(27-36)]

Jesus lifted up his eyes on his disciples, and said: "Blessed are you poor, for yours is the kingdom of God. Blessed are you that hunger now, for you shall be satisfied. Blessed are you that weep now, for you shall laugh. Blessed are you when men hate you, and when they exclude you and revile you, and cast out your name as evil, on account of the Son of man! Rejoice in that day, and leap for joy, for behold, your reward is great in heaven; for so their fathers did to the prophets. But woe to you that are rich, for you have received your consolation. Woe to you that are full now, for you shall hunger. Woe to you that laugh now, for you shall mourn and weep. Woe to you, when all men speak well of you, for so their fathers did to the false prophets."

"But I say to you that hear, Love your enemies, do good to those who hate you, bless those who curse you, pray for those who abuse you. To him who strikes you on the cheek, offer the other also; and from him who takes away your coat do not withhold even your shirt. Give to every one who begs from you; and of him who takes away your goods do not ask them again. And as you wish that men would do to you, do so to them. If you love those who love you, what credit is that to you? For even sinners love those who love them. And if you do good to those who do good to you, what credit is that to you? For even sinners do the same. And if you lend to those from whom you hope to receive, what credit is that to you? Even sinners lend to sinners, to receive as much again. But love your enemies, and do good, and lend, expecting nothing in return; and your reward will be great, and you will be sons of the Most High; for he is kind to the ungrateful and the selfish. Be merciful, even as your Father is merciful."

Thanksgiving Day

A Reading (Lesson) from the Book of Deuteronomy
[8:1-3, 6-10 (17-20)]

Moses said to all Israel, "All the commandments which I command you this day you shall be careful to do, that you may live and multiply, and go in and possess the land which the Lord swore to give to your fathers. And you shall remember all the way which the Lord your God has led you these forty years in the wilderness, that he might humble you, testing you to know what was in your heart, whether you would keep his commandments, or not. And he humbled you and let you hunger and fed you with manna, which you did not know, nor did your fathers know; that he might make you know that man does not live by bread alone, but that man lives by everything that proceeds out of the mouth of the Lord. So you shall keep the commandments of the Lord your God, by walking in his ways and by fearing him. For the Lord your God is bringing you into a good land, a land of brooks of water, of fountains and springs, flowing forth in valleys and hills, a land of wheat and barley, of vines and fig trees and pomegranates, a land of olive trees and honey, a land in which you will eat bread without scarcity, in which you will lack nothing, a land whose stones are iron, and out of whose hills you can dig copper. And you shall eat and be full, and you shall bless the Lord your God for the good land he has given you.

"Beware lest you say in your heart, 'My power and the might of my hand have gotten me this wealth.' You shall remember the Lord your God, for it is he who gives you power to get wealth; that he may confirm his covenant which he swore to your fathers, as at this day. And if you forget the Lord your God and go after other gods and serve them and worship them, I solemnly warn you this day that you shall surely perish. Like the nations that the Lord makes to perish before you, so shall you perish, because you would not obey the voice of the Lord your God."

Psalm 65 [page 672] or *65:9-14* [page 673]

A Reading (Lesson) from the Letter of James [1:17-18, 21-27]

Every good endowment and every perfect gift is from above, coming down from the Father of lights with whom there is no variation or shadow due to change. Of his own will he brought us forth by the word of truth that we should be a kind of first fruits of his creatures. Therefore put away all filthiness and rank growth of wickedness and receive with meekness the implanted word, which is able to save your souls. But be doers of the word, and not hearers only, deceiving yourselves. For if any one is a hearer of the word and not a doer, he is like a man who observes his natural face in a mirror; for he observes himself and goes away and at once forgets what he was like. But he who looks into the perfect law, the law of liberty, and perseveres, being no hearer that forgets but a doer that acts, he shall be blessed in his doing. If any one thinks he is religious, and does not bridle his tongue but deceives his heart, this man's religion is vain. Religion that is pure and undefiled before God and the Father is this: to visit orphans and widows in their affliction, and to keep oneself unstained from the world.

✝ *The Holy Gospel of Our Lord Jesus Christ According to Matthew* [6:25-33]

Jesus said, "Do not be anxious about your life, what you shall eat or what you shall drink, nor about your body, what you shall put on. Is not life more than food, and the body more than clothing? Look at the birds of the air: they neither sow nor reap nor gather into barns, and yet your heavenly Father feeds them. Are you not of more value than they? And which of you by being anxious can add one cubit to his span of life? And why are you anxious about clothing? Consider the lilies of the field, how they grow; they neither toil nor spin; yet I tell you, even Solomon in all his glory was not arrayed like one of these. But if God so clothes the grass of the field, which today is alive and tomorrow is thrown into the oven, will he not much more clothe you, O men of little faith? Therefore do not be anxious, saying, 'What shall we eat?' or 'What shall we drink?' or 'What shall we wear?' For the Gentiles seek all these things; and your heavenly Father knows that you need them all. But seek first his kingdom and his righteousness, and all these things shall be yours as well."